Marketplace Behavior —

Its Meaning for Management

Marketplace Behavior —

Its Meaning for Management

Sidney J. Levy

amacom

A DIVISION OF AMERICAN MANAGEMENT ASSOCIATIONS

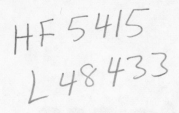

This book was set in Caledonia with Serif Gothic Heavy display
  by P & M Typesetting, Inc.
It was designed by Beata Gray
Printer and binder were Edwards Brothers

Library of Congress Cataloging in Publication Data

Levy, Sidney J., 1921–
  Marketplace behavior—its meaning for management.

  Includes index.
  1. Marketing. I. Title.
HF5415.L48433   658.8   78–19134
ISBN 0–8144–5476–3

*In remembrance of Jacob Levy
and Johl L. Adler*

Preface

This volume was prepared to provide a perspective on marketing behavior. The paucity of materials remains a general handicap despite the growing number of publications that use a behavioral science approach to understanding marketing. The purpose is to offer a discussion useful to marketing managers in search of a fundamental and integrated viewpoint. Most behavioral texts on marketing either are focused on consumers or are collections of reading held together loosely by a general theme. The chapters in this volume are interconnected in a consistent framework. It derives its coherence from a basic definition of the marketing exchange process as a *dialogue in which all actions by sellers or buyers are taken to be symbols that express something about the source of the behavior and the actor's intentions.*

If behavioral analysis is to be integrated into a meaningful concept of marketing, we need to think about the goals we have in mind and what we can realistically expect to achieve. One of the broader aims is to apply behavioral science to marketing. To some minds this approach promises unusually beneficial, if still mysterious, results, or the tangible acquisition of powerful tools that will ultimately expand successful prediction and control of marketing events — that is, getting significantly more people to buy their product. As soon as any practical moves are made in this direction there are murmurs or outcries of disillusionment and disappointment (for various reasons that include real failures — after all, even the moon-shot cameras failed on our first attempt). A major reason for doubt arises out of the unrealistic expectation that behavioral science can be applied like a poultice to an inflamed area with fast easing of pain. When goals are dictated by such expectations, we look for easy answers, even magical solutions. We search for the know-it-all expert, for the sudden illumination from a list of consumer motives, for the piercing but frustrating insight that reveals at last why consumer resistance is so great: The product obviously arouses sexual guilt or represents the bad mother. Then there is the hope that through some sort of general exposure a certain amount of behavioral science will rub off. A consultant may be hired to come in and wander around from time to time, letting osmosis or serendipity govern the results. In between these two extremes are pragmatic efforts, perhaps wary, arduous, or tentative, as some people try to take from the behavioral sciences what can be usefully applied from their orientations, methods, and findings.

As a psychologist who has turned his interest and attention to the study of marketing problems, I believe that the preferred way to bring behavioral science to bear on marketing management and study might be fully to train people within the behavioral science disciplines, then to let them go into business. But, this is not meant to imply that all businesspeople should first be behavioral scientists (J. B. Watson and Frank Stanton have set such examples), which seems an unlikely generalization. Besides, many behavioral scientists have little understanding of, or sympathy for, business problems. How much behavioral study should marketing managers have, and how unrelated or indirectly related to marketing issues can the materials be? Ideal aims will combine with expediency to produce a compromise, a hybrid — sterile or fruitful. The present volume represents one version.

Some marketing managers find opportunities and possibilities in seemingly remote materials, as one might use any knowledge gained from a liberal arts education. Others have difficulty seeing the relevance of information, even when it is translated into "implications for marketing." As a research psychologist consultant, I have often encountered three main obstacles to the constructive use of behavioral science theory. One is the charge of obscurity, obfuscation, or rarefied jargon: "I don't understand it." To this my reaction has been, "Well, try harder," or "Let's talk about it some more," or "Maybe you just don't want to."

Another questions the value or relevance of the knowledge, with a shrugging "So what?" This question can be difficult to answer. The implications of any discipline depend on the logic, imagination, or creativity of the learner, but in varying degree. Some knowledge has apparent immediate implications, given the situation, one's goals, prior understanding, and so forth. Then again, longer thought may be needed, or more information, or perhaps the learning is simply not useful.

A third charge focuses on the "obvious" character of some behavioral study or reflects the feelings of familiarity one may have when an insight is achieved: "I knew it all the time." To this we may respond that learning should reflect known realities, that in the Socratic sense *of course* we knew it all the time, but to give it affirmation or attention is valuable. In a more belligerent mood, when faced with this same reaction, one might reply, "Yes, but what did you do about it?"

Some of these objections are no longer as common as they were when behavioral science practitioners first entered the scene as intruders in the marketing field. But objections continue to arise among newcomers, and others are not receptive to the ideas in themselves, but are merely cowed by the popularity and dominance of behavioral interests and study. The alarmed reactions widely disseminated by Vance Packard's *The Hidden Persuaders* still prevail. The ethical issues are still open to debate and social conflict, as people are uncertain as to how much freedom of inquiry is compatible with how much examination and analysis of private lives.

A more particular problem is the tendency among marketing writers to limit their behavioral study to consumer or buyer behavior and to avoid a larger view of the behavioral processes operating throughout the marketing system. Further, the most popular kinds of behavioral study are strongly oriented to analytical methods, mathematical models, multivariate techniques, and an urgency to measure. This kind of work is most readily done with simple variables, which eliminates consideration of many kinds of interesting ideas whose human complexity eludes statistics and experimental design.

Comparatively little discussion is devoted to quantitative work here. This volume is frankly qualitative, relying on a holistic, interpretive approach to exploring the marketplace. I hope this approach does not discourage the researchers and managers of more structured bent, and that they will see it as a useful complement to their efforts. Certainly, I have found that many marketers are eager for such an orientation as a source of intellectual stimulation and insight, and even as a reassurance that their own deeper awareness of their symbolic lives also reflects reality.

SIDNEY J. LEVY

Contents

i

Modern
Marketing

When Robert Woodruff was Chairman of the Board of the
Coca-Cola Company, he was asked to approve a new advertising
jingle that included the following line:

> *Fifty million times a day*
> *people stop and say,*
> *There's nothing like a Coke.*

Mr. Woodruff said he could not approve the commercial because
it was not true, that 50 million people did not *say* that. One of
the advertising people, defending the idea that listeners would
understand the claim to mean that 50 million Cokes (the number
was conservative) were consumed a day, said, "But, Mr. Woodruff, that's just poetic license." To which Mr. Woodruff responded sternly, "Young man, at the Coca-Cola Company we do
not take license with the truth, poetic or otherwise."

This vignette is cited as an instance of marketing behavior. It
illustrates various points that will be developed in the following
pages. It shows that marketing behavior is not just a matter of
consumer behavior, but that managers also behave. It shows that
a simple idea of the marketing concept that focuses on meeting
the needs of consumers is inadequate because managers also
have their goals, values, and needs, and that honest managers
may differ. It shows the force of a marketing impulse coming

from above in the organization, affecting what some would regard as even a trivial matter. It shows that marketing behavior has to struggle complexly with facts, truth, values, and the symbolic nature of what is being presented. In sum, it locates people as our subject.

Enlightened managers have become increasingly aware of the complexities of operating in the modern marketplace. Management responsibilities are more encompassing, with pressures to know technical facts, to trace processes, evaluate equipment, and take account of law; to comprehend, organize, and reorganize systems; to master the financial aspects; and above all, to cope with people. This last requirement is the most difficult because the subject matter is relatively volatile, diffuse, intangible, and subtle, and the behavioral sciences are immature in the help they can give. Still, the challenge remains. To deal with the marketplace requires an understanding of the people in it, what buyers and sellers do, and why they do it.

TOTAL MARKETING

Although the management of marketing behavior might seem the province of the marketing manager, this volume is addressed to all managers, with the following logic. It is useful to distinguish between *the task of the marketing manager* and *the manager's marketing task*. The task of the marketing manager is to take responsibility for the marketing function in the most specific ways, but the other managers need to recognize how their functions contribute to the organization's marketing results. Also, most importantly, the basic guiding impulses that determine the organization's marketing thrust come from top management. In essence, top management's marketing task is to provide marketing *policy determination,* whereas the marketing manager's task is to ensure the *implementation* of that policy, and the other manager's marketing task is to provide *integration* with that policy.

Some managers resist this idea as intrusive to their domains — such internal conflict may improve the marketing goals and their implementation, but not if managers are merely competitive and unconstructive. This total marketing view was recognized by the head of the Pillsbury Company when he asserted that Pillsbury was henceforth to be considered a marketing company and he was the chief marketer. He did not mean to usurp the functions of the marketing manager, but was consciously asserting a definition that was necessary if all the company inputs were to lead to the desired marketplace output.

This point of view is a modern one. Early in the century, marketing was typically defined as those "business activities necessary to effect transfers in the ownership of goods and to provide for their physical distribution."[1] These words conjure up visions of transportation, invoices and bills of lading, and perhaps negotiations and contracts. These issues remain important, but as time passed they were taken increasingly for granted as specialized marketing activities and technical matters. As customers became more prosperous and alternatives began to proliferate in the ways people could spend their money, the requirements for marketing success became less clearly defined. By the 1970s the focus on people in the marketing system reached such a height that new definitions of marketing were called for. Contrast the previous definition with one of the most recent: "Marketing is human activity directed at satisfying needs and wants through exchange processes."[2] Here the focus is on people and their relationships. Managing this type of marketing calls for knowledge of what the relevant human activities are (and can any be irrelevant?), for a study of needs and wants, and for an assessment of one's abilities and potentialities for satisfying them. This attempt to view the marketing process through the eyes of its participants is a phenomenological approach. Its implications are developed in this volume.

Thus, it is evident that marketing management has come a great distance since the time when its content was fairly narrowly concerned with firing-line problems of salesmanship, retailing, distribution, and pricing. Now it is almost taken for granted that marketing managers will have a legitimate and urgent interest in products and their development—although there are still companies in which production and technological research units guard themselves jealously from marketing "interference."

Marketing managers who do not as yet give full and active thought to consumer behavior feel that they should be doing so. The rise of the concepts of image and positioning gives managers a handle for expressing their general communication aims. Marketing research as an entrenched activity and tool adds a pow-

erful intellectual dimension to those marketing managers who
have mastered its administration and use. Those who have not
yet achieved this competence are coming to aspire to it.

Marketing managers find their way to conferences, seminars,
evening school, books, and consultants. Where effective progress
has been made, they have come a long way from the early marketer who worked close to intuition and interpersonal, face-to-
face skills. The marketer moves toward being less just a genial
seller and more an engineer of market forces.

Recognition of the need for an enlarged perspective is reflected in attention directed toward the concept of interface,[3] in
which marketing personnel are confronted with their relationships to technology, government, and other company depart-
ments and social units. The demands for social awareness and
company responsibilities in the public sector eventuate in such
activities as U.S. Gypsum's housing program and in market research aimed at the problems of poverty and the ghetto.[4]

The marketer is urged to look toward distant horizons. Walt W.
Rostow[5] has discussed the challenge to efficient marketing institutions posed by developing countries. He points to information diffusion, to the growth of consumer goods incentives, to the
modernization of rural marketing, and to other needs in the development of national markets, calling for a new and significant
role for marketing. This enlargement and vitality in marketing
raises the possibility that some new perspectives on the nature of
marketing are needed.

BROADENING MARKETING

As modern marketing grows and evolves, some stocktaking is
useful in order to see the directions of this activity and what it
encompasses. Eugene J. Kelley points out, "Marketing is a discipline which can be researched and analyzed from different
viewpoints; it has significant managerial, social, legal, institutional, and interdisciplinary dimensions."[6] Various attempts are
being made to view this fact with some generality, to define the
structure and province of marketing thought.[7] As such attempts
seek to develop general theories of marketing, they become increasingly encompassing. The boundaries of marketing continue
to grow: Marketing executives are required to take account of

more and more variables in a field that John Howard has termed "fantastically complex." In addition, the scope of marketing is extended by the widening realization that marketing activities are not confined to the traditional economic units that have held them as their function.[8]

REASONS FOR CHANGE

1. *The selling of intangibles.* Insurance, mutual funds, travel, memberships, new credit arrangements, leasings, consultation, consortium plans of various kinds, and so forth require fresh viewpoints and perspectives on markets and an understanding of customer groups and their evolving motivations.

2. *International marketing.* New settings make novel demands for cultural sensitivity. Despite those who claim that marketing is basically the same the world over, the international marketer is forced to adapt to widely different circumstances, governments, laws, customs, and product and media mixes.[9]

3. *The growing role of government.* As a force affecting companies' marketing actions and as an organization with its own marketing functions, government modifies the commercial nexus of marketing. In both obvious and subtle ways, the government as regulator, as seller, and as customer constantly changes the character of the market and of marketing methods.

4. *A fast-moving environment.* Intense competition, mergers, jolting technology, and social changes create strong pressures for product innovation and innovation in all the techniques of marketing. The speed of economic fluctuation calls for alertness and agility.

5. *Rapid communications.* The marketplace is "tribalized," drawn closer together by the speed with which information is disseminated. The feeling of knowledge widely shared through the mass media causes bandwagon effects, allows for consumerism, and uses up ideas omnivorously.

6. *Social conflict.* The growing incidence of organized social protest against business firms, city governments, schools, and other institutions increases interest in reviewing the organization's basic purpose, its offerings, and the effectiveness of its communication with the institution's clients.[10]

THE MANAGER'S TASK

The view of marketing transactions that underlies the material presented in this book observes (and requires) that managers work with an exchange of meanings—those they are putting forth in all their marketing actions and those they interpret as coming to them from their customers.

If managers are to act in an insightful way, they should investigate several sets of ideas which together comprise their central areas of thinking. The main overall task they have is to relate all the symbols they can control to the general thrust of the organization or to their product responsibility. If marketing has focused on the mechanics and statistics of volume, sales, prices, and market demographics, then managers must look beyond such marketing to the behavioral enterprise and what it is about. This can be done by asking and exploring the following questions.

1. *What does one have to offer?* Managers should *understand* what they sell, what they might want to sell, or what their customers want them to sell. This means not merely adopting some clichés of the marketing concept, but learning about the symbolic significance of what they may be offering in the marketplace. The meaning of their offering is their central message. It is not simply the physical objects or service actions that they offer, but the import that having and using them carries for their audiences. Thus, a product has practical attributes and levels of performance. It has psychological meaning, and it occurs in a sociological context. This is true of the most mundane and simple objects (snow shovels and cotton swabs) and of the complex or rare (autos, diamonds).

2. *Who are the audiences?* Managers generally conceive of each market as a fairly specific group, as a hard core surrounded by the fuzzy edges of miscellaneous users. In some cases, the user group is quite precise—babies, newlyweds, housewives with teenage children, design engineers, business executives, possibly cross-run with, and described by, numerous demographic variables, such as age, income, education, and race. Marketing research may reveal some of the attitudes of the group and their customary behavior with regard to brands. This information is helpful in deciding on which communications are appropriate to them. The field of buyer behavior has been growing and much data is now available. Managers can draw on this knowledge and refine it to a present purpose, carrying out consumption-system

analyses and studies of the nature and sources of the buyers' (and nonbuyers') motives, opinions, and preferences, as well as how these affect their products and the market situation.

3. *What can the marketer do and say?* Choosing marketing actions is easy if traditional methods and popular ideas are followed. But each manager's case is his or her own. Later in this volume we will explore some of the various meanings that may inform the manager's thinking, but each manager must study what specific means are available and what they will accomplish in a specific instance. Awareness of overall trends may suggest a shifting toward the use of specialized media or a broad change in color preferences that could affect product, packaging, or how the company trucks should be painted (for example, the rise—and recessionary decline—in the use of lavender, violet, and purple in clothing and home furnishings).

4. *How do subsymbols relate to the goal?* All the specific subactions en route to the goal carry their meanings. Adept managers think about the goodness of fit to the brand gestalt as well as the pragmatic value of their actions. The accumulation of symbolic meanings produces more intense imagery. Friendly personnel reinforce the "Friendly skies of United" and give the slogan substance. A lawyer's toughness may reassure clients of the effectiveness of legal services being bought. A fancy binder may suggest high quality in a research report—or a waste of money on frills.

Sometimes a subsymbol seems to override the rest. The use of games by gasoline and food retailers has, at times, led to abuses and scandals. Competitive pressure led to their use, sometimes against the better judgment of individual managers.[11] Robert G. Reed III, vice-president of marketing of Cities Service Oil Co., testified in Washington that he was personally opposed to games as a promotional method: "Frankly, I believe the petroleum industry can develop other advertising and promotional methods which will do more than games to serve its long-range interests. Citgo is working to meet this goal. I have never been in favor of the use of games in our overall marketing program. I do not feel that games are a firm basis by which we may build lasting customer and dealer relationships. However, the use of them by competitors has forced us to enter the field."[12] With short supply of gasoline, the games vanished. But the subsymbols remained, as some service stations still wiped windshields, while others did not.

SUMMARY

1. The marketing output of an organization exists in the minds of its members and its customers. To be aware of this fact is to recognize that products, brands, companies, and industries are clusters of meanings or symbols, and that all the actions taken by the personnel involved have some potential part in creating the clusters of meanings.

2. Top management has primary responsibility for saying what primary cluster of meanings it wants to project into the marketplace, of itself, its products, and so on.

3. Marketing managers have the role of translating these aims into the specific marketing actions that will communicate the intended ideas. This role, which was always present but not especially noticed because of the traditional emphasis on transportation and salesmanship, has come to the fore because of the modern awareness of the importance of choice-making by customers.

4. All the managers in an organization—regardless of their function—contribute to the ultimate marketing output and its particular style, and should therefore perceive what the organization's marketing goal is and how they are bringing it about. The idea of total marketing points to this necessity.

References

1. Harold H. Maynard, Walter C. Weidler, and Theodore N. Beckman, *Principles of Marketing* (New York: Ronald Press, 1932), p. 1.
2. Philip Kotler, *Marketing Management* (Englewood Cliffs, N.J.: Prentice-Hall, 1976), p. 5.
3. Conrad Berenson, "The R&D: Marketing Interface—A General Analogue Model for Technology Diffusion," *Journal of Marketing*, Apr. 1968, pp. 8–15.
4. Frederick D. Sturdivant, "Better Deal for Ghetto Shoppers," *Harvard Business Review*, Mar.–Apr. 1968, pp. 130–139. Helen H. Lamale, "How the Poor Spend Their Money," in Herman P. Miller (ed.), *Poverty American Style* (Belmont, Calif.: Wadsworth, 1968), pp. 150–161.
5. Walt W. Rostow, "The Concept of a National Market and Its Economic Growth Implications," in Peter D. Bennett (ed.), *Marketing and Economic Development, Proceedings of 1965 Fall Conference*, American Marketing Association, 1965, pp. 11–20.
6. Eugene J. Kelley, "From the Editor," *Journal of Marketing*, July 1967, p. 11.
7. Robert Bartels, "The General Theory of Marketing," *Journal of Marketing*,

Jan. 1968, pp. 29–33; see also "The Identity Crisis in Marketing," *Journal of Marketing*, Oct. 1974, pp. 73–76.
8. **Philip Kotler** and **Sidney J. Levy**, "Broadening the Concept of Marketing," *Journal of Marketing*, Jan. 1969, pp. 10–15.
9. **James H. Donnelly, Jr.** and **John K. Ryans, Jr.**, "Standardized Global Advertising, A Call As Yet Unanswered," *Journal of Marketing*, Apr. 1969, pp. 57–60.
10. **Sidney J. Levy** and **Gerald Zaltman**, *Marketing, Society, and Conflict* (Englewood Cliffs, N.J.: Prentice-Hall, 1975).
11. **Fred C. Allvine**, "The Future for Trading Stamps and Games," *Journal of Marketing*, Jan. 1969, pp. 45–52.
12. **Advertising Age**, July 22, 1968, p. 25.

Suggested Readings

Alderson, Wroe, *Marketing Behavior and Executive Action* (Homewood, Ill.: Richard D. Irwin, 1957).
Borch, Fred J., "The Marketing Philosophy as a Way of Business Life," American Management Associations, *Marketing Series, No. 99*, 1957.
Buzzell, Robert D., "What's Ahead for Marketing Managers?" *Journal of Marketing*, Jan. 1970, pp. 3–6.
Drucker, Peter F., *Management: Tasks, Responsibilities, and Practices* (New York: Harper & Row, 1974).
Howard, John A., *Marketing: Executive and Buyer Behavior* (New York: Columbia University Press, 1963).
Lewis, Richard J., and **Leo G. Erickson**, "Marketing Function and Marketing Systems: A Synthesis," *Journal of Marketing*, July 1969, pp. 10–14.
Myers, James H., "Marketing Organization and Administration," in Frederick D. Sturdivant et al. (eds.), *Managerial Analysis in Marketing* (Glenview, Ill.: Scott, Foresman and Co., 1970), pp. 283–325.

ii

Marketing
Behavior

As sellers and as buyers, everyone manages marketing behavior. We cannot avoid doing so because we must make decisions about what we can and want to offer to other people, how to present ourselves, and what response we want in return. These necessities are the essence of marketing. Everyone is part of the marketing system. The marketplace is thus a social system in which people are constantly interacting and usually improving their results by increasing their understanding of human behavior.

This understanding of marketing behavior should be an encompassing one. We define marketing behavior as *the internal and external states and actions of customers as they learn about, acquire, and use products and services; and the internal and external states and actions of sellers as they develop, offer, and convey their goods and services.* Evidently, one can never know all of this. But that is the large goal to be pursued.

Managing marketing behavior calls for thinking about one's own behavior, how it comes about, and what effects it is likely to have. That's why this is not a book about consumer behavior alone, but one that inquires into some of the bases for, and meaning of, managers' behavior as well. Managing marketing behavior also calls for thinking about other people's behavior and such issues as these:

Who are the people I have to know about?
What special characteristics do I need to know about?
What do they do that affects me?
What do they do that I have to adapt to?
What do they do that I want to sustain? To change?
How can I bring about such sustenance? Such changes?
Why do people behave this way?

The study of marketing behavior generally focuses on consumer behavior for several reasons. Basically, the greatest felt need has been to understand the women who are the buyers of so many consumer products. The managers in companies that make and distribute these products are usually several steps removed from their ultimate customers and therefore feel less readily knowledgeable about them than do, for example, industrial managers and sales personnel, who are closer to their customers and regard them as people much like themselves. In the consumer realm, the manager is often a mature upper-middle-class white man thinking about customers who are predominantly young lower-middle-class and working-class women, white and black. This situation is changing, a fact of which this text takes account by not assuming that marketing managers are invariably male and consumers female.

Marketing behavior is a larger and more fundamental topic than consumer behavior. To study behavior in marketing requires a study of the behavior that goes on in all directions and by all participants. It means paying attention to the motives and decision-making processes of marketing managers as well as homemakers, to the psychology of purchasing agents, to the reasons why salespeople are looked down on, to what products mean in industry as well as in the home. To work and interact with these various groups requires concepts and ways of thinking about what marketing is and about what we need to know.

When marketing managers make decisions about products, packages, transportation, prices, advertisements, sales outlets, labels, names, and salespeople, they are asserting some beliefs about people in the marketplace and their likely reactions. Some managers do well (or don't do well) without knowing why. Others want to understand in order to succeed.

There are no simple answers, but there remains the need to explore and think about the complexities of human behavior, and thereby to reason toward improving marketing decisions. Theories, interpretations, and speculations about human likelihoods are needed. Decisions are ventures into the future. They require

more than rules for "how to do it." They require facts and ingenuity, information and astuteness, and an awareness that, as Ein-
stein put it, imagination is more important than knowledge.

MARKETING THEORIES

Marketing theories are of many kinds. Generally, they have not
been complex or highly developed. These theories are ways of
examining and explaining what goes on in the marketplace. Since
a theory is someone's way of saying what is important about the
events being studied, different theories have different emphases.
The commodity approach is, in a sense, a theory that focuses on
the longitudinal history of given commodities in the belief that
this will provide an orderly view of marketing processes.

Traditional marketing theory has emphasized the operation of
marketing *institutions* and the various central *functions* in marketing, such as buying, selling, storing, and financing. Usually,
the ideas and facts presented in traditional study have not been
dignified as "theories," although they are actually sets of assumptions and generalizations that do imply a theoretical framework
for organized observations in the marketplace. The character of
marketing research that a company does is largely determined by
its implicit or explicit theory of the market.

When marketing theory draws on ideas from the study of economics, attention is turned to matters of pricing and utility of
time and place, with an emphasis on rationalizing the behavior of
buyers. Managers turn their thoughts toward theories of organization and the principles that may be derived from them in an attempt to gain greater efficiency or optimal achievement of the
marketing organization's goals.

More recently, marketing theory has turned to the development of models of buyer behavior[1] and of the structure of markets. Modern attempts to do this have grown because of the
search for less purely descriptive views of the market. The goals
are to gain more dynamic understanding of marketing processes,
to explore how buyers are motivated, and to examine how the
marketing complex is articulated. One direction of study emphasizes the development of quantitative models. These provide systematic methods for relating variables, for simulating variables,
for simulating marketing audiences, structures, and processes,
and for abstracting and testing hypotheses about significant marketing events.[2]

Another important development in marketing has been the increased attention given to ideas drawn from the behavioral sciences. From the wish to gain greater knowledge about such areas as consumer motivation, reactions to products and advertisements, and factors affecting buyer decision making, marketers and students of marketing have been developing many elements of a sociology of marketing and a psychology of marketing. These elements have been more or less piecemeal, with occasional attempts at integration or a bringing together of writings.[3]

This book presents a behavioral viewpoint that relates three broad premises to ideas from many directions: (1) the marketing dialogue, (2) sources of behavior, and (3) symbols in the marketplace. Before we look into these three broad premises, it will be useful to talk about the definition of marketing that has already been implied, and that forms the underlying orientation of this book.

THE FUNDAMENTAL DEFINITION OF MARKETING

How does the market system come about? Who are sellers and buyers? The ordinary understanding of marketing mainly includes the idea of an exchange of a product for money. But that definition is neither inclusive nor basic enough. Marketing is also going on when a service is exchanged for money, or when a service is exchanged for another service. In those cases, as any action can be a service, what limit can be placed on what should be included or not included?

A basic marketing analysis begins with certain core ideas. Most central are the motive and action of the buyer. The initial impulse throbs in someone who wants something (product or service). In the search to find or get it, it may be grown, gathered, hunted, or made. This fundamental activity, in which the buyer *takes* from the soil or the wilderness and in turn spends time, energy, and skill, constitutes a prototypical exchange. Although calling this exchange "marketing" is offensive to common understanding, it might be termed archetypal marketing. In this archetypal situation, the buyers have no human intermediary who acts as seller, although in providing their time, energy, and skill, they are also sellers who lack another human intermediary as buyer. The provider of the plants or the kill is usually perceived as a deity of some kind, a seller god who accepts prayers and other offerings as the price of a successful harvest or hunt.

Then, even if only in fantasy or imagination, the exchange relationship exists or is induced.

In the primitive situation, there are, of course, people with whom other marketing activities are being conducted—intimate marketing with family and friends; the barter or trade of traditional exchanges; and conventional, commercial marketing with some form of money. As soon as other people are involved, all the components of the marketing interaction are present: that which is offered, that which is desired, the location, and the telling of the nature of the exchange contents, as well as the conditions for the transaction.

Put plainly, then, *marketing is what people do when they want to provide something to, or get something from, someone else.* Because the kinds of things offered or sought vary, as do the time, place, and participants, it is possible to distinguish many categories of marketing. The providing or getting that goes on between people in their private lives, where the content of the exchanges that occur includes parental attention, filial devotion, sexual gratification, reprimanding, and teasing, may be termed *intimate marketing.*

This category is a matter of analytical perspective. Analyzed by a religious person, marriage is a sacrament; by a political scientist, it may be viewed as a power struggle or as a unit with a particular sort of voting pattern; and a lawyer may note if the marriage is legally contracted. A marketing analyst would ask what each member of the marriage offers, provides, gives—in traditional parlance, "sells"—and what each member expects in return, whether interpreted as a price or as that which he or she "buys."

From this point of view, it is not foolish or demeaning to analyze the marriage in terms of the services the wife provides, as cleaner, cook, lover, mother, and so on, the worth of those services to the husband, their market value if offered elsewhere, and what she wants or gets in return. She is providing a type of labor and, in many societies, she is herself clearly a commodity, with defined units of value. This is less clear in modern Western society, where romance is supposed to govern. Still, many men classically dislike paying the price of saying "I love you," and in consequence, marriage deals fall through. As women pursue careers outside the home, the nature of the husband–wife exchange of services is seen in a new light because it is no longer hidden in tradition.

Intimate marketing is no less marketing for seeming relatively primitive when compared to the characteristics of the major *commercial marketing* systems with their elaborated networks of communications, transportation, and product development. Similarly susceptible to marketing analysis are the aims, actions, and interactions that occur in the spheres variously delineated as *nonprofit marketing,* conducted by various social agencies, the *social marketing*[4] of prosocial goods and ideas, *political marketing*[5] of candidates and political positions, and so forth.

All this is to say that the large view of marketing being developed here seeks to go beyond the synecdochic confusion which takes part for the whole, saying that only "bad" marketing (deceptive advertising, high-pressure salespeople) is really marketing, and that marketing cannot include truthful advertisements, sellers of well-made products conscientiously offered, sales personnel of integrity, and prices fairly made. As for exploiting motives, it is probably beyond the ability of the marketing discipline to determine whether it is more virtuous to provide receivers with *what they want* or with *what they ought to have,* especially since political scientists, moral philosophers, and students of mental, social, and economic health are unable to reach consensus on the basic issue and its many ramifications. In the basic concept of marketing under discussion, these various viewpoints are themselves commodities in the marketplace of ideas, as such seekers (and purveyors) of truth as Milton and Mill have shown us.

The fundamentally simple definition of marketing as giving and getting, providing and receiving, extends in several directions. It comprises endless units for analysis by virtue of referring to all the people involved, and their status of developing and preparing offerings, and their relative inclinations to receive; dyadic (face-to-face) exchanges; individuals vis-à-vis social units, agencies, enterprises; and such organizations facing each other. The definition is impartial to the actor, and any element or interaction may become a unit of study—contrary to the custom of most texts, which focus on the sellers' viewpoints.[6] The objective is to look in both directions or in as many directions as there are participants; not to assist us in "exploiting" another (except as superior knowledge and insight have that effect), but to examine how people come to provide and to take what they do.

Given this fundamental view—that marketing is a discipline that can examine all exchange systems for what is exchanged—

and the various attendant circumstances and processes, the social system can be approached as a marketing system. Warner and Lunt had something of this basic idea in mind when they pointed out that the social regulation of behavior consists of "(1) a division of labor necessary for manipulating tools in acquiring a living from nature, and (2) a distribution of the newly formed desirable goods. The type of social organization possessed by a group will determine the allocation of pleasant and unpleasant tasks among its members as well as the sharing of the spoils. . . ."[7]

The three underlying themes of the approach to marketing developed in this book are the marketing dialogue, the sources of behavior, and the symbols in the marketplace.

The Marketing Dialogue

The market is a system composed of individuals and groups interacting and exchanging meanings. Sellers and buyers of all kinds affect one another because of the meanings attached to their actions or nonactions. The seller sends out meanings in many ways. Similarly, the customers are expressing their meanings, initiating messages, and reacting to the meanings coming from the seller. Simply, then, the marketing dialogue can be expressed as a general statement, encompassing any sellers and buyers. Figure 1 gets the message across.

Furthermore, the roles of sellers and buyers can change, with a buyer becoming a seller and vice versa. As Figure 2 shows, among those usually regarded as sellers or as buyers, an exchange of meanings (*m*) is going on as well. These subsets of buying and selling, and therefore the exchanges of meanings, are part of the richness of events that influence the complex course of the marketplace. These diagrams may help alert us to the di-

Figure 1. The marketing dialogue.

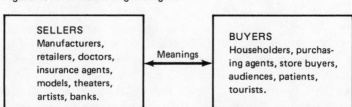

| SELLERS
Manufacturers, retailers, doctors, insurance agents, models, theaters, artists, banks. | Meanings | BUYERS
Householders, purchasing agents, store buyers, audiences, patients, tourists. |

Figure 2. Ramifications of the marketing dialogue.

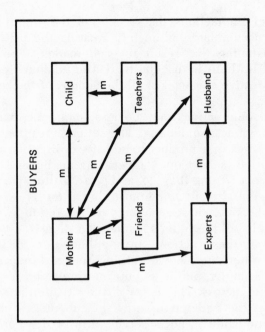

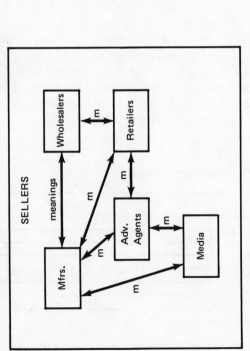

versity of interactions that occurs as the multiplicity of "dia-
logues" accumulates, ultimately creating the patterns of selling
and consuming that result in each market. The general view
summed up here is that the marketing dialogue emphasizes the
communicative character of all the actions of the sellers and buyers.

new dialogue

While some actions may be less important than others, each
adds or subtracts something. The sellers' meanings are conveyed
by the choice of a product to sell, its design, its name, package,
price, outlets, salespeople, advertising media, and messages—potentially everything they do, as Figure 3 illustrates. The product
may be central in its importance, but it too is essentially a kind
of message, one whose meanings are reacted to by customers and
modified by all the seller's marketing actions.

Some of these actions are deliberate, explicit, and direct,
whereas others are inadvertent, implicit, and indirect. But the audience (customer, public, client) interprets and reacts in terms of
what comes across. The reality of the situation may not be as important as the perception and belief about it. For example, the
Ford Foundation is not a service arm of the Ford Motor Company, but it is commonly regarded as such, hence to many people
the company seems unusually attuned to public, esthetic, and social needs. In this sense, anything a company does or appears to
do functions as a message from the company.

Similarly, from the buyers' side come actions and responses
that convey their meanings to the sellers, as shown in Figure 4.
Once again, these meanings may be direct or indirect, positive or
negative, visible or implicit.

Figure 3. Meanings from the seller.

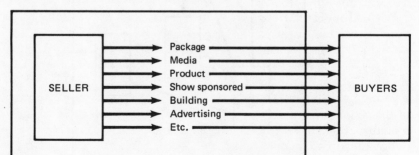

Figure 4. Meanings from the buyer.

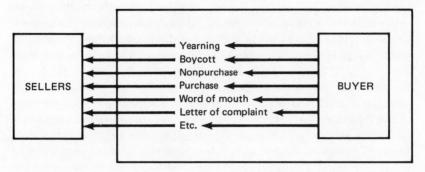

Sources of Behavior

✗ *Behavior and meaning have personal and social roots.* What are the sources of the behavior and meanings expressed by sellers and buyers? When persons behave, they are acting as individuals and are expressing something of their individual personalities. For many marketing problems it is important to study personality and its psychology in order to understand, for example, why certain consumers are eager to follow fashions, or what kinds of people are attracted to retail-store management. However, unique though they may be, people's actions are not infinitely variable to the observer. They show many commonalities and can be traced to various common circumstances. At one level, physical differences are apparent. Certain physiques and physiological characteristics are important sources of behavior and meaning. For example, size, taste buds, hair color, and amount of cholesterol in the arteries can dictate certain marketing needs, such as oversize beds, intolerance for spices, hair dye, and polyunsaturated fats.

With all their differences, people are taught and constrained by their associates in the groups they belong to. They learn to behave like proper or improper members of groups according to age, sex, social class, ethnic background, and so on. Anyone's actions will be governed to some extent by his being, for example, a young, male, Catholic, middle-class, single student, so that many of his actions will therefore differ considerably from those of, say, a mature, female, Protestant, working-class, married waitress.

But these two people could also share certain understandings and values based on overlap in personalities, for instance, enjoyment of grade B war movies. They will also share values as members of American society, having acquired broadly similar views regarding the nature of marriage, dress, government, or various social relations and customs that would mark them off in other societies as strictly American. Some forces are even more transcendental. There are outside pressures on societies, there are the effects of living in the Space Age and its changing cosmology.

Thus, behavior is a product of many sources, and any action is a distillation of the total being of a person. It reflects or expresses in a summary way the person's physical possibilities, individual feelings, ways of being a member of many groups, and cultural setting. Figure 5 depicts the origins of behavior in terms of the marketplace behavior.

Figure 5. Sources of behavior and meaning.

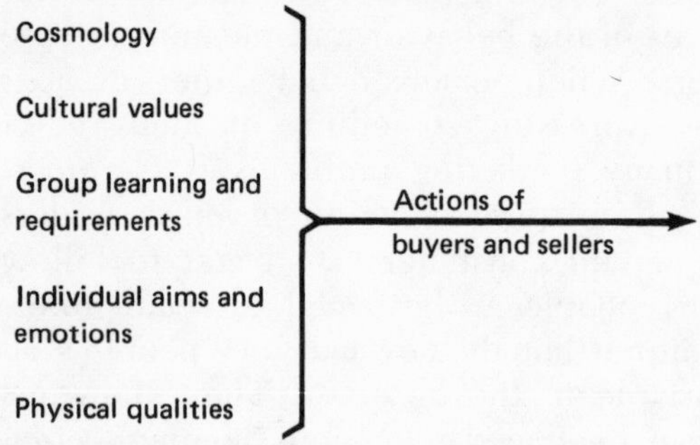

Cosmology

Cultural values

Group learning and
requirements

Individual aims and
emotions

Physical qualities

Actions of
buyers and sellers

Symbols in the Marketplace

Symbols carry the meanings that are exchanged in the marketing dialogue and that are derived from the sources of behavior. The concept of symbolism is useful because it helps us analyze and understand the meanings that are exchanged in the marketplace. Without a concept of symbolism, things just *are*, but when viewed as representations of meanings, awareness of their value and role for people is enriched.

The stress on symbolism and meaning is a dominant theme in this book in order to show the centrality of this way of thinking about behavior. It is hard to overestimate the importance of learning what things mean to people, as that is a major key to the explication of their actions. Meanings are mental attributes of objects and deeds — and people create them. Recently a court ruled that when bank customers got money from a free-standing automatic teller, it is not considered a branch bank, but if they put money into it, it is a branch bank. Rigor or consistency is not necessarily at issue, as this logic would then be extended to make all mailboxes branch banks as well. Many more examples of the ways in which marketing behavior is symbolically significant are discussed in subsequent chapters.

SUMMARY

1. Marketing behavior refers to the activities of sellers and buyers. These activities are internal (motives, logic, feelings, perceptions) and external (shopping, purchasing, storing, using, pricing).

2. All these marketing activities become represented in people's minds, thereby becoming symbolic and gaining meaning.

3. The marketing dialogue refers to the exchange of these meanings (symbols). As sellers and buyers interact, whether face-to-face or at a distance through intervening media, their actions are the resultants of the reciprocal interpretations they make.

4. These interpretations have sources in the participants' culture, group memberships, and individual personality.

References

1. Interesting examples are the comprehensive efforts by **Francesco M. Nicosia,** *Consumer Decision Processes* (Englewood Cliffs, N.J.: Prentice-Hall, 1966); **John A. Howard** and **Jagdish N. Sheth,** *The Theory of Buyer Behavior* (New York: Wiley, 1969).
2. **Philip Kotler,** "New Mathematics for Marketing Planning," in John S. Wright and Jac. L. Goldstucker (eds.), *New Ideas for Successful Marketing* (Chicago: American Marketing Association, 1966), pp. 507–528; **Arnold E. Amstutz,** *Computer Simulation of Competitive Market Response* (Cambridge, Mass.: MIT Press, 1967); and **David Aaker,** *Multivariate Analysis in Marketing: Theory and Application* (Belmont, Calif.: Wadsworth, 1971).
3. **John A. Howard,** *Marketing Theory* (Boston: Allyn and Bacon, 1965); **S.H. Britt,** *Consumer Behavior and the Behavioral Sciences* (New York: Wiley, 1966); **Scott Ward** and **Thomas S. Robertson,** *Consumer Behavior: Theoretical Sources* (Englewood Cliffs, N.J.: Prentice-Hall, 1973).
4. **Philip Kotler** and **Gerald Zaltman,** "Social Marketing: An Approach to Planned Social Change," *Journal of Marketing,* July 1971, pp. 3–12.
5. **Avraham Shama,** "Candidate Image and Voter Preference: A Theory and Experiment," doctoral dissertation, Northwestern University, Evanston, Ill., 1973.

6. **Philip Kotler** and **Sidney J. Levy,** "Buying Is Marketing Too!" *Journal of Marketing,* Jan. 1973, pp. 54–59.
7. **W. Lloyd Warner** and **Paul S. Lunt,** *The Social Life of a Modern Community* (New Haven, Conn.: Yale University Press, 1941), p. 24.

Suggested Readings

Alderson, Wroe, *Dynamic Marketing Behavior* (Homewood, Ill.: Richard D. Irwin, 1965).

Bartels, Robert, *Marketing Theory and Metatheory* (Homewood, Ill.: Richard D. Irwin, 1970).

Bartels, Robert, *The Development of Marketing Thought* (Homewood, Ill.: Richard D. Irwin, 1962).

Enis, Ben M., "Deepening the Concept of Marketing," *Journal of Marketing,* Oct. 1973, pp. 34–41.

Kotler, Philip, "A Generic Concept of Marketing," *Journal of Marketing,* Apr. 1972, pp. 46–54.

Sweeney, Daniel J., "Marketing: Management Technology or Social Process?" *Journal of Marketing,* Oct. 1972, pp. 3–10.

Tucker, W. T., "Future Directions in Marketing Theory," *Journal of Marketing,* Apr. 1974, pp. 30–35.

iii

Exploring
Marketing
Communication

If marketing exchanges are seen as a kind of dialogue in which sellers and buyers tell each other things by their words and actions, the concept of communication becomes a key idea. Ordinarily, marketing communication is understood to refer to advertising, news releases, or such messages as directives to the sales force. But here we are recognizing that all the actions taken by an organization and its representatives say things to the actual and potential members of the market. The problems of communication are many, ranging from trying to say what it is, to knowing when it is going on and how successful it is.

Never before have so many communicated with so many. The cynics wonder if it's worth all the newsprint and electricity required to make it happen. This may be a Looking-Glass Land where, to paraphrase Alice's Red Queen, it takes all the communicating you can do to stay in the same place. If you want to get somewhere, you must communicate at least twice as fast as that.

Communication can be and is studied from many vantage points. Raymond Williams notes this in the following passage:

> . . . necessarily, the communication scientist materializes in many specialized forms. He is one kind of sociologist, concerned with [these] institutions and their effects. He is one kind of engineer, concerned with [these] technologies and with the systems which are necessary to

design, understand, and control. He is one kind of cultural analyst, concerned with the meaning and values of particular artifacts and classes of artifact, from poems and paintings to films and newspapers to buildings and fashions in dress. He is one kind of psychologist, concerned with the basic units and patterns of communicative inter- action, face to face (though if we always spoke face to face, in each other's presence, the problem would be much simpler) or in the dif- ferential use of machines. Or he is one kind of linguist or linguistic philosopher, concerned with the basic forms and structures of the acts of expression and communication.[1]

In some respects, the people involved in marketing participate in all these forms of communication specialization, or can draw on them to improve their buying and selling. The institutions that the sociologist examines are in and of the marketplace, and the marketer is in them, is affected by them, and in turn affects them. Marketers are often intimately connected with the engi- neering technologies of communication and are certainly major users of the technological systems. In keeping with the central motif of this volume, the marketer (whoever he or she is—man- ager, consumer, advertising director, sales manager, purchasing agent, media buyer—and in whatever industry) is a kind of cul- tural analyst, concerned with "the meanings and values of par- ticular artifacts."

THE PURPOSE OF COMMUNICATION

According to Harold Lasswell, a convenient way to describe an act of communication is to answer the following questions:

> *Who*
> *Says What*
> *In Which Channel*
> *To Whom*
> *With What Effect?*[2]

This simple question has been elaborated into complex models of the communication process, because to answer it narrowly leaves many additional unanswered questions. If a man returning home at the end of the day is greeted by his wife saying, "I bought some lightbulbs today," to which the husband replies, "Let's try that new restaurant,"[3] what questions are aroused in our minds? The words are clear and simple. We think we know what they mean, but the husband's answer seems an odd response, which suggests that perhaps the wife was saying more than the words she said. It helps to know that the information implied by her simple declarative sentence was really telling her husband, "If you want me to fix your dinner, you will have to replace that burned-out lightbulb in the kitchen before it gets dark."

For one thing, the example implies that communication has a purpose. The purpose can be defined in various ways and at various levels, and some definitions are controversial. Communication could be limited to the idea of the transmission of a message. A frequently expressed purpose is that it provides information only. "I just wanted you to know, but I don't want you to do anything about it." But the question can be raised whether no action isn't also a kind of behavior, in this instance a compliance with the speaker's request to refrain. Furthermore, the briefest of messages carries a multiplicity of purposes, so it remains problematical whether it is possible to limit communication to just the transmission of a message.

Frank E. X. Dance, for example, asserts that the communication "in its broadest interpretation, may be defined as *the eliciting of a response*," and defines human communication as "the eliciting of a response through verbal symbols."[4] There are, of course, communications other than verbal ones, but Dance sees the eliciting of responses through verbal symbols as uniquely human.

The responses people seek to elicit through communication are as infinitely varied as each separate message may come to be. But running through them are many common threads. Joost A. M. Meerloo has listed several needs that are represented in verbal communication.[5]

The need to express. One's inner life must somehow be externalized. People speak even when no one else is around.

The need to make sounds. They are a means to achieve the purpose.

The need for contact. The crux of the matter — without other people there would be no point to it.

The need to communicate. The telling of ideas and facts, the making of words, and getting them across, form a basic human need.

The need to create. New ideas are formulated. (This is an important part of our purpose and will be returned to later.)

The need to confront the world. Communication is aggressive.

The need for individuation. Through telling and response, the person comes to achieve self-realization or self-actualization.

The need for magic control. Through communication the person is made to feel powerful.

The need to be controlled. As a participant in dialogue, one is submissive and compliant.

The more conscious need to control others. Is the response the one that was sought?

Sexual desire. Invitation, closeness, and willingness are of special importance.

The word serves as camouflage and defense mechanism. Because communication is multilayered in its implications, the apparent layer conceals other meanings.

The need to confess. The true state of affairs presses for expression, both directly and in slips, humor, and nuances.

The refusal of contact. Inhibition, withholding, and silence elicit responses to these negative actions.

When evaluating the success or failure of a communication, one criterion is how well the effect of the message corresponds to its purpose or intention. This issue is elaborated into evaluating the effectiveness of entire marketing programs, and specific advertising campaigns, of knowing whether the content of a label is accomplishing its aim, and so forth. Sometimes the intention seems simple—making a sale, getting a vote, teaching the multiplication table—but it is not always clear how any specific message is helping to accomplish that aim, and all too often no single message is adequate to achieve the goal.

It may become important to observe intervening goals: Is the audience at least receiving the message? Is the language of the message one they can understand? What does it mean to understand the message? Does true understanding include agreeing with the message? What context or preconditions are required for comprehending the message? What differences are there between those who do and those who do not respond as one would like? How can a message be evaluated when the sender's intentions are not known?

COMMUNICATION MODELS

To help study the manifold problems of communication, many approaches have been developed, and the various research workers and thinkers focus on issues of particular interest to them. One of the great steps was the development of *information theory*, a mathematical approach innovated by Shannon and Weaver.[6] By measuring the quantitative flow of information, much can be learned about relationships of bits of information to such variables as time, capacity, density of population, and structure of an information processing system. This approach ignores content or meaning, being especially concerned with the statistical probabilities of the utterance of words.

Mathematical theory is somewhat abstract as an orientation to communication. As Dance says, while information theory can tell how many bits of information are contained in the flip of a coin, it provides the same number, "whether the coin is flipped to see who buys the beer or to see who leaves the life raft so it will not sink with everybody aboard."[7] That is, most people are concerned with communication problems that must take account of the specific content of the messages.

The linguistic approach is similarly fundamental in examining relationships among elements in communication. It sometimes narrowly focuses on the writing of grammars, but more recently in the field of psycholinguistics, attention has turned to the psychological processes at work in the way language is acquired, expressed, and understood. The work of Noam Chomsky has been most influential in this field. Chomsky's central concern is of major importance to the matters discussed in this volume:

> [I take] the core problem of human language ... to be this: having mastered a language, one is able to understand an indefinite number of expressions that are new to one's experience, that bear no simple physical resemblance, and are in no simple way analogous to the expressions that constitute one's linguistic experience; and one is able, with greater or less facility, to produce such expressions on an appropriate occasion, despite their novelty and independently of detectable stimulus configurations, and to be understood by others who share this still mysterious ability. The normal use of language is, in this sense, a creative activity. This creative aspect of normal language use is one fundamental factor that distinguishes human language from any known system of animal communication.[8]

Once acquired, the everyday use of language tends to be quite repetitive and stereotyped and does not show the kind of creativity Chomsky is talking about. Part of good judgment lies in recognizing the appropriateness to a situation of repeating familiar communications because they provide the kinds of meaning (affirmation, security, chance to learn, ritual) that are called for.

Beyond such familiar routine ways in which communication serves to maintain accustomed exchanges and decisions are the possibilities for freshness, invention, novelty, and initiative. These possibilities come about because of the human ability to combine and recombine the elements of language in new ways, to move away from the content with the highest probabilities of occurrence toward more surprising ones. Sheer novelty is a basic spur to attention. Aristotle noted this in commenting that surprise was the first step to knowledge. Pavlov identified the "orienting reflex" as a physiological reaction invoked by a novel stimulus, a reaction that may disappear rapidly once the stimulus is repeated. Pavlov says:

> It is this reflex which brings about the immediate response in man and animals to the slightest changes in the world around them, so that they immediately orientate their appropriate receptor-organ in accordance with the perceptible quality in the agent bringing about the change. . . . In man this reflex has been greatly developed in its highest form by inquisitiveness — the parent of that scientific method through which we hope one day to come to a true orientation in knowledge of the world around us.[9]

This statement has broad implications for marketers. As managers of the presentation of themselves, their products, and all the means they use to provide them, make them available, and inform about them, marketers contribute to the environment of the familiar and the unfamiliar, the continuous and the discontinuous, the habitual and the surprising. To be an interesting, innovative manager, one cannot be guided merely by habit, convention, rules-of-thumb, and how-to-do-it checklists, as then the customers' orienting reflexes and inquisitiveness are less likely to be aroused.

Furthermore, as marketers who receive messages and who have to decide what to take, they have the problem of dealing with their own orienting reflexes and habitual responses and of stirring their own curiosity and creativity in handling incoming messages. The field of communications that is perhaps most directly relevant to the issues that concern marketing people is *mass communication*. Much study has been done under this heading. In his article "Mass-Communication Research: A View in Perspective"[10] David Manning White pays tribute to the many scholars who have worked to explore the nature of mass communication.

Beginning with studies of the nature of the "public" in the writings of Walter Lippmann[11] in the 1920s, studies on newspapers and their readers abounded, with special emphasis on political implications. In the 1930s, psychologists (notably Gordon W. Allport and Hadley Cantril) examined the role and impact of radio.[12] The 1940s and 1950s were a kind of golden age of communications study as psychologists, sociologists, political scientists, historians, and journalists (and many others, especially under the leadership of Samuel A. Stouffer, Robert K. Merton, Paul F. Lazarsfeld, and Bernard Berelson) delved into the various media. They explored such problems as voting behavior, media habits, the comparative effects of different media, the effectiveness of specific kinds of messages on various audiences (radio serials and housewives, television and children, Kate Smith and the purchase of war bonds), and came up with various techniques of measurement and analysis.

This tradition of inquiry continues to the present time, with persistent attention given to studying what publics, audiences, and innumerable market segments learn, under what circumstances they learn more or less, and what they do or do not do about what they learn. Such studies go on in academic institutions, the media, research companies, advertising agencies, and organizations as they try to improve their decision making.

The idea of the masses and the seeming pervasiveness and power of the mass media aroused much anxiety about what the newspapers, radio, and television might do to people. As more was learned about differential exposure and obstacles to effective persuasion, subtler theories were developed. It was necessary to take account of such elements in the communication situation as the audience's prior position, the credibility of the source, the nature of the argument, and the importance of specific kinds of appeals — fear, sex, humor. Hovland and several associates at Yale University pioneered much of this work in the 1950s.[13] Cox summarized some of the implications of the Yale studies[14] which were recently extended by Sternthal and Craig.[15]

Raymond A. Bauer pointed out flaws in the model of social communication when it acts as though "the communicator *does* something to the audience . . . [with] considerable latitude and power to do what he pleases." Bauer stresses the "transactional process in which two parties each expect to give and take from the deal."[16] Klapper dealt fully with this issue, suggesting that the joint implication of a review of communications studies casts doubt on the power of the mass media to cause (at least in any simple manner) the audience effects that often raise concern. Klapper emphasized the importance of observing the communication process phenomenologically, that is, through the perceptions of the audience, to see how the message is being processed through many "mediating variables," and serving the needs of the audience. He saw mass media as contributing to *reinforce* people's beliefs. Many problems, for example, the effects of media on socialization of children, still pose open questions.[17]

These theories and problems should probably be of interest and concern to all citizens and marketers. More specifically, since marketers have the job of presenting messages to their customers and suppliers, it is useful to them to have means of assessing or evaluating communications, a basis for raising questions and hypotheses about what kinds of messages to send forth and why. Marketers need to think about the elements available to them. If they want to do routine maintenance management that does not go beyond what is traditional and safe, all they need is a job and someone to imitate, and need think no further. However, if they want to be managers who are in tune with the changing world they work in, and who are aware that they progress toward the unknown with large or small creative steps, then they are like the artist who does not want to be a copyist, but who wants to learn the basic elements of line and color and something of how they work in order to use them in an individual way.

THE CONDITIONS OF SUCCESS IN COMMUNICATIONS

In keeping with the philosophy of this book, the heading of this section is not meant to suggest a discussion of how to be successful in communicating, any more than one could tell an artist how to paint a successful painting. (Sir Joshua Reynolds once told an audience of artists that it was not possible to paint a masterpiece with a central blue mass. Whereupon Gainsborough, who was in the audience, went home and painted *Blue Boy*, which may or may not be a masterpiece, but was certainly successful.) Rather, the purpose is to note some of the ideal conditions or general requirements that appear to play a part when communication does achieve some desired effects.

In a classic paper, "How Communication Works,"[18] one of the major workers in the field of mass communications, Wilbur Schramm, ranges across the many levels of communication, analyzing some of the complexities in conveying and receiving messages. Schramm developed a model in which sources transmit messages to their destinations by means of encoding and decoding. The communication process is viewed as cyclic or transactional in character because feedback is recognized, but the focus is on the sender's viewpoint, or on the sending phase in the communication cycle. The emphasis is on what one needs to know to judge "what a given kind of communication does to people." Despite this "does to people" idea, which seems to see the source as active and the destination as passive, Schramm goes on to discuss conditions that show that the destination is not merely a passive agent, implying that much should be known about the receiver to accomplish the goal of a particular communication.

One of the common assumptions about communication is the notion that communicating consists in reproducing the content of one mind in the mind of another. "Do you understand?" tends to inquire whether the other person now has the same mental content as the sender of the message. This is a "hydraulic" concept of communication, as though thoughts were flowing from the vessel of the source into the vessel of the destination. However, it is often apparent that there are obstacles to this flow. Perhaps the receiver of the message is unable to understand, lacking the intellectual equipment. Sometimes there is the frustrating realization that he or she simply *will* not understand. The audience resists, refuses, or possibly seems to accept and agree with the message, but will not do what is wanted. How many times does a sales pitch go this way? The prospect listens, may even nod comprehendingly and say "I see," but then says, "no sale." The community of understanding that would produce a completely successful communication falls short because there are defenses against total submission, operating as a force of competing ideas and wishes.

Still, given a specific purpose for communicating an idea (the marketer's aim in the marketing dialogue), one wants to have some way of judging what is likely to happen. As Schramm says, "Every time we insert an advertisement in a newspaper, put up a sign, explain something to a class, scold a child, write a letter, or put our political candidate on radio or television, we are making a prediction about the effect communication will have."[19] He then lists the conditions or requirements that may guide communicators toward the effectiveness they desire.

1. The message must be so designed and delivered as to gain the attention of the intended destination.
2. The message must employ signs which refer to experience common to source and destination, in order to "get the meaning across."
3. The message must arouse personality needs in the destination and suggest some ways to meet those needs.
4. The message must suggest a way to meet those needs which is appropriate to the group situation in which the destination finds himself at the time when he is moved to make the desired response.

You can see, by looking at these requirements, why the expert communicator usually begins by finding out as much as he can about his intended destination, and why 'know your audience' is the first rule of practical mass communication. For it is important to know the right timing for a message, the kind of language one must use to be effective, and the group standards in which the desired action will have to take place. This is relatively easy in face-to-face communication, more difficult in mass communication. In either case, it is necessary.

Let us talk about these four requirements.

1. *The message must be so designed and delivered as to gain the attention of the intended destination.* This is not so easy as it sounds. For one thing, the message must be made available. There will be no communication if we don't talk loud enough to be heard, or if our letter is not delivered, or if we smile at the right person when she isn't looking. And even if the message is available, it may not be selected. . . . The designing of a message for attention, then, involves timing, and placing, and equipping it with cues which will appeal to the receiver's interests.
2. *The message must employ signs which refer to experience common to both source and destination, in order to "get the meaning across. . . ."* In designing a message we have to be sure not only that we speak the 'same language' as the receiver, and that we don't 'write over his head,' but also that we don't conflict too directly with the way he sees and catalogs the world. There are some circumstances, true, in which it works well to conflict directly, but for the most part these are the circumstances in which our understandings and attitudes are not yet firm or fixed, and they are relatively few and far between. . . .
3. *The message must arouse personality needs in the destination and suggest some ways to meet those needs.* The first requisite of an effective message . . . is that it relate itself to one of our personality

needs—the needs for security, status, belongingness, understanding, freedom from constraint, love, freedom from anxiety, and so forth. It must arouse a drive. It must make the individual feel a need or a tension which he can satisfy by action. Then the message can try to control the resulting action by suggesting what action to take. . . .

4. *The message must suggest a way to meet those needs which is appropriate to the group situation in which the destination finds himself at the time when he is moved to make the desired response.* We live in groups. We get our first education in the primary group of our family. We learn most of our standards and values from groups. We learn roles in groups, because those roles give us the most orderly and satisfying routine of life. We make most of our communication responses in groups. And if communication is going to bring about change in our behavior, the first place we look for approval of this new behavior is to the group. . . .[20]

Schramm's paper provides a good beginning for a perspective on communication in the marketplace as well as for the rest of this volume. He points out that the message (anything the marketer does in the marketing dialogue) must offer a way to meet the audience's needs in a manner appropriate to the group situation in which the person is found at the time. This means that the human setting for the receiver's actions is important. The setting expresses group membership and participation.

The word "group" can be understood in two fundamental ways: in terms of the immediate situation and in terms of certain forces. It may refer to the people in the "immediate" environment, whether the customer is watching television, walking through the supermarket, driving a car, or sending a written complaint to the marketing manager. In each of these instances, only those things will be done that are regarded as fitting to the setting. For example, some consumers are conscientious about using coupons to buy the brand that sent them to the store. On the other hand, if the grocer isn't fussy about it they might try to use the coupons as money to buy any brand. What about the letter of complaint? The marketing services manager may send it to the customer relations department because that is what the other people in the office expect, or may just file it because the others will not notice.

A broader interpretation of the "group situation" refers to those forces that act upon buyers of the same age, ethnic background, occupation, social class, or other population. To the extent that they adhere to the standards and requirements of these groups (whether other people are present or not), a communication must fit these standards and requirements if it is to coincide with the aims of both the customer and the source of the message. The general principle to which Schramm refers in his fourth point, then, underlies the necessity to study the nature of group membership, how being part of a culture, a society, or any social group affects the behavior of buyers and sellers. Chapters IV through VII discuss the kinds of analysis and input that bear on this issue.

Schramm's third point concerning successful communication states that the message must arouse personality needs and must suggest ways to meet those needs. Some knowledge of psychology is essential if communicators are to be aware of what they are doing and the means to achieve their goals. It is not enough to identify the groups that make up the market. Their personality needs and dynamics and how these are expressed in the social roles they play have to be studied in order to think sensibly about their marketing behavior and how to deal with it meaningfully. A simple list of human needs won't do the trick. Discussion and readings about the social and psychological context for marketing activity help the marketer assess the kinds of people sellers and buyers are. Knowing this, one can formulate *what* to say to them. Chapter VIII explores some of the problems and possibilities of psychological analysis.

This leaves the basic issue of *how* to say it. It is the crux of adept marketing management that what comes across should have a "goodness of fit." Schramm says that to do this "the message must employ *signs which refer to experience common to source and destination.*" The "sign" may be the product or service itself, its pricing, distribution channels, advertising — any means of coming to know about it. The critical question is, what does it mean to the receiver? The answer to this question entails a study of signs and symbols, of how people perceive and interpret what they encounter in the marketplace. Symbolism and the issue of meaning must be addressed throughout the discussions of culture, group influences, and psychological dynamics. They are explored more specifically in Chapters IX and X in terms of their role in the commercial marketing situation, especially as sellers' tools.

SUMMARY

1. All marketing actions are communications. They carry implications and are interpreted by customers.

2. It is therefore imperative for managers to study marketing communications in order to conceptualize the meaning of successful communication and how it is to be achieved.

3. Communication involves all human needs, and the nature of both familiar and novel messages requires analysis and creative application. There has been much study, but the astute use of communication remains an open and competitive challenge.

4. Schramm's criteria for evaluating the effectiveness of communication specify a desired response as well as the major conditions for eliciting it. These conditions are highly ramified. They reinforce the necessity to think about behavior at all the levels summed up in Chapter II and taken up in more detail in the following chapters.

References

1. Raymond Williams, "Communications as Cultural Science," *Journal of Communication*, Summer 1974, pp. 17–18.
2. Harold D. Lasswell, "The Structure and Function of Communication in Society," in Lyman Bryson (ed.), *The Communication of Ideas* (New York: Cooper Square Publishers, 1964), p. 37.
3. George A. Miller, "Human Communication," in Eugene H. Kone and Helene J. Jordan (eds.), *The Greatest Adventure* (New York: The Rockefeller University Press, 1974), p. 259.
4. Frank E. X. Dance, *Human Communication Theory* (New York: Holt, Rinehart and Winston, 1967), p. 289.
5. Paraphrased from Joost A. M. Meerloo, "Contributions of Psychiatry to the Study of Human Communication," in Frank E. X. Dance (ed.), *Human Communication Theory* (New York: Holt, Rinehart and Winston, 1967), pp. 153–155.
6. C. E. Shannon and W. Weaver, *The Mathematical Theory of Communication* (Urbana: The University of Illinois Press, 1949).
7. Op. cit., p. 292.
8. Noam Chomsky, "Form and Meaning in Natural Language," in John D. Roslansky (ed.), *Communication* (Amsterdam: North-Holland, 1969), p. 65.
9. I. P. Pavlov, *Complete Works*, Book IV (Moscow-Leningrad, Academia Nauk, 1940–1947).
10. Lewis A. Dexter and David Manning White (eds.), *People, Society, and Mass Communications* (New York: The Free Press, 1964), pp. 521–546.
11. Walter Lippmann, *Public Opinion* (New York: Macmillan, 1922); see also Walter Lippmann, *The Phantom Public* (New York: Harcourt, Brace, Jovanovich, 1925).

12. Gordon W. Allport and Hadley Cantril, *The Psychology of Radio* (New York: Harper & Row, 1935).
13. Carl I. Hovland, Irving L. Janis, and Harold H. Kelley, *Communication and Persuasion* (New Haven, Conn.: Yale University Press, 1953).
14. Donald F. Cox, "Clues for Advertising Strategies," *Harvard Business Review*, Sept.–Oct. 1961/Nov.–Dec. 1961.
15. Brian Sternthal and C. S. Craig, "Fear Appeals: Revisited and Revised," *Journal of Consumer Research*, December 1974; see also Brian Sternthal and C. S. Craig, "Humor in Advertising," *Journal of Marketing*, Oct. 1973, pp. 12–18.
16. Raymond A. Bauer, "The Obstinate Audience: The Influence Process from the Point of View of Social Communication," *American Psychologist*, May 1964, p. 516.
17. Joseph T. Klapper, *The Effects of Mass Communication* (New York: The Free Press, 1960).
18. Wilbur Schramm (ed.), *The Process and Effects of Mass Communication* (Urbana: University of Illinois Press, 1955), pp. 3–26.
19. Ibid., p. 12.
20. Ibid., p. 16.

Suggested Readings

Berlo, David K., *The Process of Communication* (New York: Holt, Rinehart and Winston, 1960).
Cherry, Colin, *On Human Communication* (Cambridge, Mass.: MIT Press, 1966).
Davison, W. Phillips, *International Political Communication* (New York: Frederick A. Praeger for the Council on Foreign Relations, 1965).
Duncan, Hugh D., *Communication and Social Order* (New York: Bedminster Press, 1962).
Hertzler, Joyce O., *A Sociology of Language* (New York: Random House, 1965).
Katz, Elihu, and Paul F. Lazarsfeld, *Personal Influence: The Part Played by People in the Flow of Mass Communications* (New York: The Free Press, 1955).
Meier, Richard L., *A Communication Theory of Urban Growth* (Cambridge, Mass.: MIT Press, 1962).
Reusch, Jurgen, and Gregory Bateson, *Communication* (New York: Norton, 1951).
Schramm, Wilbur L., *Mass Communication: A Book of Readings* (Urbana: University of Illinois Press, 1960). *The Science of Human Communication* (New York: Basic Books, 1965).
Smith, Alfred B. (ed.), *Communication and Culture* (New York: Holt, Rinehart and Winston, 1966).

iv
Culture
and
Meaning

The types of explanation (or search) for understanding in marketing vary according to the necessities posed by different problems. Thus, physical distribution systems are analyzed if goods are to move, demand curves are studied to help marketers work out prices, and color research provides useful information for making decisions about package visibility on shelves. Areas of inquiry also depend largely on the taste and characteristic orientation of the various marketers and on the kinds of knowledge they find congenial for their approaches to problems.

In Western society, a practical, rationalistic approach predominates, with much reliance on the security of quantification of analytic elements.[1] The inferences made tend to stay close to the facts of overt phenomena and measurements that seem related by rather conventional reasoning. Even in the behavioral sciences, which generally focus on social psychology and radiate especially to attitudes, social stratification, and psychographics, attention again goes to scales, classifications, and the adding up of discrete items.

By comparison, the discipline and traditions of anthropology play a small role in marketing thought. Some lip service may be given, but there is little elaboration, development, or study. And when an anthropological approach is considered, it usually does not seem useful. The anthropologist's level of generalization is seen as too broad and encompassing a view to help with the multitudinous small marketing problems that come up in daily life.

From another perspective, if anthropology is the study of humankind, then everything we do and all forms of study are, by definition, aspects of anthropology — ways of working closer in on components of the total problem. Thus, like the man who was so pleased to learn he spoke prose, we can be gratified to recognize that in studying marketing, we are already "doing anthropology." However, anthropology also exists as a set of specialties[2] which vary in their interest for marketers.

THE CONCEPT OF CULTURE

The behavior of sellers and buyers can be analyzed at many levels. How people act, what they tend to think about and find important, and what their customary ways are can be partly understood at one level as a reflection of the nature of the society in which they grew up and where they live. What is the role and influence of the culture? "Culture" refers to the broad matrix of a society, to those aspects of its life that govern the kinds of objects it has (its material culture) and that govern its characteristic language, morality, art, and science.

There are many definitions of culture. According to a very broad definition, "Culture is the sum total of what human beings learn in common with other members of the group to which they belong."[3] This definition allows us to refer to Western culture, the culture of poverty, the culture of any given society.

The study of culture — a pursuit ordinarily considered the province of anthropologists — may seem a remote activity for marketing people. But is its value more than academic? Here are some of the reasons why marketing managers should definitely study culture.

1. Culture is one of the ways of explaining how and why consumers, buyers, clients, and publics behave in their interactions with marketers. The action of the American who refuses to eat snails or who buys guns may be accounted for by a personal aversion to seafood or by an enjoyment of being a hunter. But these are not isolated attitudes. They are learned, and they prevail in a society that generally discourages the eating of snails, but admires the skillful hunter.

2. Most generally, the study of culture enlarges thinking and perspectives. It fosters an awareness of the large contexts of action and of the fundamental themes that underlie behavior. In effect, marketers who study American culture are learning about themselves and about areas that might otherwise be overlooked because they are so obvious and taken for granted in this environment. It is hard to take a fresh look at familiar objects, but that is just what is needed to come up with new marketing ideas.

3. Marketers who understand something about their culture are in a position to appreciate the influence of broad social processes on marketing. Someone who is immersed in a social process without understanding the larger scene may merely become its victim. An example might be a merchant who rents a store in a changing neighborhood without being aware of the urban blight that is creeping in and apt to overtake the enterprise within the next few years. Many marketers show no particular sensitivity to the characteristic values of the American people and how they are being modified. Others use personal observation, general reading, analyses reported in the media, and the findings of research to maintain a sense of perspective on their society.

4. Commercial marketing is itself not only profoundly affected by the cultural processes in which it is embedded, but it is also a force that changes the culture. Many firmly believe that marketers cannot be indifferent to that fact. Marketers must think about the effects their actions may have on the social system, on minorities, on child development, and on the environment. This belief fuels controversy about control of energy resources, pollution, violence on television, pressing such corporations as General Motors and J. Walter Thompson to evaluate their sponsorship policies.

5. The growth of international marketing tends to reward those who can adapt to the demands made when different cultures meet. To study a foreign market is to study a foreign culture, to encounter its strange customs, its novel laws, its different ways of thinking and talking. This knowledge aids, but is not a substitute for, judgment and freedom of action. As Joseph McGuire points out:

> A cultural approach to business behavior uncovers the obvious patterns and interwoven structures which serve as guidelines for and limits to business actions, and often discloses those subtle and underlying means and goals of behavior. . . .[4]

Cultural theories are informative only of "proper" or "normal" cultural behavior, and do not serve as precise guidelines for action. In any given business situation there may be several alternative courses of action which are satisfactorily within the cultural framework.[5]

Understanding a culture contributes to a sense of the possibilities within its framework. Once you have a grasp of the current stage of the society, your marketing expectations may be tempered considerably. Marketing and cultural settings interact, just as culture and technological progress do. Robert L. Heilbroner points to the state of readiness that varies in different cultures.

> The Kalahari bushmen or the tribesmen of New Guinea, for instance, have persisted in a neolithic technology to the present day; the Arabs reached a high degree of proficiency in the past and have since declined; the classical Chinese developed technical expertise in some fields while unaccountably neglecting it in the area of production ... the system of interchangeable parts, first introduced into France and then independently into England, failed to take root in either country for lack of government interest or market stimulus. Its success in America is attributable mainly to government support and to .its appeal in a society without guild traditions and with high labor costs.[6]

6. Not the least of the values of cultural perspective is its potential benefit in putting to rest or easing the prescription that marketing should concern itself with satisfying needs — not with products and advertising that arouse unnecessary wants, a distinction of dubious reality. It may be that scarce resources and an impossible population will eventually put everyone at a subsistence level. But even then, people in different areas and of different historical backgrounds will probably not subsist in the same way. They will insist on having a culture, having wants and trying to satisfy them in their own peculiar ways. Beyond survival, there are only wants — to do it, whatever it is, one preferred way or another.

A BROAD LEVEL OF ANALYSIS

A culture is the net result, the aggregation, accumulation, and interaction of preferred ways among any given group of people. When we look back and try to reconstruct the pattern of a culture from the traces of its passage — its artifacts, its movements, its skeletons, its refuse, and its environment—we call it archaeology. Modern marketing study may be thought of as the archaeology of contemporary life, learning about the meaning of current objects while the users and what they have lying around are available to tell us about them. It is still a detective's task, the piecing together of a puzzle, but there is a lot more data around. A special recent example of a rather literal sort is the examination of household garbage.

Anthropologists, like others, are in a constant struggle against the problems of deciding what level to generalize on. Comparing many societies, one can be oriented toward the largest generalizations—What are the most profound and most general characteristics of humankind? Or one may be more impressed by, or more eager to demonstrate, human diversity. The only ultimate truth possible is that humans are both fundamentally the same and obviously different. Both emphases have their partisans and are used to advance or to fight ethnocentric biases. The weapons used are as varied as the subspecialties in anthropology: race, linguistics, the size of baboon brains, decorations on shards of pottery.

An overview of the meaning of culture can be gained from various directions. A useful place to start is with the environment, since cultures represent the ways in which human groups adapt to and use their environment. A people may do little to protect themselves from their environment and may be casual in gathering food if the elements are mild and growth plentiful. Another group may have to cultivate the soil arduously or hunt long and hard. Different conditions will influence the language spoken (Eskimos understandably have many words for different types and states of snow); the complexity of the economy; the social relationships; and the technology of tools, weapons, and machinery. In an elaborately developed culture it is possible to control the very air with cooling, filtering, and dehumidification and to have a market system that is far-flung and abstract in the nature of its exchange, rather than local and face-to-face.

We find cross-cultural study generally intriguing because it feeds curiosity about exotic ways and permits members of one culture to feel superior or inferior to another. Just as we say that the bland person has no personality, despite the psychologist's contention that everyone has a personality, so we call one group uncultured, even though it does have a culture in scientific terms. These views reflect values being placed on vivacity or sociability in the individual as well as on some preferred elaboration and cultivation of esthetic experience in the society.

However judged, among the contents and forms of cultures are the objects and behaviors, the providing and receiving which comprise their marketing. Margaret Mead once commented to the effect that 15 minutes in the commercial marketplace of a strange people was enough to tell her what the people were like, implying the intimate relationship of the market to the character of the people (and Dr. Mead's perspicacity).

Here are excerpts from two classics which bring out the way anthropologists approach the content of marketing. The first is by Franz Boas on the *potlatch* of the Kwakiutl Indians.

> Before proceeding any further it will be necessary to describe the method of acquiring rank. This is done by means of the potlatch, or the distribution of property. . . . The underlying principle is that of the interest-bearing investment of property. . . . Possession of wealth is considered honorable. . . . But it is . . . the ability to give great festivals which make wealth a desirable object . . . rising in the social scale . . . may be done by inviting the rival and his clan or tribe to a festival and giving him a considerable number of blankets. He is compelled to accept these . . . he must repay the gift with 100 per cent interest. . . . The rivalry between chiefs and clans finds its strongest expression in the destruction of property. A chief will burn blankets, a canoe, or break a copper, thus indicating his disregard of the amount of property destroyed and showing that his mind is stronger, his power greater, than that of his rival.[7]

Similarly, Bronislaw Malinowski provides an extensive analysis of the *kula*.

> The Kula is a form of exchange, of extensive, inter-tribal character; it is carried on by communities inhabiting a wide ring of islands, which form a closed circuit. This circuit joins a number of islands to the North and East of the east end of New Guinea. Along this route, articles of two kinds, and these two kinds only, are constantly travelling in opposite directions. In the direction of the hands of a clock, moves constantly one of these kinds — long necklaces of red shell, called *soulava*. In the opposite direction moves the other kind — bracelets of white shell called *mwali*. Each of these articles, as it travels in its own direction on the closed circuit, meets on its way articles of the other class, and is constantly being exchanged for them. Every movement of the Kula articles, every detail of the transactions is fixed and regulated by a set of traditional rules and conventions, and some acts

of the Kula are accompanied by an elaborate magical ritual and public ceremonies.[8]

Both Malinowski and Boas go on to discuss at length the systems of exchange they are analyzing as they indicate the various rules, regulations, requirements, rewards, and losses involved.

A DEEP UNDERSTANDING

The largeness of view taken in a perspective on a culture may seem either superficial or not at all helpful to the marketer who wants analyses that appear more immediately actionable, more immediately results-oriented. In actuality, the large view may also be a deep one, as it looks for the underlying values that can explain otherwise disparate bits of behavior. An expansive concept is also essential for interpreting general phenomena, such as the relative failure of the bidet to diffuse into American plumbing. It is not enough to say that American bathrooms are too small. There have to be cultural reasons for rejecting the bidet, since it is a permanent fixture in many French bathrooms.

It is a relatively superficial use of cross-cultural study to learn not to make foolish mistakes, such as advertising beefburgers in India; using the wrong color for mourning; or using *shi* for the number 4 in Japan, when it also is the word for death. After all, one can't pretend to know everything about any group—one's own or anyone else's (and many Indians do eat beef). However, such information is an improvement.

A further and more penetrating orientation among social and cultural anthropologists involves analysis of meaning. Many anthropologists are distinguished by their attention to things that are important to the people being studied. These workers want to learn the significance of the cultural events. They become involved in analyzing relatively basic themes, searching for what binds them together in a coherent pattern. Of special fascination to these anthropologists are such notions as creation, birth, child-rearing, kinship, incest, deference and degradation, the role of the gift, the sacred and the profane, the beautiful and the ugly. Commonly, such themes infuse the minutiae of everyday life with implications and bases for marketing action.

One of the traditionally unfortunate deficiencies of formal marketing lies in its reluctance to deal with the less tangible realms of explanations of human behavior. Given to a narrow sense of realism and practicality and the tenacious grip of the economic mind, marketers tend to resist areas of understanding that have to do with symbols, myths, legends, arbitrary belief, and fantasy. Marketing texts make a few gingerly references to symbolism or handle it largely as a technical aspect of communication. Despite the avid involvement of humanity in song, dance, pictures, movies, fairy tales, folktales, novels, science fiction, and Agatha Christie, marketing studies are likely to restrict themselves to a narrow concern with product features and pricing variations.

But everywhere yearnings, aspirations, and interpersonal relations are laden with magical, superstitious, mystical, and religious significance, with private imageries, sentiments, cosmic theories, and ways of relating to nature. Malinowski sees the *kula* ring as comparable in meaning to the crown jewels of England and the collecting of sports trophies, according to the forces of tradition, sentiment, and pride that most people experience.

Perhaps the closest that marketing comes to an appreciation of these vital forces is in the field of advertising, in which fantasy, song, and dance are given play, with some awareness of the mythic intrigue inherent in these forces. The repressive forces of the Federal Trade Commission, obsessed with literalness, will probably be unable to do much to protect us from the strange power of Mrs. Olson, Marlboro Country, and the Real Thing.

INTRACULTURAL CONFLICT

Generalizations about a culture are made up of abstractions about the nature of human beings as they structure their society to encompass the particular forms of institutions and processes such as education, advertising, health care, and the treatment of offspring. These issues are translated into products and services. In turn, the products may also become the issues, being transformed from social issues into commercial marketing practices that are themselves controversial. For example, attitudes toward the elderly and the role they play in society have brought about Social Security, Medicare, new institutional arrangements, medical profiteering, and new health services.

All products and services have a moral component, reflecting a challenge to the society's position on their existence. Campbell's vegetable soup is a benign example with few who would condemn it. More dramatic examples are contraceptives, cigarettes, abortions, lotteries, and Sunday hours. Marketing research surveys may show the proportions of people who take one position or another, but the statistical results are usually offered with little analysis or interpretation of the cultural situation. However, the fact of such cultural conflict has gained more attention of late, stirred especially by problems of consumer protestation, pollution, and the assertion of demands by groups in the society pressing for liberation.[9]

Social marketing and commercial marketing problems interact, as they are really different ways of looking at the same phenomena: What may be sold in the society, and how? Social marketing conflict is not merely a matter of competing ideologies. As with other entities in the marketplace, the ideas have partisans, come from ideological entrepreneurs or sympathetic organizations, have sellers who hawk them, and have media outlets suited to various marketing segments.

Social marketing differs from competitive commercial marketing because the response of the audience is not easily converted into monetary units that allow conventional calculation of gain and profit (although often money contributions are also sought, making the fund-raising a marketing activity in itself). Social marketers seek to profit in other ways, to triumph in achieving, or moving toward, their goals of support, legislation, and social change, against the groups in society that oppose these goals or prefer others.

In endless contention, the infinitely segmented population sustains these conflicts. No position is so virtuous in the eyes of all or so universally approved that others will not disagree with it, find it imperfect or evil, and seek to prevent its dominion. Consequently, some consumers are apathetic about efforts on their behalf, and some oppose consumer advocacy, finding the proposed cure worse than the disease.[10] Many women do not want the Equal Rights Amendment passed. Some blacks fight against busing. Thus, every situation contains multiple values that can be emphasized to incline those affected in different directions.

The following pages are devoted to an extended example of how a specific object—the tree—is regarded by various members of society. The analysis was originally made at the behest of the Southern Forest Products Association to communicate to its members why some people are opposed to the cutting of trees.

REACTIONS TO THE CUTTING OF TREES

One way of analyzing reactions to the cutting of trees is to examine the rhetoric people use in putting forth their views and their formal opinions. People's choice of language, its tone, the kinds of words that recur, and the figures of speech they use to express their feelings clothe their ideas with implications and justifications that will make their positions plausible. Whatever the emotional sources of the positions taken, a thought structure arises, with values being stated and reasoning offered to defend them. Thus, each position has not only its rhetoric, but its logic of appropriate ideas, its claim to certain facts, and recommended actions. In the background are deep-seated beliefs and emotions, some of which will be interpreted here.

People who most differ often refuse to debate on the same ground. They confine their attention to the elements that are most meaningful to them. This attitude is apparent in the literature on forests and tree cutting, in which three main positions emerge, with several variations.

Woodsman — Chop That Tree

On the one hand are those who clearly believe that tree cutting is essential, that demand is outstripping supply, and that almost any means are justified to obtain the needed lumber. The basic view these people have of trees and forests is cut-and-dried: the tree is an economic resource. Concerns are with the number of feet of lumber, the changing distribution system, and the various bases for increasing yield and rate of return. A typical article of this kind in *Forest Science*[11] reports a study of two criteria — net present value versus internal rate of return — to determine which is preferable. The article concludes that in the Southern industrial forest, the optimum rotation age is more sensitive to changes in factors, such as stumpage rates and annual fixed costs, if the rate of return criterion is maximized. This language and these ideas are a far cry from those of concern to the environmentalists and conservationists, and show no interest in the issues they raise.

Wide open spaces. Moving along the continuum, there are those who do take notice of the people who object to tree cutting, and speaking as silviculturalists or as industry spokesmen, assert directly opposing views. Fred C. Simmons is especially vigorous in this direction. In two characteristic articles,[12] one of which was titled "Woodsman–Chop That Tree," Simmons argues that the natural way is bad, that leaving forests alone results in an ecological desert. It is better to let in more sunlight than the wilderness permits, and better to use the forest for needed wood products. *Commerce Today*[13] fears for the industry with so much competition coming from highways, dams, cities, and suburbs. Even more eager to show that tree cutting is a good thing, Hagenstein[14] says that "clearcutting is silviculturally sound," for one thing, because it provides esthetically pleasing open spaces in forests.

Woodsman–Spare That Tree

At the opposite end of the spectrum are those who seem relatively indifferent to the consumers' need for lumber, paper, and wooden products. Partly, this group assumes that the forces that will provide the products are strong, especially as they are apt to believe that the government either does not know how to control the industry or is on its side. They see several villains: the Executive Office with its complex economic dealings that dominate smaller companies, the Forest Service, and "narrowly oriented forestry school" graduates who seek to deny that U.S. forests are being abused. In his discussion of "Our Export Forest,"[15] Robinson maintains that unless exportation of private timber is controlled, enlightened forestry practices stand little chance of implementation. *Business Week*[16] examines the struggle and notes the polarity, saying that the industry practices of clearcutting, regeneration with single-species supertrees, and unregulated use of private land fly in the face of conservationist and preservationist interests.

Ecological purism–through thick and thin. The extremists of these interests reason that "enlightened practices" in forests are impossible. They are not merely skeptical of their success–they believe that any interference with the forest is detrimental to it. Michael Thomas[17] and Clifford E. Ahlgren[18] perceive the forest's own cyclical destruction and renewal as essential patterns and any human intervention as a serious threat to the sensitive equilibrium established over thousands of years of continuous natural development.

Forest Management Takes a Stand

As might be expected, between the extreme positions has developed a middle ground in which the main issues center around forest management to find ways of resolving the need to chop down the trees, yet preserve the forest. Even here, the controversy is active, with vigorous voices proclaiming the advantages or the hazards of forest management. Robert W. Upton[19] says, "You can't preserve a tree forever, but you can manage a forest." Marlin C. Galbraith[20] concludes that wood-product crops are compatible with other environmental values. Somewhat triumphantly, Charles W. Bingham[21] relates that thinning, fertilizing, selection, and crop rotation help regenerate logged-over land. He says that managed forests increase yields per acre, the amount of available oxygen to meet the trees' biological oxygen demand, watershed, and wildlife, and provide recreational parks and scenery. Putting his faith in enhancing the environment through science and technology, Bingham maintains that intensified forest management is the key.

But it is apparent that many cautions are needed. Maki[22] looks at the pros and cons of clearcutting and points out that practices should be tailored to fit soil, landform, climate, and species. Similarly, Resler[23] finds that clearcutting has benefits for wildlife resources, but requires the careful application of scientific knowledge. To many, the benefits of clearcutting, even-aged management, and prescribed burning do not offset the aspects detrimental to wildlife resources. Pengelly[24] writes that the benefits may not be compatible with intensive forest management, especially with scarifying, tree planting, fencing, and poisoning. Since we have discovered that forests need fires, the notion that we may as well help them along with prescribed burning does not serve to reassure those who are skeptical of humankind's record of controlling our environment.

The Protection of Trees

Cutting trees used to be an immediate necessity to pioneering, clearing a space, and building a home. The imagery of Lincoln the rail-splitter raised no clamorous protestations from his contemporary tree lovers. The tradition of the lumberjack, of Paul Bunyan, of log-rolling contests, of the exciting cry of "Timberrrr!" was an all-American part of childhood lore. The connection between tree cutting and the necessity for shelter, warmth, and safety was strong enough, when joined with the magnitude of the forests, to overcome resistance to tree cutting.

But resistance to tree cutting is not a new phenomenon, as witness the old story of George Washington and the cherry tree. George Pope Morris wrote his classic little poem, "Woodsman, Spare That Tree!" more than a century ago. Now the resistance has grown greatly. Not long ago, the following item appeared in the newspaper:

> *Vienna (AP)* Which comes first, the animals or the trees? The latter won out in a referendum in which voters decided against plans for a zoology institute to be built in a Vienna park. The construction would have required chopping down about 70 trees.

Despite our widespread lethargy in the face of conservation issues, this incident and the many others in which citizens have chained themselves to trees to thwart the bulldozer point to the potential support available to environmentalists and conservationists. As leaders, they can sometimes awaken in others a not very dormant impulse to protect the trees, as suggested by the rest of the Morris poem:

> *Woodsman, spare that tree!*
> *Touch not a single bough!*
> *In youth it sheltered me,*
> *And I'll protect it now.*

To understand this desire to protect the tree, let us analyze it on several levels. First, what are the meanings of trees and forests as interpreted by tradition in folktale, myth, and religion? Second, what do people say about trees? What are their specific associations? Third, how might these ideas relate to the people who are especially anxious to preserve the wilderness?

The Tree as Symbol

Forests have a notable place within the general symbolism of landscape. Cirlot[25] connects forest symbolism with the idea of the Great Mother. It is a place "where vegetable life thrives and luxuriates." Free from any control or cultivation, dense and dark, obscuring the sun with its foliage, the tree also represents the unconscious impulses that threaten in the shapes of snakes, wolves and, as in a Disney cartoon, trees that reach out to tear at someone racing terrified through the forest. Forests, harboring dangers, demons, enemies, and disease, were among the first places in nature to be dedicated to the cult of the gods.

The forest is also a challenge in humanity's endless contest with nature, to its capacity to survive in the face of the worst. As in the Dickey story *Deliverance*, the forest raises the question, Can humanity contend with the primitive nature of the wilderness and emerge unscathed from the awful forces of wild waters and uninhibited sexuality? The answer may be "no," but people still want to go off to the woods where civilization does not make its demands for sobriety, shaving, proper dress, and language.

The mythology of the tree is, if anything, even richer than that of the forest, being "one of the most essential of traditional symbols."[26] The tree has been interpreted as standing for the life of the cosmos—sometimes the idea of life without death, since people are often impressed with the longevity of individual trees as well as the continuity of the family of the tree. The relationship to the tree is a holy one. It stretches from the most ancient times, when each tree was animated by a divine spirit, to a contemporary comic strip in which the cartoon character Ziggy plants a tree and proclaims:

> Planting a tree is a sacred trust . . . trees last through the ages . . . empires may crumble, but trees remain . . . a tree is a measure of time. . . . A calendar for the changing seasons. . . . This tiny sapling will grow to become a sanctuary for birds . . . where they can build their nests, and raise their young to grow, and begin the cycle anew. . . .[27]

This scene is in keeping with the old idea that a man has asserted his manhood most fully when he has "built a house, planted a tree, and fathered a son." In relating to the tree, he respects its mystic principles. The tree works in a transcendental way to connect the three worlds of Hell, Earth, and Heaven, through its roots, its trunk, and its aspiring foliage. Numerous trees have been identified as special symbols: the Tree of Knowledge, or of Good and Evil; the Tree of Life, taking form in different societies and cultures as the Cross of Redemption and the Nordic mythological cosmic tree, Yggdrasil.

The Tree as Projection

As we interpret the meanings of trees in terms of our present needs, we may wonder whether the ancient ideas still persist. As part of a projective test, a picture of a tree in a landscape was shown to a large sample of people, with the invitation to tell a story about the picture. Some excerpts indicate the kind of tales they told.

There was something beautiful about that old tree that Gene liked. It has been there as long as he could remember, but it had never ceased to fascinate him.

Along all rivers and through all valleys, one tree always stands out and above the rest. This is as true in life (humans) as it is with the trees. For example, in a family the father is the "tree."

Here I see a depiction of the timeless fundamental struggle between good and evil. Good is the black shape which looks like a tree. Evil is represented by those white flames licking around the base of the tree, threatening to engulf it . . . the tree of good must be constantly vigilant and aware of those dark and terrible forces that threaten to destroy it.

There's the old tree and there's the house. How I used to love that old tree. How proud I was when I learned to climb it. Funny, it seemed bigger to me when I was a kid than it does now. I used to feel so warm and secure and satisfied when I touched that tree. . . . You always feel funny going back to something that you once knew well. . . . Wish they hadn't cut off that big branch.

These stories (and many others) show that the tree retains important basic meanings. Great yearnings become visible when people talk about the tree. They often reminisce about childhood. They envision escape from stress, finding again the peace and protection of being a child taken care of by the secure adults, with the tree acting like a strong, successful father or mother, allowing shade, rest, and calm.

It is easy to identify with a tree, to see our lives paralleled in its struggles to survive winds and storms, to bemoan its loss of a limb, damaged as if we had lost one. We feel obligated to that great tree, for to protect it is to reciprocate the favor and, in a way, to be protecting our inner being, our sap.

The Tree as a Positive Life Force

In some people this benevolent attitude toward the goodness of the tree and its identity with the Life Principle takes special hold. They are willing to fight, to protest, to keep the wilderness, to enlist in the cause to maintain the natural character of the environment. Their specific goals vary. Some are ardent about the wilderness, while others are more concerned about using resources in a reasonable manner with due thought for their future survival.

Others are interested in an equitable use of trees and forests so that they are not consumed for products alone, but are also available for other kinds of enjoyment. Those who stress ecological interactions are apt to put forth the values of the watershed, air-cooling and -cleansing, wildlife protection, while avoiding problems of flooding and erosion. Some emphasize the human comforts, in an effort to watch out for tree screens and shelter from climate extremes, reduce noise, and retain or develop opportunities for recreation. Their persisting devotion is to esthetics, to the beauty of the landscape, its scenic quality, and its sheer excellence as a visual, atmospheric experience.

In a review of studies, Thomas J. Steele[28] summarizes a pattern of characteristics displayed by wilderness enthusiasts. He shows that "wilderness lovers consistently value solitude, independence, and companion groups consisting only of family or very close friends." Steele pursued the hypothesis, which suggested that people who tended to fit the David Riesman model of highly "inner-directed" people and those who fit the Karen Horney description of highly "detached" people would have significantly more favorable attitudes to the concept of wilderness than would those who are either other-directed or compliant. Steele's study supported this hypothesis, indicating that people who lead the way are likely to be rather individualistic and self-sufficient, non-compliant, and intent on their own inner values and standards for guidance in a rapidly changing society.

Examination of all the data points to two primary sources of devotion to trees. One is the wish to turn away from the destructive forces of modern industrial society. This affiliation with the grandeur of the past expresses itself in reference to Paradise, the Garden of Eden, in emphasis on the enduring nature of trees, to fears that we will be "devoid of the ancient trees." Continuity with ancestors is implied by use of the word "legacy" and a life pact destroyed by "betrayal" by the U.S. Forest Service. An article by David Holstrom[29] in *The Christian Science Monitor* urges, "Give a gift of part of the forest in order to save 500,000 years," suggesting something of this participation in the kind of immortality signified by the forest.

The life cycle of the tree, with its vitality and grand growth, both mysterious and religious, calls forth the sexuality of the tree as a second primary source of involvement with, and inspiration from, the tree. The tree summarizes in its life cycle and its nature both male and female principles, with its phallic trunk and its maternal foliage. Protests against tree cutting are hurled at the problems that come about—the loss of seed and the interruption of natural reproductive processes. To cut a forest is to violate it, to destroy its virginity. In their biological community, trees come to a climax. These are, of course, technical terms that do not in themselves imply any peculiar sexuality of aim toward the tree. Still, the way the word rape is used, in defense of the forest, and the common attribution to trees of nurturant motives toward the birds nesting in their hair, illustrate the anthropomorphic life people give them. Trees are like people, but nice people. They evoke the melancholy yearning to be a child again, carefree and protected. The tree's quiet, modest nonanimal sexuality has even been a source of envy to Sir Thomas Browne, who wrote in the seventeenth century:

> I could be content that we might procreate like
> trees, without conjunction. . . . (Religio Medici, pt. ii, #9)

As we have seen, emotional reactions to tree cutting vary historically, depending on what people need from them. In early days, their religious significance was both frightening and awesome, and one could believe that trees spoke with the voices of gods. Humanity has been attributed to trees, since it is hard to believe they do not suffer anguish from the buffets of the storm and the cut of the ax. They seem giving of life, of shelter, to be grandly sexual, and thus capable of our intense identification with them. Areas without them seem exposed and desolate, with no motherly oasis to protect from the harsh blaze of the Sun-father. They can be sacrificed—and presumably willingly die—for the essential housing, firewood, and sailing craft of those who build, plant seeds, and beget and bear children. But it is no wonder that so many of us feel desperate when it seems we could perhaps destroy them all.

MEANING AND MARKETING

The point is not that belief in arboreal demons should be substituted for scientific inquiry. These are the implications:

• Marketing is not only an impersonal economic activity, but in addition to its conventional considerations about exchanges, buying and selling values, income, budget, outlets, and transportation, it is inevitably interwoven with other personal, noneconomic relationships in society.

• Objects in the market have meaning and are part of the meanings in people's entire life patterns. They reflect, superficially or deeply, enduringly or in passing, the kinds of inner life described in the example of trees.

• A richer appreciation of the significance of marketing will come about if more attention is given to interpretations and relationships at levels not usually studied. As many marketing research questionnaires will testify, a typical arsenal of values includes cost, durability, convenience, and delivery date, presumed to be best when they are low, strong, easy, and fast. Certainly these are common desires, but preoccupation with them leaves problems usually omitted from marketing texts: the desire for transformation and epiphanies, restoration of loss, revenge, or even simpler preferences for satisfaction with expensiveness, fragile things, troublesome dealings, and late arrivals.

The ideal market is like a Heaven—perfect but dull. The real market is the human one on Earth, fraught with emotion, strivings, and the symbolic investments that make us care about what and how we market with others.

CULTURAL DIVERSITY AND MARKETING

Comparing different cultures has value beyond the intrigue of exotic tidbits. It challenges the obviousness and familiarity of being immersed in our own culture. The sense of surprise we feel is a jar to preconceptions, a necessary stimulation if we are to have fresh perceptions of the kinds of products, consumer behavior, and distribution situations routinely dealt with. Whenever questions of possibility arise, many in an organization are quick to be cynical about what people will or will not do, because they are so strongly impressed with customary behavior. It is therefore therapeutic to observe the wide range of possibilities in human behavior. Maneck S. Wadia, an anthropologist who has shown interest in consumer behavior, comments:

> This diversity of human behavior may be illustrated in almost every activity in which human beings engage. Social organization, toilet habits, religious ceremonies, food habits, all vary endlessly. The Eskimos of the Arctic live almost exclusively upon meat and fish in contrast to the Jains of India who are strict vegetarians to the point of wearing masks so that they do not "eat" or "kill" germs. Dog and horse meat is eaten by many people. Some Mexican Indians breed a

special variety of dog for food, and in Russia horse meat is still a part of the diet. Yet there are many people, like ourselves, who find the idea of eating dog meat or horse meat nauseating.[30]

An interesting way to gain a sense of the increasing complexity of marketing development that occurs with increasing development of societies is to observe various kinds of historical and contemporary societies. For example, Eugene Burdick's "The Invisible Aborigine"[31] is a "non-marketing" article that makes fascinating reading as a starting point. It is vivid in its evocation of a way of life that is extremely distant from the American suburb. Although it may seem too distant to be more than a curiosity, and one may protest that there is no point in examining a group so unlikely to form a market for us, its value lies in its demonstration of an extremity of the human condition, how people can live at a level close to subsistence markedly dominated by the barrenness and aridity of the environment. One might envision a continuum of human existence with the aborigine at one pole.

The anthropologists say he is the simplest person in the Pacific and the world. He travels light. The possessions of a whole family, of a lifetime and sometimes many lifetimes, will amount to no more than twenty pounds. A stone worn smooth by handling and sweat and throwing, no bigger than an apricot, will serve as both a weapon and a religious object. A woman's hair is valued not for romantic reasons, but because it is the best cordage the family will ever have.

The aborigine probably walked into Australia centuries ago when that continent was connected to the mainland. For a long time he ranged down the coastline, moved up the banks of the rivers, followed water wherever it existed. He never developed money, arithmetic, tools, or villages. No one is sure why. Even when it was possible to build habitations and settle down, the aborigine did not. He roamed endlessly and grew lean and spare in the process.[32]

At the other end of the spectrum are the countries of the West, with their electricity, supermarkets, automobiles, money, and complex social organizations. Growing up in this type of environment makes it hard to grasp what it is like to make a snack of ants, to drink mare's urine, to wear white for mourning, or to move into foreign markets where radios play music that seems weird or unmusical, where women are secluded, or where a casual manner is taken as offensively impolite.[33] Being aware of, and tolerant of, these differences does not come easily, as Margaret Mead has pointed out:

Our ability to think about other men and their culture has proceeded slowly and haltingly, with occasional flashes of sophistication and periodic returns to floundering in various morasses of ethnic self-centeredness.[34]

But even the invisible aborigine demonstrates the presence and importance of basic human attributes and needs. The great emphasis on conserving energy may remind Americans of their own labor-saving devices and their frequent wish to take the easy way, and arouse some fresh thoughts in the light of the widespread and growing anxiety about energy resources. The aborigine's skill in throwing, the ingenuity of the boomerang, and his adaptive manner of running arouse admiration and appreciation. No matter how far away and strange the aborigines may seem, they show the need for family life, dancing, and the important satisfaction found in fantasy—imagining, storytelling, religious explanation, and so forth.

Moving along the marketing continuum, we might look at the ways of life among the Sioux and Yurok Indians, as described by Erik Erikson.[35] Most societies focus strongly on certain objects they regard as having very special meaning. These objects may be gathered, fished for, killed, captured, grown, mined, or manufactured, but they are main sources of motivation, gratification, and incentive to the people. The kangaroo and the boomerang to the aborigine, the salmon to the Yurok, the buffalo to the Sioux, the yam to the Dobu, the blanket to the Kwakiutl are intensely meaningful. Daily life and its ordinary demands make it seem practical and reasonable that food and tools would be so dominating. But humans go beyond this level of practicality and become deeply involved in their identification with these objects. They imitate them, love and hate them, squander or hoard them, and build complex rituals and interpersonal networks around them.

More familiar marketing systems, with the usual characteristics of money, trade, selling, stores, wholesalers, and retailers, are found in contemporary underdeveloped and developing countries. An examination of how such systems work can fill in more points along the marketing continuum. For instance, Egypt has made many changes since the 1952 revolution that brought Nasser to power. But, as pointed out by Boyd[36] we are still able to see a particular system in operation, the ways money is spent, and the assumptions made about the various people in the market system. For example, at one point the authors state that "most wholesalers, however, regard selling as simply transferring physically the goods from the seller to the ultimate buyer."[37] Other issues could be raised about the attitudes of the people, the outlook of the government, traditional contrasted with modern cultural forces, the role of the Moslem religion, and so forth, in determining the type of market system that is present and evolving.

Similarly, in such disparate parts of the world as Mexico and modern Australia, forms and levels of marketing development show interesting local characteristics. In discussing discount houses in Australia and Mexico, John S. Ewing highlights similarities and differences among these two countries and the United States, referring to traditions, history, and specific recent occurrences. Again, we can observe the complex network of attitudes at work among the groups involved in the country, the sources of resistance, the interests of government and specific companies, and the relations of producers to distributors. The situation in Australia, with its tradition of price maintenance, led to manufacturers' boycotts and powerful retailer resistance to discount houses. In Mexico, the Aurrera Company was successful with its new discount houses, which were basically in keeping with the Mexican tradition of price-cutting after bargaining, despite similar resistance from industry.[38]

A continuum might be set up for different societies, ranging from the aborigine to the modern American, with Egypt, Australia, and Mexico suggesting a few of the many possible development points along the way. Each point on the continuum suggests a complex set of features, such as hand-to-mouth buying, buyers' aims, role of personal selling, interest of producers, and role of government in a typical blend.

In thinking about the different dimensions that underlie such a continuum, we should bear in mind its cross-sectional nature. The continuum is used as a convenient device for making comparisons that may remind us of pertinent variables. It does not mean that all marketing developments tend toward the U.S. model nor does it suggest that all countries do, should, or will recapitulate the historical development of the American marketing system. However, general trends are probably visible when there are movements toward rising income, education, growth in consumer emphasis, shifts from rural to urban dominance, increase in advertising, decline in personalized relations, new forms of credit, and so forth.

As sellers or buyers, people have to express what their culture teaches them to believe, allows them to choose, or insists they articulate. The social organization can be thought of as a kind of "invisible machine," as Lewis Mumford has conceived of it, with people acting as interlocking parts. The culture is a source of designs for living, a matrix of intangibles and tangibles that determines handling of space, time, and attitudes toward work, sex, and material goods. Marketers who appreciate the complex interweaving of physical environment, technology, economic life, and social structure are better equipped to plan around and adapt to the culture in which they work.

SUMMARY

1. The cultural context can provide the marketing manager with perspective. The organization, the product, the sellers, and the buyers are all "embedded" in this context, which governs their marketing actions.

2. The moral component of products and services is shown in society's attitude of acceptance, permission, controversy, criticism, and condemnation toward them.

3. These attitudes are determined by the structure of values in the society, and what meanings the goods and services have in relation to them. The complexity of this situation is illustrated by the special analysis of trees and their relationship to humankind.

4. Each society is in a stage of cultural development, which the marketer acts to reinforce or alter. Marketing planning will be affected by the marketer's awareness and insight.

References

1. Robert S. Weiss, "Alternative Approaches in the Study of Complex Situations," *Human Organization*, Fall 1966, pp. 196–206.
2. Sol Tax (ed.), *Horizons of Anthropology* (Chicago: Aldine, 1964).
3. Conrad M. Arensberg and Arthur H. Niehoff, *Introducing Social Change: A Manual for Americans Overseas* (Chicago: Aldine, 1964), p. 15.
4. Joseph W. McGuire, *Theories of Business Behavior* (Englewood Cliffs, N.J.: Prentice-Hall, 1964), p. 223.
5. Ibid., p. 240.
6. Robert L. Heilbroner, "Do Machines Make History?" *Technology and Culture*, July 1967, pp. 342–343.
7. Frank Boas, "The Social Organization and the Secret Society of the Kwakiutl Indians," *Annual Report, 1894–1895* (Washington, D.C.: U.S. National Museum, 1897).

8. **Bronislaw Malinowski,** *Argonauts of the Western Pacific* (New York: Dutton, 1961), p. 81.

9. **Sidney J. Levy** and **Gerald Zaltman,** *Marketing, Society, and Conflict* (Englewood Cliffs, N.J.: Prentice-Hall, 1975).

10. **Ralph Winter, Jr.,** *The Consumer Advocate versus the Consumer* (American Enterprise Institute, July 1972).

11. "Which Criterion? Effect of Choice of the Criterion on Forest Management Plans," *Forest Science,* Dec. 1972, pp. 292–298.

12. **Fred G. Simmons,** "Wilderness East? – No." *American Forests,* July 1972, p. 3; see also **Fred C. Simmons,** "Woodsman – Chop that Tree," *The New York Times,* Dec. 14, 1970, p. 43.

13. "Woodsman, Manage that Tree," *Commerce Today,* Dec. 25, 1972, pp. 11–15.

14. **W. D. Hagenstein,** "Clearcutting is Silviculturally Sound," *Forest Industries,* Dec. 17, 1970, pp. 26–29.

15. **Gordon Robinson,** "Our Export Forest," *Sierra Club Bulletin,* Jan. 1973, pp. 10–17.

16. "Timber Industry's Struggle for Wood," *Business Week,* Nov. 25, 2971, pp. 72–76.

17. **Michael Thomas,** "Down in the Forest," *Geographical Magazine,* Nov. 1972, pp. 135–141.

18. **Clifford E. Ahlgren,** "The Changing Forest: Part I," *American Forests,* Jan. 1973, pp. 40–44.

19. **Robert W. Upton,** "You Can't Preserve a Tree Forever but You Can Manage a Forest," *Pulp and Paper Magazine of Canada,* July 1972, p. 99.

20. **Marlin C. Galbraith,** "Environmental Effects of Timber Harvest and Utilization of Logging Residues," *Environmental Affairs,* Fall 1972, pp. 314–332.

21. **Charles W. Bingham,** "Enhancing Environment Through Science and Technology," *Journal of Forestry,* Feb. 1971, pp. 72–76.

22. **T. Ewald Maki,** "Clearcutting and Soil Depletion," *Forest Farmer,* Oct. 1972, pp. 12–15.

23. **Rexford A. Resler,** "Clearcutting: Beneficial Aspects for Wildlife Resources," *Journal of Soil and Water Conservation,* Nov.–Dec. 1972, pp. 255–259.

24. **W. L. Pengelly,** "Clearcutting: Detrimental Aspects for Wildlife Resources," *Journal of Soil and Water Conservation,* Nov.–Dec. 1972, pp. 255–259.

25. **J. E. Cirlot,** *A Dictionary of Symbols* (London: Routledge and Kegan Paul, 1962).

26. Ibid., p. 328.

27. **Ziggy,** *Chicago Sun-Times,* May 27, 1973.

28. **Thomas J. Steele,** "The Marketing of the Wilderness Cause," unpublished paper.

29. **David Holstrom,** "Give a Gift of Part of the Forest in Order to Save 500,000 Years," *The Christian Science Monitor,* Dec. 20, 1972, p. 1.

30. **Maneck S. Wadia,** "The Concept of Culture in the Analysis of Consumers," *Proceedings of the 1967 American Marketing Association Winter Conference,* Dec. 1967, p. 189.

31. **Eugene Burdick,** "The Invisible Aborigine," *Harper's Magazine,* Sept. 1961, pp. 69–76.

32. Ibid., p. 69.

33. **Edward T. Hall** discusses some of the problems created by cultural variations in his *The Silent Language* (New York: Doubleday, 1959).

34. **Margaret Mead** and **Nicolas Calas** (eds.), *Primitive Heritage* (New York: Random House, 1953), p. xxiii.

35. **Erik Erikson,** *Childhood and Society* (New York: Norton, 1963), Part II.

36. **Harper w. Boyd, Jr., Abdel Aziz El Sherbini,** and **Ahmed Fouad Sherif,** "Channels of Distribution for Consumer Goods in Egypt," *Journal of Marketing,* Oct. 1961, pp. 26–33.

37. Ibid., p. 32.

38. John S. Ewing, "Discount Houses in Australia and Mexico," *Journal of Marketing,* July 1962, pp. 37–41.

Suggested Readings

Blishen, Bernard R., et al., *Canadian Society* (Toronto: The Macmillan Company of Canada Limited, 1961).

Buchanan, William, and Hadley Cantril, *How Nations See Each Other* (Urbana: University of Illinois, 1953).

Hacker, Barton C., "Greek Catapults and Catapult Technology: Science, Technology, and War in the Ancient World," *Technology and Culture,* Jan. 1968.

Heilbroner, Robert L., "Do Machines Make History?" *Technology and Culture,* July 1967, pp. 335–345.

Herskovits, M., *Economic Anthropology: The Economic Life of Primitive Peoples* (New York: Alfred A. Knopf, 1952).

Kluckhohn, Clyde, *Mirror for Man* (New York: McGraw-Hill, 1949).

Kluckhohn, Clyde, and Henry A. Murray, *Personality in Nature, Society, and Culture* (New York: Alfred A. Knopf, 1955).

Kuhn, Alfred, *The Study of Society: A Unified Approach* (Homewood, Ill.: Richard D. Irwin–Dorsey Press, 1963).

McClelland, David C., *The Achieving Society* (Princeton, N.J.: D. Van Nostrand Company, 1961).

McGuire, Joseph, *Theories of Business Behavior* (Englewood Cliffs, N.J.: Prentice-Hall, 1964).

McGuire, Joseph (ed.), *Interdisciplinary Studies in Business Behavior* (Cincinnati: South-Western Publishing Company, 1962).

Mumford, Lewis, *The Myth of the Machine: Technics and Human Development* (New York: Harcourt, Brace, Jovanovich, 1967).

V
Cultural Change and American Society

In tradition-bound, static societies, marketing problems are few and familiar, since most ways of producing and distributing products and services follow established and routine patterns. But in the modern world rapid change is a dynamic force with profound effects. This fact is of special importance to marketers, because they initiate change and they also have to react to it.

All the many factors that lead to cultural change have an impact on marketing. Technology constantly alters the pattern of available goods, production costs, competitive challenges, and the interests of customers. Numerous outstanding examples can be found: computers, transistors, miniaturized components, synthetic fibers, new drugs, and miraculous chemicals, with no end in sight for laboratory inventiveness. The diffusion of cultural influences through international movies, fashions, foods, art, and travel, leads to new viewpoints, clothing styles, esthetic awareness and preferences, and ways of living. As W. Lloyd Warner has pointed out:

> The whole American society is rapidly growing into one *primary* community, in which corporations along with other complex hierarchical structures play their significant and necessary roles. Change is built into the very nature of this social system, most innovations originating from within, not from without; yet to maintain order and still change,

this society continuously incorporates its persistent past into its moving future.[1]

The sources of change may be debated, and the growth of the single primary community Warner envisioned is being slowed by fresh waves of immigration and reintensification of ethnicity. How does the persisting past join the moving future? To gain perspective on the process, it is necessary to give thought to both historical and contemporary events, and to observe those factors that resist change and those that foster it. This is a vast subject covered by many disciplines, each of which offers theories that are in some respects inadequate. Some emphasize geography, economics, or political circumstances, while others focus on social relations, genetics, technology, or moral philosophy. The theory of moral corruption and decadence frequently cited to account for the decline of the Roman Empire has lately taken blows from evidence that the true cause was inadvertent, but systematic, lead poisoning of the elite Romans, who ate food cooked in lead pots. Then again, this fact may be insufficient to explain the triumph of Christianity over Roman paganism.

There is a great temptation to explain social change by simple formulations, since each instance to be accounted for probably has some attractive and distinctive feature. But a more general theory of social change must take many variables into account, given the great diversity of societies and their detailed variety with respect to social change. Social theory has to consider the physical environment with its potentialities and obstacles, the kinds of cultural phenomena that occur, social structures, the kinds of personalities typical in the society, relationships with outside groups, population size, existing levels of skills, and so forth. Each of these aspects acts interdependently to explain the rate of change observed in a particular area through sufficient analysis of their interaction.

Everett E. Hagen's theory of social change is based on a detailed analysis of the factors that cause a traditional society to enjoy a period of economic prosperity. Hagen sees cultural, social, and psychological elements as the more profound sources of economic behavior. Rapid change and special features are dramatic and conspicuous, but Hagen points out that these can be misleading, and that long-run forces are at work:

Other instances of the bursting of barriers and probable discontinuity in the pace of economic change might be cited. Serious business recessions during the period of the transition have also affected the pace of change. But if we emphasize the moments of change, we shall be deceived by their apparent suddenness and apparent importance. Underlying them and preceding them were forces and sequences of change, operating over longer periods, which become manifest to the casual historical observer only when the pace of overt action changes. Their importance becomes apparent only when we ask ourselves what the mechanisms at work may be and construct an adequate theory of the functioning of the society.[2]

The changes that take place in a society are not just abstractions. Robert Redfield describes what happened in the Yucatan village of Chan Kom when new technology was introduced:

Since 1938 the women of the village have had the opportunity of bringing their corn to be ground at a motor driven mill, and since the autumn of 1947 they have had their choice of two mills. I was told that everyone now eats mill-ground corn and found no reason to doubt the statement. The cost is fifteen centavos (three cents) for the grinding of about eight quarts of meal. . . . In a good many cases some time is freed for the woman of the house, and another errand is to be done by some child of the household. We were told by one concerned with the finer points of cooking that mill-ground corn makes less savory tortillas.[3]

The idea that the new way tastes less good than the old way is quite conventional. The same thing happened in the United States when instant coffee, cake mixes, and frozen orange juice concentrate were first introduced, although the generation that grows up with these products uses them to set its own norms. Tradition-minded people see new ways as corrupting. Redfield cites one of the elders of the village who complained about some of the changes that were taking place all around him:

Things will be bad for the children of Chan Kom when they grow up, he says, for two reasons; the land does not produce as it did and the people are taking up vices and bad habits. People are drinking more than they did, he thinks. He says that when the present leaders of Chan Kom are dead, without their good example the people will become drunkards, as they are in some other villages. Cigarette-smoking and chewing gum—even the recent fad of wearing dark glasses—he sees as "vices," as wasteful and corrupting customs unsuitable to sound people.[4]

It is interesting to note the broad tendencies in cultural change that suggest the direction peoples are likely to take given the development of their economic resources and technology. For example, the desire to improve diet through increased animal protein is a major human aspiration. Figure 6 correlates income with the amount of animal protein ingested by people in 30 countries. It shows how the eating of meat correlates highly with increasing income.

Alan R. Beals points to the type of impact on the marketing behavior of Indian villagers made by a wartime influx of British and American soldiers and money. New forms of production developed among the villagers and farmers, and consumption moved to include more of familiar, desirable products and services; higher-quality, higher-status versions of familiar products; and the adoption of new products and services.

> The war period was a time of great prosperity in Namhalli. The environs of Bangalore were crowded with British, American, and Indian soldiers. Many villagers, both male and female, found jobs in military camps. For Namhalli's middle-school graduates there were highly paid jobs as clerks and factory laborers. There were opportunities for windfall profits from smuggling grain, misappropriating military property, or engaging in prostitution. The farmer also prospered. Officers in charge of procuring food for military establishments toured Mysore State in trucks offering high prices for "English" vegetables. Farmers began growing carrots, tomatoes, beets, cauliflower, and cabbages. Iron plows and improved livestock were purchased. New houses were built. Children were sent to high school riding on newly purchased bicycles. European-style haircuts became universal among the menfolk, and everyone who considered himself educated purchased a cotton, or in extreme cases a woolen, suit which could be worn on trips to Bangalore. . . . An ever increasing percentage of the grain, milk, and vegetables produced in Namhalli was sold in Bangalore. The money obtained in this way was used for new purposes such as paying doctor bills, betting on horse races, buying tailored clothes, paying electric bills, and attending motion pictures.[5]

Most of the changes that arose out of wartime prosperity did not endure in Namhalli. Twenty years later, an observer comments that most of the Namhalli people still do not eat these "English" vegetables, get European haircuts, pay electric bills, or ride bicycles.[6]

This chapter explores some of the content of cultural change in America. Many U.S. marketers are not directly involved in marketing in other countries. Their central necessity is to understand the workings of their own society and culture and the modi-

Figure 6. Income and supply of animal protein per person in selected countries.

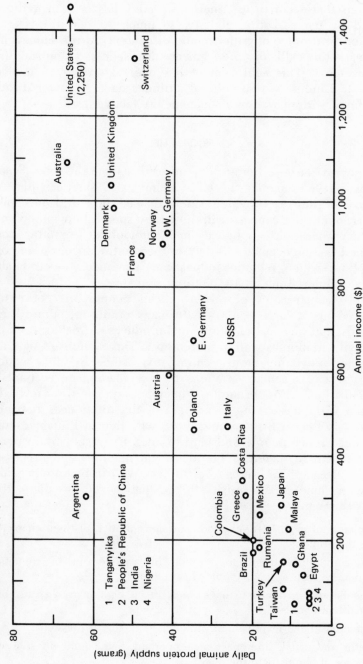

SOURCE: U.S. Department of Agriculture, Economic Research Service.

fications that occur in it. American society has been heavily affected by its marketing activity, so much so that this fact is frequently a source of criticism and discontent. At the same time, the marketing skills of Americans are also seen as an outstanding achievement. This achievement has been described as a challenge to Europe, where cultural attitudes have characteristically interfered with marketing management effectiveness.[7]

AMERICAN LIFE

It is not my purpose here to defend or disparage the role of marketing, but to recognize the basic character of American life. An analysis of the way in which Americans see the world must take into account their concern with how they spend their money, not only on household appliances and automobiles—so often condemned as a preoccupation—but on their entire spectrum of consumption, which includes education, insurance, travel, health services, entertainment, art, clothing, and sports.

The characteristics of the American people are not easily summed up. A large country with many traditions, ethnic backgrounds, and physical environments produces a great array of individual variation as well as stereotypes. Descriptions of national character inevitably arouse controversy, since by their nature they cut across actual variations or take inadequate account of contradictions. For example, Americans generally view the French without showing awareness of the differences between those who live in Brittany and those who live in Provence—differences French people find hard to miss. Even so, certain broad themes exist in societies. The dominant qualities and processes typical of American life can be studied. We can begin our analysis with some broad brush strokes that assert the distinctive American pattern:

Richness of manufactured goods and consumption of them characterize the economy.

The country has strong agrarian roots, but a modern urban orientation to money, salaries, and complex institutions.

The population tends to have long life, a high marriage rate, and small households.

The educational level is high, although its quality is debated.

Status and racial differences are important, being both divisive and sources of pluralistic pride.

Religion is deemphasized by separation of church and state and general growth of secularism.

Values tend toward moralizing and twofold judgments.

Work and play tend to be separated.

"Time is money" dominates actions, philosophy, and scheduling.

Effort and optimism are greatly valued and spur achievement.[8]

All these elements can be studied fully and qualified in detail. Despite the general truth of the first point, for example, there is a growing literature and concern about the poor in America and the kind of marketing that reaches them.[9] The high level of education in America is distinctive and widespread. However, it varies according to social class and does not itself solve the problems of dropouts and so-called hard-core unemployables, and the growing criticism of the public school systems. Nevertheless, the fact that the country has these concerns can be taken as evidence of the affluence and rising expectations among many members of society, encouraging them to press for more improvement.

A list of static statements isn't enough to grasp the vital process that characterizes American life. How have people's living habits changed? What new attitudes toward consumption and lifestyle are emerging? Some speculations on the nature of modern living may help understanding by focusing on the changing viewpoints of consumers. Looking back to the 1930s, the Great Depression seemed anomalous in the face of the nation's vast resources. It led to political activism and implementation of Keynesian philosophy, which called for vigorous governmental economic intervention. With the post-World War II surge of productivity and the consequent affluent buyers' market, there was a general sense of a process coming to fruition. Life in the United States seemed bountiful, and merchants were bent on filling the role of providers. Products were increasingly designed to make things easy, comfortable, colorful, and varied. The vision of the Good Life for All, with almost universal education and the proliferation of single-family dwellings in suburban idylls, came to dominate the fantasies and aspirations of the mass market.

During the 1950s, fresh difficulties began to emerge. One harbinger was the popular identification with David Riesman's *The Lonely Crowd.*[10] Its lament at the emergence of other-directedness as the predominant American personality trait met with widespread agreement, even by those who echoed sadly to the title and didn't read the book. But other-directedness can also be taken as an essential feature of rapid economic development, as McClelland says,[11] making for orderly social behavior, flexibility in adaptations to change, and a market morality that is responsive to public opinion.

More generally, other-directedness is interpreted as a loss of stable traditions and autonomy, as an impersonal and alienated dependency on passing currents. The individual's vulnerability to "others" thus became the occasion for alarm, expressed and spurred by Vance Packard's widespread success, *The Hidden Persuaders*, a book that purports to expose the presence of insidious forces seeking to manipulate the consumers' desires.[12] Another sign of the marketing system being viewed as generally inimical to the interests of the community was Galbraith's *The Affluent Society*. Designed to reveal some of the ills of the day, he developed the idea that advertising had a squirrel wheel effect in making the people want the things the corporations wanted to produce, at the expense of public sector benefits.[13]

Whether Galbraith is correct in this or not, the public is capable of generating desires for things in the search for an improved standard of living and in emulation of elites, as they have since time immemorial. Through the 1940s and the 1950s, people moved from self-denial as a necessity and a puritan principle to self-indulgence as a way of life. Their ethic came to dictate consumption as a virtue where once it counseled conservation, and many still yearn to gratify themselves. Even those who protest the profligate use of credit make more actual and relatively casual use of it than their forebears were able or apt to do.

The changes in the mid-century American scene were expansive in character. There were more people, with increases in both the birth rates and longevity. These "more people" had more of all kinds of things—they had more leisure time, more money, more objects, more pleasures, and more worries. In the 1960s a reaction flared up, with a surge of conflict in values as people (young and middle class, especially) protested the Vietnam War and expressed rebellion against materialistic values, pollution, waste, hypocritical morality, and so forth.

It should be said that in many basic ways there is little doubt people have also *not* changed. When they are interviewed about how they live nowadays and how these living patterns compare with those they wanted when they were young, and with those of their parents, they are able to see many differences. But mingled among these differences are still threaded the yearnings for a stable family life, freedom from illness, wishes for the betterment of one's children and for finding a way to happiness in a troubled world. Within this framework, thinking not about the broad picture of goods moving in the market and the dramatic implications of income and sales curves, but about the people in their homes, struggling with raising their children to be reasonably clean, obedient, and affectionate, they can hardly find the changes implied by frozen foods and microwave ovens as particularly significant.

Nevertheless, the redistribution of values goes on, a swinging of the several pendulums that direct social and psychological energies. Through history, there is movement between emphases on pleasure or austerity, permissiveness or restraint, realities or fantasies; and countries wax and wane as their energies are practical or philosophical, guiding or following. So, too, in the day-to-day living of ordinary people there are shifts in emphasis on work or pleasure, on getting or spending, on building or laying waste our powers.

For a long time, the American pattern was one of pioneering, of adventure, and of self-denial for the fabulous rewards over the long haul, even if these arrived only in an afterlife. Security was less important than severity. The aim of Americans was to acquire or develop resources, whether personal or economic. For the average consumer, this meant struggling to make a living to meet fairly basic needs. Necessities took the major share of the income, and luxuries were for the rich or the wasteful.

THE CAKE EATERS

The extremes are hard to sustain, so a kind of centering movement takes over. People do not want to save. They do not want to waste. They want to consume judiciously. They are "cake eaters" because they want to enjoy their material objects without using them up. This tendency is exemplified in many ways, perhaps most strikingly by those who save money in the bank while buying major appliances on credit. It is summed up as a philosophy by the woman who said she wanted to "save a little, spend a little, and enjoy a little."

American consumers (and strivers the world over) are heavily engaged in living out what might be called a consumption fantasy. They want security, possessions, and pleasure, and they want to have these goals satisfied immediately. They ask: What will it cost me per month? One consumer said about friends: "They bought a house out in Harvey for $25 down on GI and $97 toward their own home in payments. What if they have to pay for 32 years? By laying it out, they have their own." Everybody still worries about money—the most frequently named concern in most surveys—but they are not sure about how to worry about it. The sharp inflationary pressures of the 1970s coupled with anxiety about constricting forces in the economy raise many problems about saving, investing, borrowing, and spending. These factors ultimately affect what people believe they have coming to them.

The orientation to possessions is very strong. Despite consumerism and criticism, their faith in the manufacturer is great, resting on a foundation of research, the spurs of competition, and an implicit acceptance of the fact that society revolves around making new things, better things, miraculous things in a casual way. Beneath the fashionable cynicism and sophisticated carping about the inadequacies of the marketplace, specific hopefulness remains. People know that NEW in an advertisement is not to be scoffed at, no matter how overworked, because the world of science seems to innovate as easily as invention was once arduous. The pervasive belief is that everything is different nowadays. The words "All the things they make for babies that they didn't have before" greet every new parent.

In his well-known theory, Abraham Maslow suggests that human aims move upward in a hierarchy from the need to satisfy physiological functions, through needs for safety, love, and self-esteem, to "higher" forms of needs, such as self-expression, understanding, and esthetics.[14] In reality, these needs become interwoven and the hierarchy is not a simple one. Some develop the act of eating to a high art, while others take up fasting for the sake of self-expression or social causes.

A variation on Maslow would show that often people do not rise to supposed high-order interests when they might, but display another principle instead. Generally, the less we have to worry about basic things, the more we worry about peripheral issues. Translation: If the object itself can no longer be improved in the way it functions, tastes, satisfies nutritional requirements, or eases handling, or if some new product cannot be invented that will make the object totally outmoded and inefficient, the marketer turns to minor variations in size, combinations of ingredients, or redesigned packaging.

There may also be variations in the esthetics of presentation. Consumers make esthetic discriminations (even if of a minor sort) and often elevate their attention to a product above its basic function. For example, if toilet tissue can be chosen for its relevance to the color scheme of the bathroom, people may stock up on several more rolls for coordination with sets of towels. But when there are shortages, and the price is rising rapidly, one may do without, or be quick to take whatever is available, especially if there is some saving involved. Still, the purple tissue is missed.

The consumption fantasy presses hard. Partly it is a fantasy because it cannot be entirely gratified—and even as parents lavish on their children all the things they missed as children, they still fret about whether they are doing the right thing. The Puritan Ethic is not totally eclipsed. One woman compared herself with her mother:

> I like to cook just as my mother did. My husband tells me I am pretty good, but I am not as good a trainer of children as my mother was— too easygoing. I think I was better as a child, too. If Mother told me not to go anywhere, I never argued with her. Times change [sigh]. Now they dance and all. Because they have had so many things, they want so much. They had a lot as children. Sometimes I think it isn't good. They got more than they needed. Things come too easy for them. We had to go without. I try to get things for my kids. There are so many more things to want now. Styles change. You've got to keep with the times. Coats become outmoded. They don't want to wear them anymore, even if they're still good. One of the girls says, "Where did you get that old-fashioned coat?" It belonged to her sister and was new 2 years ago. The idea is, they are sisters, so why can't she wear a coat that's 2 years old?

Her remarks reflect some of the new imperatives at work under the Consumption Fantasy.

Convenience is an aim in itself. To say that something is convenient (quick, easy) serves to justify it to a fair degree. Behind this justification is, of course, some other logic: being a generally busy person; being a working woman with no time to cook; being entitled to convenience because one is just as good as anyone else; and so forth.

Style may be almost as important as basic function. If any automobile will get you there, you may as well make your choice on the basis of color, shape, or trim. Over time, style distinctions become more elaborate. At first, novelty in style tends to be modern—the design seems radical, bright, variegated, regarded as "smart." Then it tends to retrench itself somewhat, to darken without becoming drab, and to elevate itself toward the sleeker, more severe modes regarded as "elegant." And all the better for obsolescence if those shifts can be made rapidly.

When pragmatic issues arise, a new trend emerges. For example, the gasoline crisis of the winter of 1973–1974 forced many automobile manufacturers to turn out small cars. Meantime, the elite tried to hang on. By the winter of 1974–1975, although car sales were down, large-car sales were surprisingly strong. Manufacturers soon intensified their efforts to combine elegance with smaller size.

The enjoyment of human life is worth more than the value of toil or of money. At the heart of the pressures toward convenience, style, pay later, and permissive parenthood is this most fundamental right of the consumer. As has often been noted, the less people must slave to subsist, the more they can be self-expressive and humanly individual. There can be growing concern with the human individual. It lies at the heart of the American dream, and is the important idea that tends to become obscured in the urge to accumulate objects. Having a degree of wealth and enjoying its fruits liberates energies that tend otherwise to be bound up in the bitternesses and intensities of struggle to survive. The fact that these liberated energies create new problems should probably not be blamed on the wealth. The notions that (1) saving oneself justifies the acquisition of appliances and (2) exhausting oneself needlessly is foolish, find increasing currency. In an interview with a housewife, she bolsters her intention to insist on doing less work: "I keep telling my husband that I'm worth more than the washing." At one point, Ann Landers, who counsels the troubled, admonished a husband as follows:

Confidentially—Old-Fashioned Husband: I have a different name for it, Dad. Your wife would rather have a washing machine than silver handles on her casket. Stop comparing her with your mother.

But there is much more involved here than the labor-saving advantages of major appliances, even if these are not to be sneezed at. As human energies are freed from work, they need new occupation. Part of the frenzy in the Consumption Fantasy is that it has to take some form, and people want it to have a well-composed form. However, for consumption to have a pleasing and harmonious pattern requires an integrated way of life, a sense of living in a manner that satisfies a personal system of values.

In the present period of rapid transition and world revolution, with the new levels of automotive and geographic mobility, with the agonizing struggle to turn the American city into something manageable, it is not easy to find such harmony and satisfaction. Certainly, mass education reaches more and more people, the working classes have surpassing incomes, the persisting vision and reality is of a home of one's own; and the unity of family ("togetherness") is grasped for more intently as it seems to get more elusive. But crime and delinquency rise and personal discontents continue to proliferate. Parents worry about drugs in the high schools, vandalism in the suburbs, college girls taking the pill and "shacking up," and try to take comfort from the fact that most premarital sex is said to be nonpromiscuous and between engaged couples, or that one's child can do it and still be a nice person.

The direction of modern times has been toward liberation, toward liberation of women, of peoples, of children, but the net effect has been a kind of internal and external violence as the liberated are uncertain about what to do with themselves. The traditionalists are appalled at the freedom of working women, 18-year-olds who drink and vote, and the rates at which marriages decline and divorces increase.

As modern science and technology have undermined traditional notions of work and property,[15] and as society shifts its orientation away from agriculture and production to distribution, government, and services, there are many repercussions. By their magnitude and their intensity, by the problems they pose as well as the opportunities they provide, they may be regarded as crises.

THE INTELLECTUAL CRISIS

The intellectual crisis is a major one. Modern events place great demands on people for revising their views of the world, their capacity to understand and act upon the environment. The necessity to adapt, to take account of new circumstances, and to revise old assumptions and stereotypes presses upon people. After Sputnik, this pressure found expression particularly in educational ferment. It made buyers and sellers feel at the mercy of science, but also eager to command it and to gain its benefits. The intellectual crisis demanded a revised curriculum, that more people be educated, and that they be educated more intensively, at length or in accelerated programs for those more capable. Vast educational complexes made some time in college seem like a higher high school. Many consumers are not released from this prolonged juvenile status until past a third of their allotted life span.

Not only did this mean "college for all," but the importance of education as a value, as a modern competitive requirement for achievement and earning, pushed toward continued learning, adult education, and even the dream of learnings that will allow workers to change their occupations to fresh ones when in their forties and weary with what they have been doing. People shop for courses at evening schools, take brush-up courses and summer workshops, seek to learn the language of computers, and gather in innumerable conferences, seminars, and talky conventions.

Having to reach out this way to encompass reality more thoughtfully than ever places a premium on all experiences that can be interpreted as educative. Some of the commercial results are apparent. Educational manufacturers and publishers thrive, audiovisual materials grow, people buy devices and courses to foster more rapid reading like verbal sponges who are not sopping up the words fast enough to keep up with their flow. Variety stores, drugstores, and airport terminals sell books, including workbooks to help first-graders practice arithmetic and reading.

In the seventies, the school population declines and there is disenchantment with formal education and its vocational values. Pragmatism is urged and how-to-do-it thrives. The drive to use an intellectual approach to life in the desire to be knowing and self-conscious about it pushes people toward the magazines that discuss theories of family relations, how to bring up difficult children or live with a demented aunt, and what recent surveys show about such matters as the public's attitude toward doctors. Research becomes one of the magic words of this era. There seems no end to the variety of new ways of putting things together, of taking them apart, of breaking them down and reconstituting them, of using sound, magnetism, crystals, transistors, infrared, magic chemicals, and clever mechanics to change the way things are made, and how the world will shelter, clean, and feed itself. Sometimes the consumer has had enough, and there is nothing left to marvel at. It is all too much to absorb. Nutritional information comes apace, warning against cholesterol in meat, eggs, and butter, against even poor old spinach for interfering with calcium utilization in the body, against water in ham, against the charring on a barbecue, and against sugar, calories, and insecticides in everything.

In such a situation marketing communications can work toward clarification, to help consumers out of the polyunsaturated maze, not to take too much understanding for granted when attention has to strain in so many directions already. Should we dry clean our own clothes? Humidify the house? Try a food that is frozen, dried, or sprayed, on a no-grease skillet? Or buy an electric shaver that takes lather and rinsing? In sum, a big problem of the intellectual crisis is how to make the new technical world comprehensible, to pass it from the innovators through old-fashioned adults to the youngsters who will hopefully and casually survive this crisis.

As the energy crisis ("if there is one," the public wonders) becomes more urgent, there is pressure to solve it with solar energy, wind, hydraulics, clean and safe nuclear energy, or—it is hoped—some great new scientific breakthrough. The variations in confidence. in the marketplace that come with fluctuations in availability of goods, sharp changes in prices, an uneasy stock market, and the uncertainty that leaders know what to do to solve problems, are a challenge to the intellect of marketers. People who have never had enough food, clothing, and shelter tend to be passive, but those who feel actively deprived of what is due them, with the "winds of rising expectations," or who feel forced to settle for less than they have been used to, are likely to be frustrated and angry, and to look for someone to blame. "Marketing" tends to be associated with material values, but it is inescapably concerned with fostering intangible values and new ideas, part and parcel of the intellectual life of the community and the struggle to learn new ways of thinking.

THE MORAL CRISIS

Another area of changing meaning is bound up in the moral crisis. What kinds of morals and ethics are Americans going to have? They are clearly going to be different, but in what ways is less clear. The many problems with a moral aspect take up much modern energy. What to do about segregation, nuclear weapons, where to live, sexual freedom, propriety, delinquency, and violence on television, are only a few of the issues that make life a debate with conscience.

In terms of the problems of everyday living, these uneasy

moral issues take the form of questions about how to be a good husband, wife, or parent, what values to pursue in child-rearing and how to implement them. People need to determine what basis for goodness will motivate them. Perhaps never before have so many people had church membership without believing in a God or a hereafter. Still, they make choices. In their purchasing behavior they express values. In eighteenth century England everyone who could afford it wanted to build. As one Englishman wrote at the time:

> Every man now, be his fortune what it will, is to be doing something at his place . . . and you hardly meet anybody who, after the first compliments, does not inform you that he is in mortar and heaving of earth, the modest terms for building and gardening . . . necessities of life without which a gentleman of the smallest fortune thinks he makes no figure in his country.[16]

Today it is still regarded as good to be involved in mortar and the heaving of earth. We still have a sense of social prestige and moral substance, complicated by problems of whether to build or buy, to go to a condominium, or just rent in the face of mortgage costs, and whether to garden flowers or vegetables in the face of food costs.

Moral crises tend to find particular expression in women, since as mothers and schoolteachers they have been given so much of the obligation to teach the young and to produce the kinds of people the society gets. Today's fathers have become more aware of their share in this process. But however it comes about, parents marvel at their children's precocious development, their eagerness to grow up fast, to join their peers, to date and learn the world sooner. This reaching out makes young people a more significant market than they have ever been, since despite extending their education, they are being provided with relatively more money and greater freedom than ever in spending it. Toys, endless snacks, school supplies, clothing, and a wide array of indulgences including cars, travel, and easy access to contraceptives are all part of giving the children what they want and often what the parents never had.

One of the areas of moral conflict is how to use one's money, how much credit to take advantage of, how much security to buy with savings, insurance, stocks, and real property. Anxieties in this area are affected by how people live beyond their current means, the role of corporate benefits, government subsidy of education and aid to the aged, time payments, mortgages, and charge accounts insured against default. The moral crisis is not likely to be resolved in favor of being provident unless apocalyptic events overtake man's ingenuity. Yet even a brief recession has a sobering effect, providing a righteous basis for self-discipline and reining the family. Similarly, marketing managers review the product line, reduce variety and inventory, and cut research budgets.

Many profound forces are at work to produce the current temper and attitude, forces beyond present knowlege or insight. Cake Eaters do not want to offend or rock the boat. The Consumption Fantasy thrives on an outwardness of self-expression. Current trends are shaped by the mass media. In one sense, it may be said that the media have helped turn people's psyches inside out. How people live and how they ought to live has become a matter of public record. By word and by picture, by splashing before us the golden fantasies of how a more abundant life can be lived, the media have defined for millions of people a public conception of how kitchens, living rooms, and backyards ought to be. Suburban homeowners, who lack the urban apartment dweller's privacy and anonymity, fret about their window lamps and their lawns, self-conscious as in a fishbowl.

But it is shallow to suggest that the mass media force this view on people as if only from the outside. The mass media are also ourselves, holding up a mirror to our invention, production, and perpetual capacity for elaborating the gratification of our imaginations.

The Consumption Fantasy is a dream of a way of life. Like the old symbolic murals of civilized mastery of the world with dirigible, ocean liner, locomotive, and car, the mass media project a vision of the American home with appliances in every corner, the family enjoying gracious meals prepared with instant products, with a motorboat at the dock, a barbecue pit alongside the swimming pool, and the faint holographic image of a not-so-far-off private airplane (or even a flying belt) hovering lightly in the purified atmosphere over the front lawn.

ECONOMIC CRISIS

It has been suggested that these fantasies will have to be quelled, that the United States may be in the process of shifting from the status of a "have" to a "have-not" nation. If so, this change would have momentous consequences as it contradicts the traditional view of "America the Bountiful," the land of opportunity, of new frontiers of land, the mind, space, and social progress. Questions arise concerning the allocation of resources—labor, materials, money—through governmental programs, handling of unemployment, rationing of goods, control of wages and prices, and so forth. The impact of economic crisis affects people variously and at different rates; certainly it affects the marketing activities of all, with changes in discretionary income, and the kinds of policies individuals and organizations seek to implement. There will be fundamental changes in values, basic orientations, and goals, and varied emotional reactions ranging from panic to apathy, with many more constructive possibilities in between.

THE NEED TO INTERPRET SOCIAL CHANGE

The above discussion illustrates in general ways how one might interpret some elements of the changing American scene. Marketing managers may not seem to engage in such cultural analysis, or even wish to, but their thinking and decisions inevitably express their interpretation of what is going on and what is likely to occur, as well as what they would like to see. While many businessmen were swearing at Ralph Nader and consumerism phenomena, the Whirlpool Company studied housewives' criticisms of appliances and advertised a hot line to cope with them. A Hong Kong banker expresses the belief that the blue jeans vogue is declining and he is wary of lending money to related enterprises. Some managers are actively planning what to do about conserving energy—while others are waiting unaware for the government to guide them. The greater their awareness of their society, the more insightful managers can be in raising questions about the possible effects on their products, their lines, their approach to their customers and their suppliers, and so forth.

To say that is not to make it easy. The facts do not speak for themselves, and there is constant controversy over what is "truly" happening, as well as over what ought to happen. The manager needs to analyze and interpret. The composition of American society—especially its homogeneity versus its heterogeneity—has been the subject of much debate. In the late 1950s, the general sense of rising affluence led some interpreters to suggest the United States had become a relatively homogeneous mass of middle-class people. As Daniel Seligman wrote in *Fortune:*

> The increased bunching of Americans around the middle-income levels, the increased blurring of occupational distinctions, and the increased adoption of middle-class living styles by families of diverse occupational background, have all tended to make the U.S. a much more homogeneous society.[17]

Of course, Seligman grants that status differences among people still remain, but sees the decline of the influence of national background, religion, and geographic separation as blue-collar workers move into the suburbs and socialize with junior executives.

Along about the same time, however, other writers were noticing the pluralistic aspects of our society, the new ethnic influxes, and the returning interest in Old World cultural roots. As sources of some differences fade, others are intensified and new forms of distinction arise. Herbert J. Gans scoffs at the supposed homogenization of American life, and instead sees a widening range of choice. The historical view that Gans sketches points especially to a classic pattern of change that has occurred in America with the shift of attention from the ethnic, working-class immigrant forebears, through their Americanized lower-middle-class-white-collar children, to their college-trained professional, managerial grandchildren.

But clearly, that is not the entire story, particularly given the marketing manager's interest in market segments that have not traversed this process, which is evident in the fact that the majority of the population do not have a college education. Gans agrees that regionality and ethnicity may not be the powerful forces they once were, but sees class differences as the single most important source of diversity.[18] This view did not prevent Gans and others from continuing to study the characteristics of cultural subgroups such as the Italians in Boston, and in New York City the negroes, Puerto Ricans, Jews, Italians, and Irish.[19]

By the mid-1970s the emphasis on the importance of ethnicity had gained greater stress, as reflected for example in the writing of Michael Novak,[20] to the point of some anxiety being expressed that the ethnic phenomenon was being exaggerated.[21]

Glazer and Moynihan also note the rise of the term *ethnicity* and wonder Why ethnicity? and Why now? They observe the conflicts among ethnic groups in different countries and reach the following conclusion:

> To us, however, it seems clear that ethnic identity *has* become more salient, ethnic self-assertion stronger, ethnic conflict more marked everywhere in the last twenty years, and that the reasons include the rise of the welfare state, the clash between egalitarianism and the differential achievement of norms, the growing heterogeneity of states, and the international system of communication . . . there is a phenomenon here that is, in ways not yet explicated, no mere survival but intimately and organically bound up with major trends of modern societies.[22]

A compromise position on just how effective the melting pot has been and is now, may not resolve the matter, but one is offered in a *Chicago Sun-Times* letter to the editor from Patrick McCallig, criticizing an editorial which stated that "Americans don't live in a melting pot, and never have."

> To go from one gross oversimplification (that the U.S. is a melting pot) to another, is not, I submit, either helpful, or worthy of a major newspaper. To what degree the United States has managed to assimilate its varied roots into a new culture is a subjective decision and one of continuing scholarly debate. . . . To state the United States is a society of rigid ethnic groups is to cloud further a subject much in need of careful analysis. More than that, it is an affront to the great number of Americans who do indeed come from varied cultural, ethnic, religious and racial backgrounds.[23]

LEVELS OF CHANGE

In searching out and interpreting the broad changes in the physical, social, and attitudinal environment, marketing managers wrestle with the fact that many trends are simultaneously going on in different directions and at different levels. Deep and broad trends are visible to those concerned with interpreting the general swings of history. They talk in terms of the spirit of the age, new spiritual orientations, alienation, or upheaval. These ideas refer to important background factors that modify the marketing environment and suggest something of its direction.

Analysis pitched at a less general and philosophic level may take up specific phenomena and try to understand either how they have come about or how they are apt to affect future events. For example, Mihaly Csikszentmihaly examined the hippie phenomenon for its core elements, the values held by hippies, and how these values effected their style of life. He pointed to some of the antecedents and sources of hippie style in Eastern mysticism, French existentialism, and the flowers and love of St. Francis, and he speculated about the possible influence of the hippie movement. He believed that the hippie world view might well make inroads into the present majority view if the current view shows no greater success in accommodating to the new facts in human awareness. Among these he included both negative and positive events.

> On the negative side, we're faced with the need to "make sense" of things like Nazi atrocities, the Bomb, continuing wars, the threat of overpopulation, never-ending social problems. On the positive side we find it equally difficult to adjust our world-view to things like space exploration, human organ transplants, computerization of non-creative thinking, scientific exploration of the human unconscious, and the technological promises of unlimited energy, food, and other utopian benefits.[24]

The same hippie phenomenon and its potential effects on the general society were taken up even more specifically by Fred Davis. He analyzed the hippies as representing ideas echoed in the larger culture and which will find increasing expression there. Davis identified three problems of this kind.

1. *Compulsive consumption.* The hippie is seen as reacting against the glut of material objects made possible by manufacturing skill, affluence, and a philosophy that urges their acquisition. Davis assumes that this greed cannot go on indefinitely, and that a model for new behavior is being developed by the belief that "happiness and a meaningful life are not to be found in things, but in the cultivation of the self and by an intensive exploration of inner sensibilities with like minded others."[25]

2. *Passive spectatorship.* The hippies may have exemplified a movement away from submissive acceptance of an audience and toward expressiveness for its own sake. Each person can cultivate his or her own performance, whether talented or not, with disregard for conventional or professional standards of excellence.

3. *Timescale of experience.* The new viewpoints require a reorientation to perception of, and use of, time. The presumption is

that there will be less point to focusing on what will be, with a radical shift in time perspective to what is.

Davis may be absurd in looking to the day when everyone will be a hippie. It seems an unlikely eventuality to most people, and certainly a long way off.

In the meantime, his predictions are somewhat borne out in the vogues for sensitivity and encounter groups, transcendental meditation, est, and marijuana; in the sharp increase in do-it-yourself and physical fitness activities; and in the growing number of people who are egocentric, impulsive, and narcissistic.

But all forecasting is open to the risk of contradiction—possibly Csikszentmihaly is rethinking his 1968 reference to the technological promises of unlimited food, energy, and other utopian benefits, and demographers are surprised to see that in the 1970s the rate of population growth is now greater in nonmetropolitan areas: "The most dramatic demographic change I've seen in this country, except for the increase in the birth rate in the 1950s and the decline of the birth rate in the last few years."[26] But difficult or not, marketing planners must nevertheless lay their chips on some concept of the near or long-range future.

Some workers have tried to measure the extent to which differences between generations exist and their rate of change. Some researchers find more of a generation gap than others, and much seems to depend on the variables and levels of analysis. Daniel Yankelovich found substantial changes in the way young people look at sex, religion, and their relationship to nature. Today's youth is more accepting of premarital sexual relations, more skeptical of organized religion, and closer to nature.

The value orientations identified by Florence Kluckhohn as basic to every culture include human nature, the relationship of people to nature, the nature of time, the basic modality of human activity, and the way in which people relate to one another. Table 1 shows some of these dimensions. Baldwin compared traditional middle-class-culture orientations with current youth-culture orientations as shown in Table 1.[27]

These abstractions translate into marketing issues. For example, today's young people's diminished interest in reading historical materials or studying for future careers, in the movement toward natural foods, outdoor experiences, and in the housing of communal living experiments. Cynics find these trends less than profound, and vulnerable to the traditional interpersonal realities that break up the communes as well as to the economic pressures that again make business and law careers attractive.

Table 1. *Value orientations of traditional middle-class culture and current youth culture.*

Dimension	Traditional Middle Class	Current Youth
Time	Future	Present
Activity	Doing	Being
Humankind–Nature	Dominance over nature	Harmony with nature
Basic human nature	People as neutral (neither good nor bad)	People as good
Relational	Individualistic	Collateral

Adapted from Florence Kluckhohn, "Dominant and Variant Orientations," in C. Kluckhohn and H. A. Murray (eds.), *Personality in Nature, Society, and Culture* (New York: Alfred A. Knopf, 1954).

CHANGE AND FASHION

But there seems no doubt that values and behaviors have shifted to create new patterns of consumption that are recognized by marketers of clothing, yogurt, sports, media, and so forth. As large-scale social and economic changes translate into marketing events, as they inevitably do, they lead to new patterns of spending, whether on guitars, drugs, and worn blue jeans or gold bars, new homes, and expensive porcelain birds.

Observing these patterns, some authors think about the trends called fashion, trying to relate the specific alterations in products to general principles. A classic attempt is by Dwight E. Robinson.[28] He seeks to show how the outlook of a period is transformed into the formal design of houses, cars, and clothing. William H. Reynolds[29] offers criteria for detecting fashion trends. It is clear that doing so is not a simple matter. It requires great awareness and sensitivity of judgment about the needs to be met and how genuine they are, the context of long-term trends in which the fashion may go on, past cycles that offer a model, concurrent trends that produce interactive effects, factors that are self-limiting to a fashion, and how the fashion may fit with norms, values, and existing techniques in the group. It is so hard to truly encompass these variables, or to know which are the most significant for the fashion one has in mind, that predictability is not apt to be very great or very systematic. But futurologists speculate about, and researchers try to find the key data that may help in venturing into, the unknown.

Chester R. Wasson is optimistic about predictability. He limits the variables that he considers important for effective foresight about trends. He discusses the kinds of learning that are necessary and which can be studied, identifying them as

Use-systems learning: learning a new sequence of motor habits.

Value-perception learning: perceiving new benefits as worth paying for.

Role-perception learning: adapting to the change in one's role that is implied by the new product.

He concludes that:

Not only fashion, but product acceptance in general is far more predictable than is generally thought, providing we make full use of the basic concepts of a product as a compromise bundle of desire attributes, demand as a desire set based on social conditioning, and motives as existing in a dynamic hierarchy and constantly restructured in the very process of their appeasement.[30]

The physical fitness trend might be an example, with its new motor habits (jogging), and the predictability of the purchase of new kinds of vitamins, sports shoes, and clothing.

To fulfill this optimism about seeing changes and predicting their nature clearly requires more than large ideas about where a society is going, in general. The desire attributes, demands, and motives Wasson refers to are ideas that characterize market segments in ways that need to identified.

In looking for patterns of relationships and the forecasting of trends, experts within specific fields speculate about the phenomena they deal with. For example, Jack Denst, a Chicago artist-designer, related decor colors to significant social and news events.

The religious aspects of the "baroque" period in the late seventeenth century resulted in the introduction of soft tones of pink, white, and gold.

The Edwardian era, placid and prosperous, encouraged the use of white, soft green, and black.

A decade rampant with riots, drug scenes, and social revolution, the 1960s also saw space and lunar exploration. Thus, in the middle of mind-boggling reds, yellows, intense blues, and gold green came the clear gleam of silver, inspired by technical advancements.

Pastels of the 1970s will cool the scene, and before long the earth colors will take over, reflecting the public's serious involvement with ecology.

Another set of relationships is suggested for clothing and music. Table 2 points to nuances that are visible to those close to

Table 2. Relationship of fashion to music styles.

Period	Fashion	Music Style
1950s	Pompadour hair, leather jackets, motorcycles, cuffed jeans.	Elvis Presley: the hillbilly heart-throb and the Teen Angel.
1964	Long hair, mod clothing.	The Beatles and The Rolling Stones: the heralds of Carnaby Street.
1967	Very long hair, beards, beads, flowers, and medallions.	The San Francisco Sound (Jefferson Airplane, Grateful Dead, Janis Joplin): Psychedelia meets Flower Power.
	Flared trousers and the union-made undershirt.	The British Blues Invasion: the influx of heavy blues groups brought glamorous rock personalities to these shores who wore exaggerated bell bottom pants called "loon" trousers. During casual jam sessions the musicians relaxed in their jeans and undershirts. Eventually they took this style onto the stage.
1969	Platform high-heeled shoes.	Mick Jagger, Rod Stewart, Joe Cocker: the superstar song stylists tried to dress as kinky as they sounded. Python boots became the rage.
1970	The "scruffy look": Jeans faded and otherwise, lumberjack flannel shirts. Organic foods and organic living. Communes.	Acoustic music: the shift to folk-country styles in music and dress began as a reaction to the sustained cacophony of hard rock. It became an attempt to find one's roots exemplified by Bob Dylan, The Grateful Dead, and others.
	Western shirts, studded jeans, and work shirts.	Country Rock:-the fusion of country and rock initiated in part by the musical meeting of minds of each: Johnny Cash and Bob Dylan.
1972	Camp and decadence. Lurex and glitter tops, superchunky shoes.	Glitter Rock: the bizarre rockers (David Bowie, Alice Cooper, Marc Bolan). Try to out-outrage each other and the audience.

Adapted from *Men's Wear,* August 1973.

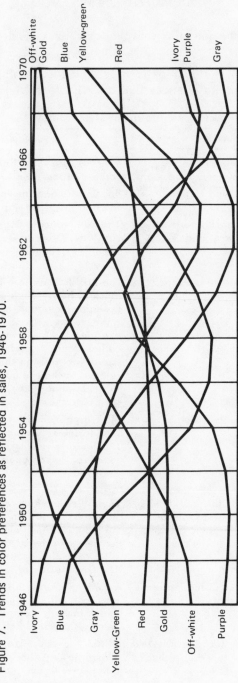

Figure 7. Trends in color preferences as reflected in sales, 1946-1970.

Reprinted with permission from The House and Garden Color
Program, House and Garden Colors® (Condé Nast Publications, Inc.).

the rock scene, and may exaggerate them, especially as no broader sense of explanation or trend is provided. Taking even broader sweeps of time pitches the problem at another level, ignoring what individuals like Alice Cooper or Mick Jagger are doing, to track more generally characteristic cycles and phenomena. The curves in Figure 7, with their long fundamental character, flow past the overtones of seasons and jogs of certain years, suggesting only a coming and going of color preferences, unrelated to other events.

SUMMARY

1. Through their decisions, marketing managers act to implement or change their culture. They conform to its central character and do what is expected of proper managers (urge profit, belong to the Kiwanis) or they may move with new trends (urge the exercise of corporate social responsibility, speak for risky innovations).

2. They struggle with the difficulties of interpreting where the society is going, but ignore the issues at their peril. In trying to understand what their customers and the people who supply their wants are doing and saying, they take account of what is demanded by society and the forces of economics, technology, philosophy, and so forth, as these affect the culture in a grand sense.

3. From the broad level of generalization, and the necessary armchair sociologizing, managers infer where they think the marketplace is specifically moving and how that movement might be translated into new products, ways of communicating, and mechanisms of exchange.

References

1. W. Lloyd Warner, *The Corporation in the Emergent American Society* (New York: Harper & Row, 1962), p. xv.
2. Everett E. Hagen, *On the Theory of Social Change* (Homewood, Ill.: Dorsey, 1962), p. 23.
3. Robert Redfield, *A Village That Chose Progress* (Chicago: University of Chicago Press, 1950), p. 36.
4. Ibid., p. 174.

5. Alan R. Beals, "Interplay Among Factors of Change in a Mysore Village," in McKim Marriott (ed.), *Village India* (Washington, D.C.: The American Anthropological Association, 1955), Memoir No. 83, pp. 97–98.
6. Personal communication from **Ruby Roy Dholakia.**
7. J. J. Servan-Schreiber, *American Challenge* (New York: Atheneum, 1968).
8. For a fuller exposition of these points, see **Conrad M. Arensberg** and **H. Niehoff,** *Introducing Social Change* (Chicago: Aldine, 1964), Ch. 6.
9. David Caplovitz, *The Poor Pay More* (New York: The Free Press, 1963); **Michael Harrington,** *The Other America* (New York: Macmillan, 1962); Task Force on Economic Growth and Opportunity, *The Concept of Poverty* (Washington, D.C.: Chamber of Commerce of the United States, 1965); **Frederick D. Sturdivant,** "Better Deal for Ghetto Shoppers," *Harvard Business Review,* Mar.–Apr. 1968, pp. 130–139.
10. David Riesman, Reuel Denney, and **Nathan Glazer,** *The Lonely Crowd: A Study of the Changing American Character* (New Haven: Yale University Press, 1950).
11. David C. McClelland, *The Achieving Society* (New York: Van Nostrand, 1961), pp. 192–197.
12. Vance Packard, *The Hidden Persuaders* (New York: Pocket Books, 1957).
13. John K. Galbraith, *The Affluent Society* (Boston: Houghton Mifflin, 1958).
14. A. H. Maslow, *Motivation and Personality* (New York: Harper & Row, 1954), pp. 80–98.
15. Gerard Piel, *Science in the Cause of Man* (New York: Alfred A. Knopf, 1961).
16. J. H. Plumb, "The Noble Houses of Eighteenth-Century England," *Horizon,* Nov. 1958, p. 41.
17. Daniel Seligman, "The New Masses," *Fortune,* May 1959.
18. Herbert J. Gans, "Diversity Is Not Dead," *The New Republic,* April 3, 1961.
19. Herbert J. Gans, *The Urban Villagers* (New York: The Free Press, 1962); **Nathan Glazer** and **Daniel P. Moynihan,** *Beyond the Melting Pot: The Negroes, Puerto Ricans, Jews, Italians, and Irish of New York City* (Cambridge, Mass.: MIT Press, 1963).
20. Michael Novak, *The Rise of the Unmeltable Ethnics* (New York: Macmillan, 1972).
21. See review of Novak's book by Howard F. Stein, *Society,* Sept.–Oct. 1974, pp. 94–96.
22. Nathan Glazer and **Daniel P. Moynihan,** "Why Ethnicity?" *Commentary,* Oct. 1974, p. 39.
23. Patrick McCallig, "Complexity of U.S. Society," *Chicago Sun-Times* Nov. 9, 1974, p. 33.
24. Mihaly Csikszentmihaly, "The Hippy As Revolutionary," *The University of Chicago Magazine,* June 1968, p. 16.
25. Fred Davis, "Why All of Us May Be Hippies Someday," *Trans-Action,* 1967, p. 13.
26. Calvin L. Beale, quoted by William Chapman, "Back-to-Towns Trend Growing," *Chicago Sun-Times,* Sept. 9, 1974, p. 32.
27. Cited as adapted from **D. C. Baldwin, Jr.,** in a useful overview of the literature by **L. Eugene Thomas,** "Generational Discontinuity in Beliefs: An Exploration of the Generation Gap." *Journal of Social Issues,* 1974, pp 1–22.
28. Dwight E. Robinson, "Fashion Theory and Product Design," *Harvard Business Review,* Nov.–Dec. 1958, pp. 126–138.
29. William H. Reynolds, "Cars and Clothing: Understanding Fashion Trends," *Journal of Marketing,* July 1968, pp. 44–49.
30. Chester R. Wasson, "How Predictable Are Fashion and Other Product Life Cycles?" *Journal of Marketing,* July 1968, p. 43.

Suggested Readings

Eisenstadt, S. N., *Modernization: Protest and Change* (Englewood Cliffs, N.J.: Prentice-Hall, 1966).

Etzioni, Amitai, *Studies in Social Change* (New York: Holt, Rinehart and Winston, 1966).

Galbraith, John Kenneth, *The New Industrial State* (Boston: Houghton Mifflin, 1967).

Greer, Scott, *The Emerging City* (New York: The Free Press, 1962).

Loomis, Charles P., *Social Systems* (Princeton, N.J.: D. Van Nostrand, 1960).

Potter, David M., *People of Plenty* (Chicago: University of Chicago Press, 1954).

Schon, Donald, *Technology and Change* (New York: Delacorte Press, 1967).

Tiryakian, Edward A. (ed.), *Sociological Theory, Values, and Sociocultural Change* (New York: The Free Press, 1963).

Warner, W. Lloyd, *The Living and the Dead: A Study of the Symbolic Life of Americans* (New Haven, Conn.: Yale University Press, 1959).

Zaltman, Gerald, et al., *Processes and Phenomena of Social Change* (New York: Wiley, 1973).

vi

Market Segments

Industrial marketers and retailers think a lot about specific customers, and face-to-face selling tells marketers a lot about individual customers, but mass market selling forces marketing managers to think in terms of market segments. All other considerations are related to this central interest and are instrumental to it, as all decisions about the market are essentially statements about some group or groups.

Somehow or other, marketers conceptualize or generalize about the groups or aggregations of customers they have or would like to have. Marketing managers may feel that they are tuned into these groups, especially if they are of the same social status, sex, or age, or think they have something to learn about them. The manager may attribute many specific characteristics to them or think about them in vague terms. Sometimes the segments are seen as "just people" who can be expected to react in ordinary ways to the messages sent to them. Other times they seem relatively unpredictable and need to be studied to learn about specific reactions. Somewhat removed from the customers, the average marketer is not visualizing the people in the segment, or is sticking with narrow stereotypes that may or may not fit the situation. In the consumer goods field, the manufacturing marketing manager, who is often several steps removed from the end user, is likely to be receptive to marketing research and its findings, whereas the retail or industrial marketing manager's market is more visibly tangible, so research seems less necessary.

MARKET SEGMENTATION: A FACT OF LIFE

Market segments are subgroups in society.[1] They are groups of people who buy and sell in particular ways that set them off from the others. The actions that distinguish them as a segment derive partly from the larger culture—those actions that are permitted, approved, disapproved, or prohibited, that are given general definition. Cultural prescriptions filter through the cultural subgroups unevenly. For example, patriotism is expected of all, but some are traitors, others are superpatriots who buy lots of flags, and most reserve their patriotism for special occasions. Furthermore, the behavior of the segment is part of its identity. The needs and patterns of buying and selling that make up a market segment are the commonalities that go with that identity. The collection and interaction of the segments form the society. It may be seen as a fabric with infinitely variegated aggregations of kinds of people and endless strands of attributes serving as bases for categorizing and grouping.

The history of market segmentation thinking can be broken down into four phases. At the beginning of this century, segmentation was not discussed as an opportunity to exercise marketing skills. Customers came to get what others had to sell or one went out to find or persuade someone to buy what they were offering.[2] For various historical reasons having to do with changes in market size, costs, production agility, competition, and communication capacity, as well as the growth of intellectual content and self-consciousness in marketing, the second phase grew out of the idea that markets should be recognized as being segmented. The third phase addressed itself to discussions concerning what the bases for segmentation should be. In the fourth phase some critics see signs of an overworked segmentation concept, which can be a false or poor basis for marketing and social policy.

While these four phases have had consecutive emphases, they are also concurrent and contemporary. Some people are just beginning to learn about the importance of segmentation in their company or industry, others are already pooh-poohing it, and still others argue about the use of demographic variables over behavioral variables.[3]

The point is, no matter what position was taken, and even before market segmentation per se had become conceptualized, it was always with us in one form or another. Market segmentation is an inevitable and fundamental aspect of economics. There have always been users and nonusers, light and heavy users, frequent and occasional users, and happy and dissatisfied users. Whether they were called segments or not, they were, and remain, segments — subsets of larger or total populations. This fact is not altered because some segments are very large or very small. It remains even though specific individuals straddle different segments or move into new segments through time.

Perhaps it should be pointed out that the segmentation that exists in the marketplace is not there for the convenience of the marketer. At times, people will group themselves to make it easy to sell to them, or to help them buy more efficiently, but they are usually busy just being who they are. The segments they form are abstractions which depend on how you look at them and what you want from them. The reality of market segments does not provide that their behavior be stable, nonvolatile, repetitive, exclusive, or gross. This fact creates problems because many marketers have a more difficult time when market segments are changing or are unreliable,[4] or when the basis for segmentation is subtle and not easily related to familiar demographic variables.

Of course, other marketers strive to bring about, or to take advantage of, such lively conditions. For example, the makers of Tylenol were relatively comfortable with their market of over-the-counter analgesics until Datril came along to stir things up. In another instance, Vitalis and Vaseline split the men's hair-grooming market until cream oil was invented. Later, men's hair took on renewed social significance, and the market segmented again, with protein sprays, the Dry Look, and other products that appeal to the new trend.

People are kinds of consumers because they are kinds of people. That they segment in their market behavior reflects and expresses the varied social fabric. Patterns of market decisions and actions accumulate because individuals make up certain groups that share specific, explicit memberships and participation in social units. This makes it possible to generalize about them as kinds of people who do similar kinds of things and buy the same things insofar as their particular memberships require it.

Buyers and sellers are members of many groups by virtue of their physical being, their location, their age, stage in the life cycle, and social status. They belong to interest groups, to occupational groups, to ethnic groups. They may take any number of kinds of people as reference groups, that is, as sources of belonging, of standards, and of aspirations. Thus, a person's behavior may be an expression of the fact that he is lower-middle-class, Republican, Baptist, a skier, college-educated, a suburban dweller, a member of the PTA, of an investment club and the YMCA, and an assistant product manager. He is male, tall, a Midwesterner, married, comes from a small family with mixed Western European forebears, is in his thirties, and belongs to the Naval Reserve. All these memberships, states of being, and characteristics (and many more) interact in varying degree to dictate his actions, the situations he will seek out, and how he will react to those he encounters.

Because the same person also lacks many characteristics and memberships, there are many behaviors he is not likely to show. For example, we can safely say that he will not become pregnant and is unlikely to wear hippie gear, go to mass, till the soil (depending on his house lot), work on a scavenger truck, or read *The New York Review of Books*. Like most people, he will adhere, in the main, to the behavior that fits reasonably with the people he is like and wants to be like. Studies show that people who associate together come to be more alike. This general tendency makes it possible to study and think about the characteristics of the endless array of kinds of people there are, whether they exist as actual groups or form a group in an abstract sense.

But this is only another way of expressing the elementary fact that market segments are "specific homogeneous groups" within a market. The trouble comes from trying to decide what there is about the segment that is homogeneous besides the marketing behavior itself. It seems reasonable that there would be some commonalities, some shared qualities or variables among people who are classed together for marketing reasons, but it can be hard to sort out those which are related to your specific product.

The subject is difficult to generalize about because different product areas pose different problems. The level of concern with segmentation varies greatly and the relevant variables tend to shift not only with logic, but with the marketer's intellectual taste. The possibilities for sorting segments are infinite because buyers and consumers are complex, and what sellers want to know about (who, how many, where, why) changes over time.[5]

SEGMENTATION PROBLEMS

The study of market segmentation raises many questions not easily answered. Numerous studies have sought to determine relationships between particular consumer variables and specific purchasing behavior. All too often, these studies are frustrating because they mainly indicate that the variables most highly correlated to the behavior are also those which are so close to it as hardly to explain much at all. A classic example was the finding that people who were most likely to respond to the introduction of a new coffee were those who tended to buy a lot of coffee.

Diversity—almost a perversity of diversity—is the easiest generalization to fall back on. You can start with a user group and find that it includes varieties of people, scores, and dimensions. You can also start with sociological categories of groups and find that they include varieties of user behaviors. People who score high on innovativeness may not show initiative in the area you want to study, or dramatic examples of people in a research sample who display high-status values and philosophy may turn out to be of lower status. While these may be exceptional cases, there are surely enough of them to muddy the waters and reduce correlations sharply. However, these exceptions to the rule should not be dismissed, since science has the task of covering the exceptional cases in terms of a theory as well.

Clearly, trying to classify people as types of buyers comes up against the refusal of so many people to be consistent buyers—or at least consistent in the ways we seek to order their behavior. The study of market segmentation—and the behavioral sciences in general—have a hard time explaining any human actions. Behavioral study is not easy, and much work needs to be done. But marketing has an even harder task, because fewer people are working to develop the multitudinous series of specific studies designed to test variable against variable that are persistently presented in social science journals.

But as complicated and difficult as all this may be, marketers deal with it because they must. They reason and plan about the market segments that concern them. They may do it unwillingly, they may do it eagerly, they may do it unknowingly, well or poorly, or they may even deny that they do it, but all their actions are implicitly or explicitly predicated on ideas about the nature of market segments. Marketers have faith that there are kinds of people out there to whom they can reach out with their product. They expect that some kind of audience alignments will occur because certain interests, beliefs, feelings, wishes, and tastes will for a time (whether brief or sustained) resonate in positive chorus to the marketing message.

For some marketers, reasoning about markets is not a strain because broad generalizations serve their purpose. Their products are widely used, the relevant general appeals are well known, and their brands are successfully entrenched. They may have less incentive than others to inquire about segments. But let troublesome competition arise, changes occur, and innovations fail, and suddenly the casual generalizations no longer suffice. When new products are being developed, what is the rationale behind them? Whose needs will they serve? Toward whom should the promotion be directed? Whom should the salesperson call on? What should the advertising messages say? Such questions cannot be answered nor can action be taken without some knowledge or belief about the nature of the various groups "out there."

An appliance company recently inquired into the suitability of a hand mixer proposed for the prototypical housewife. However, a study suggested that its most likely appeal was, for various reasons, to working women, bachelors, brides, small families, and indifferent cooks. Marketing research showed the product was evaluated as having low appeal to the more mature, experienced, and prosperous cooks, but was positively evaluated by the young, inexperienced, and poor cooks.

These kinds of people are just a few of the many varieties that turn up in market studies. From the viewpoint of research rigor, they irritatingly mix up dimensions that are economic, social, age-graded, and attitudinal, making measurement difficult. But almost any qualitative investigation of the market that gives people a chance to speak freely and fully tends to reveal attributes and dynamic processes that help explain the purchase behavior of people in different social classes, at different stages of the life cycle, in different interest groups and consuming moods, and pursuing different patterns of lifestyle.

As business becomes more variegated and objects and ways of living increasingly proliferate, the ease of generalizing about the marketplace is steadily reduced. Thinking of the marketplace as inevitably segmented can lead to a subtler, more penetrating understanding, more precise rationales for actions, and a discriminating awareness of the complexities in choice and decision making that affect buyers—all in all making for a more penetrating marketer.

This kind of awareness develops out of being alert to the currents in the modern scene and out of studying the groups and variables that have meaning for a marketer's product and brand. To help bring out the many approaches and points of view to be derived through studying different groups, examples of various patterns that result from the many segmenting forces are discussed in the following section.

EXAMPLES OF SEGMENTS

Of the many kinds of market segments, marketers are most interested in what the user groups and nonuser groups are. Sellers and buyers like to define the segment in terms of the purchase or use of a particular product or service, perhaps a specific brand. Often, the distinction is as clear cut as beer drinkers, owners of General Electric coffeemakers, subscribers to *Seventeen* magazine, and so forth. In each of these cases, if the marketers are sellers, they may want to know the reasons why these people drink beer, bought that coffeemaker, buy that magazine. They may want to know what other characteristics the segment shows in age, education, income, what other things they buy or read, and innumerable other answers that might help in relating to that segment more effectively. If the marketers are buyers, they may want to know what brands other beer drinkers in the group prefer, if other owners have had good experience with their GE coffeemaker, whether other readers of *Seventeen* saw the same ad or illustration or read the same article, and so on.

In other instances, the category of *person* is more general. Here, a user group is examined for a pattern that cuts across many products, services, or brands, as would be found among vegetarians, patients, and purchasing agents. In the search for greater understanding of who the people in the marketing world are, what they are doing, and why, the segments of interest may initially be defined less by a pattern of consumption than by a social role, life-cycle stage, or lifestyle pattern, such as young marrieds, middle-class people, black executives, cosmopolites, perhaps with the buyer aim of knowing how to be an appropriate member of such a group, or with the seller aim of improving communications.

An inquiry into the characteristics and outlook of given market segments might start out rather generally. Say an advertising agency wants to study the attitudes of housewives toward food products and meal planning. But they also want to ask broader questions about the group to pick up on the typical viewpoints and feelings about their lives and their reactions to living in a relatively abundant society. Interviews with a sample group of housewives indicated that they had to observe characteristics of both the women and their perception of the environment. Furthermore, the dimension or context of time orientation governed many aspects of their reactions. Here is a summary of some of the main findings.[6]

The Modern Era

When respondents talk about what things are like nowadays, they speak from their sense of historical perspective. They make comparisons to other eras and decades and to when they were young. They speculate about what is going on in the world and in America. Their views cover a familiar range of ideas. Essentially, they see a world of rapid change, complexity, and conflict, in which science and invention have produced some amazing consequences. These often have a transcendental quality of having gone beyond the ken or coping of ordinary men and women in daily life. The great consequences are large metropolitan networks, large governments, businesses, and unions, carrying with them their benefits in prosperity and their side effects in pollution.

As citizens and consumers, people tend to translate these ideas into concrete and immediate terms. The modern era makes available dishwashers, nursery schools, and new foods. It produces a rat race that fosters the sale of alcohol and pills. New social and personal relations are stimulated, such as early teen marriages and delayed marriages, feelings of insignificance in large work units, a new breed of sophisticated working women, the intensity of educational demands on young people, and the civil rights ferment. The large view makes people feel troubled, as the following comments would indicate.

Things are moving too fast. Everything is getting bigger and more complex to solve. Government is trying to lay its hands on all facets of life. Everything is bursting at the seams.

The generations don't understand each other. There never is enough money. There is uncertainty about the future, the possibility of catastrophe, a lack of spiritual and moral security. No leadership, no sense of direction.

It wasn't such a rat race as it is today. If things get any worse, I don't know. The momentum of life today, trying to keep up with the times—no wonder people have to take all kinds of pills and sedatives to relieve the tensions they're under.

It is like the fall of the Roman Empire. This country is going to end up like Rome.

Traffic congestion, noise, litter, fumes—I've come to accept them. They are serious. If we don't have clean water and clean air, all of us will die. They are serious, but I can't change them so I accept them.

Life is compartmentalized and lived at various levels. As the last speaker says, what she thinks she cannot change she accepts. Most people quit clucking at the amazing and recalcitrant epoch in which they live and reorient themselves to the features of the narrower span of time that is the present.

The Present

The present is the larger era made manifest in specific current events. It refers to the way things are going right now. It means a current election; the state of the economy in the current year; strikes by teacher, doctor, coal miner, and transit worker; and the severity of the weather as compared with last year. Views on such matters affect public mood and spending. The world may be going to pot or bursting at the seams, but in the meantime what will affect our own situations in the economic climate? What kinds of plans can be made, given the course of public events that might impinge on our private lives?

There is a mixed sense of uneasiness at this level. People are glad when an advance seems to be made in a tax that did not rise, or in a change in school policy that promises educational benefits for children. Not uncommonly, many people feel distant from or somehow untouched by public events. For example, one person shrugged off a question about the President and his programs, saying:

His programs have no effect at all. I go on living as I did, have my bills to pay and my son to raise.

Wariness and anxious feelings prevail. Inflationary pressures are complained about. Problems of the day seem unusually unsolvable because of intransigent, inadequate, or negative leadership.

I'm worried about the irresponsible leaders. They are the ones who will instigate violence, hatred. The racial problem really worries me.

The prices will just get higher and higher unless something is done.

Within these two large contexts of the era and the present, variations in response come about for many reasons. Whether the times are exciting or oppressive depends not only on their force, but on individual resources.

Personal Mood

Everyone has a personal, characteristic frame of mind, one that gives self-expression in a recurring way. It is a fundamental theme that endures through the overtones of temporary fluctuations in feelings. In the study being reported, the pace and tempo of the women's rhetoric or semantics showed a rhythm, a typical beat. By observing each woman in this way, it becomes possible to classify her by her emotional or temperamental rhythm.

Upbeat women are involved, "on the ball." They are alert to both traditional and new values, to changing practices and products. Upbeat women have a sense of rising perspective about their personal development. They understand the language of the day; they revel in their present abundance; they seek out stimulation and experience. They feel, or aspire to be, creative and initiating. They feel a sense of resiliency and vitality, which allows them to take things in stride rather than to set up routines and yield to them. They feel they understand young people and can sympathize with their needs, their revolts, and their desires for and against conformity. These women want to sustain their youth, to share with young people the willingness to experiment, to try new products, and to see another point of view.

We are emotionally happy. Nothing has happened to me that would form the basis of the Great American Novel, but every time I meet someone new, it's an interesting experience. I have become a Girl Scout leader. . . . I love to try new foods, and do so frequently. . . .

Right now decorating is being done in the Mediterranean mood, but coming up fast is Colonial American again.

Things have been good for us. . . . There have been many illnesses, but thankfully we've survived. We moved into a larger house, more to our liking. . . . I have many new small appliances, which I enjoy.

Cooking is still a creative art.

Onbeat women are conscientious planners, devoted to maintaining the stability of home and family. These women seek quality and appropriateness, keeping in step, and working for lifestyles becoming to the family's status and the neighborhoods in which they live. Self-control and optimism, support from religion, and constructive thinking orient them toward sensible mastery of their ups and downs.

Well, as could be expected, everything seems normal. No sickness or financial worries over the past three–four years. My husband is an average man, makes an average income. He is in the piano business, he buys and sells. I taught piano until a few years ago, but now I have less time to spend foolishly. . . . This is a troubled world, and there are times when everybody is unhappy. . . . But a woman gets along if she keeps current with the news, politics, wears nice clothing, has a good hair style. It is really the Joneses' world. Everybody is trying to get ahead.

Downbeat women show feelings of disorganization, heavy responsibility, and fatalism. They do not feel able to cope adequately with their destinies, families, or husbands. They find life either troubled or dull. One woman, asked about how she viewed her situation, said:

Let's say fair. We haven't had any real problems. We live here because my husband can drive to work. He feels lukewarm about his job—doesn't mind it though. What else is there to say? Some days here are just hectic cooking. I just stagger throughout the day. Nothin' in particular I like. I would like to get away by myself for a vacation. I lead a dull life, we haven't done much of anything. I guess we have achieved some of our goals, but you are never satisfied.

Besides the women who are upbeat, onbeat, and downbeat, there are those who are just plain *beat*. These women feel that coping is almost beyond them, that demands and circumstances have defeated them or exhausted their resources. Sometimes, the answer lies in yielding, perhaps to a rest cure or to a retreat back home for awhile. The words of a woman who had reached this point sum it up:

It has been hectic—you know, the usual things when you have five children. My husband is a Navy man and isn't home like other fathers. I'm tired, and don't like the place we live in, so I'm going back home. I want to be near my family and I want my mother now—I'm never out. I haven't been out now for six years. I hardly ever get a chance to go anywhere. I'm so tired at the end of the day I just don't want to go anywhere. I'd like to go to an island by myself and not even talk.

Individual personality thus affects how people can or cannot use abundance. Upbeat and onbeat women are more apt to seek it, use it, master it, and enjoy it. Downbeat and beat women, even in comparable financial circumstances, feel harassed by plenty and the demands it makes for striving, for going out to get it, and then making active use of it.

Stage in the Life Cycle

An important consideration in market segmentation is the life stage of the group. Capacity for awareness, the level of affluence, and the directions and quality of interest in products and services all undergo great changes with age. The developmental tasks confronting children and adolescents and young, mature, and aging adults have peculiarities that guide what meanings consumption is likely to have for them. A few typical outlooks can be illustrated by dipping into points in the age stream. For example, a 16-year-old girl indicates the testing-out, trying-out venture into an increasingly adult world of choices.

Sixteen is lots of activities, always on the go. You are in the prime of life. It is happy years. You don't have the worries other people have, you don't have to worry where your dinner is coming from. It is sometimes hard to make decisions: what to wear, the right thing to wear when you are going someplace, and sometimes you have so many places to go you don't know where to go. It is hard to decide.

An 18-year-old confronts herself decisively, coming to terms with herself, her career, her financial situation:

I am very sensitive and easily hurt, but I know my friends say how petite and cute I am. I now work at two jobs and get the money I need for school and clothes. I will graduate high school—I'm not smart enough to go to college. I'll probably get a job in an office.

A sophisticated 20-year-old suggests her enlarged view of the world.

I used to be nervous around men, but now that I work with them, we discuss general things, world situations, work, other people, TV, books, what movie they have seen lately, sports, and eventually other (on a more personal basis) specific things.

Young people generally show a reaching out, a sense of their own broadening horizons, and a wish to be somewhat more liberated and expressive than their parents, although there is less of an intergenerational gap than the publicized rebels suggest. In the words of a conforming daughter, who takes for granted the numerous products available and expects to make use of the familiar ones:

I'll do the same thing with my kids that my mother does, make them take turns doing housework. In basic things, like food, I'll probably stick to Campbell's, Hunt's, Del Monte, Chicken of the Sea, and Cherry Valley. Mostly in detergents I'll stick with Tide and Ajax. Basically, you will use what your mother used.

Some women embark on a career. Others work to increase family income. The young wife with a growing family modifies what she learned from her mother, feeling that new ways of child-rearing and new household goals teach her how to be modern. Visible in the early years of marriage is an adaptation to new things, a growing and searching, and a general orientation to mobility through the many avenues available. Foremost among these is the husband's progress. At this life stage, the mantle of hope has traditionally rested on his shoulders. Men make innumerable references to going to school to get more credits, to prospects for advancement, to getting a job with a future with diversified opportunities to learn and to broaden their knowledge. Trends in the seventies show that women are coming to express the same desires.

There are also more personal wishes. The young, maturing, traditionally prototypical housewife dreams of being rich, staying young, being slim. When she looks beyond feeling preoccupied and absorbed with her children she makes frequent references to "after my children are in school," "now all I want to do is to raise a family," "after my child is older"; she thinks about a career or self-expressive activities she might undertake, like getting involved in art, dancing, tennis, writing, volunteer work, and starting a business.

The more mature families convey a sense of reaching a peak, of settling in with a moderation of the breadth of possibilities. Commonly, the men are working pretty close to their capacity, doing the work they are likely to continue with, with not much more than a few systematic raises to be expected. Ideas of future gains tend to be replaced with acceptance of, and hopes within, the status quo.

I doubt that he will go any further in his job than he is now. He makes good money and I have no complaints.

My husband will continue as he has been doing for twenty years until we are on Social Security.

Concern mounts with figuring out how to get through the tighter period when income is settling down, prices keep going up, and the needs of older children for food, clothes, education, weddings, and the like, seem to be reaching a crescendo. There is talk about savings, fringe benefits, investments, insurance, as thoughts turn to ways of making it through the later years.

The stock and pension plan that the company set up helps our future. We have some insurance. We will manage.

We have savings and then of course there is the insurance program, which will go toward the children's education. Clothing for the children is more expensive. They want more at this time and are more influenced by what the others have.

We save whatever we can spare. We are buying bonds and have a nest egg for the children's education.

The group in their fifties and sixties tend to be in a quieter period when some responsibilities are being reduced, major goals have been met and are being enjoyed, disappointments are solidified into bitterness or resignation, and strivings are less intense. The man's retirement is a major consideration, with thinking oriented to changes in housing and new lifestyles. Society presses people to remain youthful, to keep up, to be active and independent. Those who manage to do this reasonably well may turn to a new, more convenient home, a new car for travel, new furnishings, new clothes, and reawaken in a kind of carefree blossoming. Income limitations often thwart the aims of older people. Those who feel left out are resentful, seeing those who are gratified as grasping and ungrateful.

> *No matter where I look for a job I have it thrown in my face that I am too old. I am very lonesome, my life is very lonesome. It's just like being in a prison—you can't go out if you have to watch your pennies. It worries me now that the individual is taxed to death. Young people ought to be paddled. . . . They are spoiled. It is gimme, gimme all the time. They get what they want and then get into mischief.*

Family Situation and Outlook

Putting together the various sources of reactions suggested here produces the complex that governs each family's economic situation and outlook. Nor are these matters simply related. It is possible to feel that trends are unhappy in the world while remaining optimistic about the material things that will be bought. As one person put it:

> *There has to be an end to the high cost of living. Costs keep rising, and I don't think things are going to change. Farmers are going broke. Small stores are being pushed out. I can't feel good about anything.*

Later in the interview, the same woman said:

> *During the next six months or so I will want a new car, a new rug, a new living room suite of furniture. Linoleum for my kitchen, a new lawn mower, and new shoes and clothes. I would like a lovely wedding for my daughter. I will probably have enough money to get them.*

It is probably no news that the more people have, the more they want. This seems intrinsic to some people, who are frankly acquisitive. For others, the growing wants appear to be more related to a desire to maximize the nature of their goals, so that they constantly absorb more money as it becomes available. The man who can now afford more insurance for his family considers it reasonable to carry a larger policy. Those who want to travel try to take the longest, most diverse, and in a sense, costliest trips they can squeeze in. Devout homeowners, who include vast numbers of Americans, engage endlessly in pouring money into the walls, basements, appliances, gutters, and sewers of their houses. Each home improvement project may engender another. People who value dining out and living it up do so in ever more opulent style. Another way of expressing this insatiability is to say that few consumers feel able to satisfy themselves on all fronts. They usually feel that some expenditure is being deferred to permit another, and more discretionary funds would make more experience possible. Those who are retrenching are making the same tradeoff, but with a feeling of backing into a negative direction.

RACIAL SEGMENTATION

Race is one of the broader categories that affect marketing behavior. Many specific studies are made to find out how blacks react to certain advertisements or buy certain brands, and what media are used. Commonly, such studies lack sufficient background or context, making the results narrow and fragmentary. It is useful first to generate an overview, as well as to dig into the subtler elements at work in the group, to be able to make the judgments about the group's probable responses that Schramm's communication criteria require.

One of the early articles dealing with racial aspects of the market is Henry Allen Bullock's "Consumer Motivations in Black and White." He believes that marketing approaches to blacks have been distorted by misunderstandings about the best means to solicit patronage. Bullock provides an overview. He aims for a sense of direction that will be rewarding to sellers and be morally defensible as well. By and large, he emphasizes aspects of common humanity among blacks and whites that support integrated communications, or techniques that avoid stimulating a consciousness of racial differences. He addresses the problem of what sellers should do if they are to win one racial group without losing the other. Bullock prefers to avoid the extreme of treating blacks as a special group.[7]

Others find the approach suggested by Bullock either idealistic or bland, feeling that many blacks want to have their own characteristics recognized and addressed, as is the case with various other segments of society. This is not an either/or situation, as obviously many marketing approaches are made that are indifferent to race. But there are also situations in which it seems reasonable to think about, and to orient to, issues of special meaning to blacks.

Many people have concerned themselves with clarifying these issues. In a pragmatic manner, Donald Sexton examines black buyer behavior, suggesting that many of its characteristics are mainly the results of some restraints, but that there may also be some motivational differences between black and white buying behavior. He summarizes a common finding—that as among whites, higher-income-level blacks are more status-conscious than lower-status blacks, so that having the best products and brands is an important consideration. This attitude leads to an emphasis on thinking that goods and services offered by white institutions are probably better; with further indication that this attitude may be changing as new loyalties to black enterprises grow.[8]

Sometimes, ethnographic studies suggest a richer understanding of a cultural subgroup than do traditional market research studies. An example is found in the work by Ulf Hannerz on "What Negroes Mean by 'Soul.' " He examines the meaning of this distinctive concept for its importance to the black community; its derivation; its expression in music, food, a way of life, and a style; and its relation to the issue of achievement in society. He concludes:

> By talking about people who have soul, about soul music and about soul food, the soul brother attempts to establish himself in the role of an expert and connoisseur; by talking to others of his group in these terms, he identifies with them and confers the same role on them.[9]

Even a cursory look at a cultural subgroup as large as the black population shows the difficulty of generalizing. Soul may be an issue that has to be dealt with by all blacks, but it is not the same to middle-class blacks as it is to working-class blacks. Burleigh B. Gardner notes the tendency to overgeneralize when thinking about blacks. He points out that the negro market is not one but many markets.

> First there is the slum culture or culture of poverty so prevalent in the ghetto. This culture (which in terms of Warner's social class structure is the Lower-Lower Class) is neither exclusively black nor urban. It does reach its height as a social problem in our urban slums. This culture of poverty has a pattern of interrelated values, attitudes, beliefs and behaviors which are passed on from generation to generation. For example, the Negro boy in the slums learns from his parents and from other adults and children that:
>
> 1. Poverty is a way of life for most people and that in his home there is no expectation that it will ever be different. Nor does he get to know well any other way of life. Even in school, his contacts with

children from even moderately prosperous families are rarely intimate.

2. As a Negro, he will have little opportunity to better himself. Even if parents try to tell him he has a chance, the evidence around him, the other adults and children, all say 'no.'

3. School is a pointless burden and the teachers are indifferent. The other children teach him that to be one of them he must dislike school and avoid it if possible.

4. Violence, delinquency and crime are part of this way of life. He must learn to fight others either individually or in gangs. His friends will steal partly to get things they want and partly to prove themselves. And if the law doesn't get them, there is no real social disapproval—rather there is admiration and approval among his peers and older teens.

Although this culture pervades the slums, there are residents who do not succumb. There is a high proportion of families who are striving to have a better life, who are responsible about jobs and family, who want their children to do better and to escape from the slums. When these families do manage to improve themselves financially, they are apt to move to better neighborhoods in search of better homes, schools, and social environment.

Formerly trapped in the ghetto, but now rapidly moving out, is the growing group of stable white-collar families. They are very similar to the white-collar, lower-middle-class whites. They are striving for a stable and orderly life, to own their own modest homes, to see their children through college.

At a higher economic level are the Upper-Middle Class of professionals and business executives and owners. Many have high incomes and are able to own large homes, send their children to private schools, live well and enjoy expensive luxuries. Such people were formerly trapped in the ghetto. They had homes or well-kept apartments, but could not escape far from the poverty all around. As a result, any ghetto neighborhood might contain a complete social range, from the poorest to the most affluent. Now that the successful can escape, we have the gradual process of sorting out, with these affluent moving into non-slum neighborhoods.[10]

OCCUPATIONS AS MARKET SEGMENTS

Members of occupations are segments of the market in at least two senses. They sell their goods and services in some typical or characteristic ways and they also show some homogeneous elements in their buying. For example, carpenters are likely to wear certain kinds of work clothes, use certain tools, drive typical vehicles, patronize hardware stores and lumber yards; they cluster in the working class, although some are middle class as well.

Similarly, physicians are a general subgroup who sell specialized services within the boundaries of defined occupational conduct. Unlike carpenters, their vehicles are not emblazoned with their names (although they may flaunt a caduceus), their advertisements do not appear in the local newspapers. They cluster in the upper-middle class, although some are lower-middle and working-class professionals.

All market segments can be broken down into further segments. Looking more closely at any group shows the bases for further subgrouping. The main variable is cut across by other variables, so that new groups can be examined that may be of particular interest to some marketer. For instance, physicians may be subdivided by sex, if one is interested in appealing to women doctors. In another case, a research study was carried out to answer this question: What were the social processes which intervened between the initial trials of a drug by a few local innovators and its final use by virtually the whole medical community? In the course of studying a sample of physicians to explore this question, it was found useful to classify physicians as either profession-oriented or patient-oriented, with the profession-oriented doctors being quicker to prescribe the new drug than were the patient-oriented.

The results were even more interesting when the doctors were classified for their social integration in the local medical community, with the more socially integrated doctors being much faster in prescribing the new drug than the less socially integrated doctors.[11] Thus, from physicians in general emerged the various categories relating to profession, patients, and other doctors, each being a market segment with its own marketing challenges. Then there are the further possibilities of segmenting physicians by specialization, length of experience, work setting, and so forth.

In the marketing system, people are not interested solely in consumer behavior. For example, a large manufacturing company carried out an investigation of the personnel who were its suppliers, wanting to know about their personalities, their attitudes, and their problems in dealing with the large customer and its purchasing agents. They thought that by understanding what the relatively small suppliers were like, the marketing relationships might be improved. In another case, a large distributor of appliances wanted to learn more about small retailers, their characteristic outlook and types. The situation of the retail dealer may be summed up with excerpts from a memorandum based on the study.

A manufacturer's dealer set-up is often the most-discussed aspect of the company distribution arrangement. Dealers are hard to live with, complain the suppliers; and so they are. But the trouble with dealers often lies neither with orneriness nor with the complex lines of contact and report, as one might grasp from the observations of suppliers. A good part of the trouble with dealers lies instead in the fact that they are basically small independents in an unhappy position of dependence on a supplier or suppliers eager to contact the powerful consumer.

The notion of being in business for oneself holds an appeal compounded of freedom, opportunity, self-realization, and respectability. It is somehow vaguely equivalent to being grown up, and suggests that there is a glamor in the idea that not only can, but often does, blind the dreamer to many facts. The aspirant all too often overlooks the controls held by the supplier *and* by the customer, who has many alternatives to almost every purchase.

Complaint is the most common tone when retailers are asked to sketch their situations, even among the successful ones. As the dream implies, they resent most of all their apparent lack of control over the firm's activities and their feeling of being trapped between the demands of the supplier and the public. Most small, independent businesspeople have to face these contradictions to the myth of autonomy that attracted them. The biggest differences are in the vitality and resources with which they reorient themselves to use the facts advantageously.

Psychologically, dealers are a mixed and complicated lot. They strive, of course, for self-direction, but at the same time, they seek controls and guidance to ease the unexpected burdens of responsibility. Automobile dealers, for example, may berate their supplier for exercising too much control, for "dictating" to them. At another time they resent the supplier for not giving enough support in running the dealer's business. Going deeper, there are many dimensions, covering a range from the most successful and happiest dealers to the least successful malcontents.

The Solid Citizen Dealers. One cluster is made up of dealers who are positively oriented toward their work and who have the drives and skills to do a good job. They are content with having achieved a certain degree of success. Dealers of this type are fairly isolated in the community. They put in long, devoted hours at work, spend their spare time at home, and return early to work the next morning. Their private and public lives are separate, and they make no conscious effort to integrate the two (a clue that they are content with lower-middle-class social status).

The Socially Active Dealers. Another group consists of dealers striving to be considered successful entrepreneurs by the community-at-large. On the job, they are very sales- and public relations-minded. More active and striving than the solid-citizen dealers, they emphasize the professional nature of their job and are guided by the ideals of efficiency and service. As they become increasingly professionalized and approach their ideal of a respected social status, they become active in local clubs and associations and move toward the typical upper-middle-class pattern.

The Economically Ambitious Dealers. A third configuration is seen in dealers who look at their dealerships almost purely as ways of making money. They are relatively well educated, are usually efficient, shrewd, and calculating, and they do not permit their dislike of the work or of customers to interfere seriously with well-run, profitable operations. In the short run, they are valuable assets to the supplier, but may not remain very long in a particular field.

On the basis of their response to various psychological testing materials, one can characterize these dealers as rebellious against authority and society, and as out to get what they can. Their desire to make money quickly and easily is controlled more through their fear of customer or supplier retaliations against them than because of their scruples against cutting corners. This is an entrepreneurial type also found in a Montgomery Ward study of its store managers.[12]

Resigned, Stolid Dealers. This type makes up a large and important dealer group. They seem to have approached the occupation with less initial vigor and with fewer expectations than any of the energetic, accomplishing dealers. They seem also to have reduced their expectations once they discover the efforts required to fulfill them. Having mastered the essentials of the business, they are content to coast along, depending on old answers and settled routines. The physical appearance of their place of business often shows their tendency to let things go.

In general, they are a congenial lot, who enjoy meeting people on a crackerbarrel basis. In some neighborhoods they build up quite a loyal following among friends and neighbors who enjoy dropping in to shoot the breeze. Most of these people are upper-lower class in their life ways.

Unstable, Erratic Dealers. This is a group of bosses by default. Their motivations are largely negative, and they seem to have become dealers as an escape from unpleasant aspects of a previous job. They want more to avoid a boss than to become one. Freedom from bothersome restrictions, rather than freedom to find greater self-expression, led them to become dealers.

Anticipating little satisfaction from their work, they find little. Almost immediately, they fasten onto its many negative possibilities. Harboring resentment against their duties and the customers, they perform unreliably. Frequently, their lack of energy, business ability, and technical knowledge produces a run-down business. Add to this the fact that they are often inadequately financed and it is not difficult to see why so many of them locate in neighborhoods with little objective opportunity. Once they discover that they are not in an easy spot, they let things go. Often, no sooner do they start operating the business than they are thinking of a new field. They leave the industry in the same manner as they entered it—on the spur of the moment.[13]

SUMMARY

1. Market segments are challenging to understand. Marketing managers want to know not only what the segment is like, but its members' specific attitudes toward some object or action being contemplated or going on in the marketplace. These goals increase the complexity of the information sought. What do dog owners think about dry versus moist dog food? This question can be limited to some views about the food, but it will be more meaningful if the dog owners (subcategorized in what ways?) are studied as well. Similarly, learning what airline passengers think about flight personnel uniforms is enhanced by learning something about the airline passengers themselves.

2. The possibilities for thinking about the group sources of buyer and seller behavior are endless. The social fabric may be infinitely fragmented or patterned, depending on the particular marketing situation one wants to know about. Consequently, marketers have to expand their awareness and information about themselves, the marketing system of which they are a part, and the various groups to which they relate. Frequent explorations

are required in order to remain alert to the bases for grouping that change in the marketplace and to the significance of variables that ebb and flow in affecting their tasks.

3. Examples of housewives, blacks, and dealers illustrate general segmentation and further subgrouping.

References

1. Henry J. Claycamp and William F. Massy, "A Theory of Market Segmentation," *Journal of Marketing Research*, Nov. 1968, pp. 388–394.
2. William H. Reynolds, "More Sense about Market Segmentation," *Harvard Business Review*, Sept.–Oct. 1965, pp. 107–114.
3. Daniel Yankelovich, "New Criteria for Market Segmentation," *Harvard Business Review*, Mar.–Apr. 1964, pp. 83–90.
4. Robert Mainer and Charles C. Slater, "Markets in Motion," *Harvard Business Review*, Mar.–Apr. 1964, pp. 75–82.
5. Steven C. Brandt, "Dissecting the Segmentation Syndrome," *Journal of Marketing*, Oct. 1966, pp. 22–27; Robert D. Hisrich and Michael P. Peters, "Selecting the Superior Segmentation Correlate," *Journal of Marketing*, July 1974, pp. 60–63.
6. Sidney J. Levy, "Psychosocial Reactions to the Abundant Society," paper presented at Allied Social Sciences Associations Meeting, Washington, D.C., Dec. 1967.
7. Henry Allen Bullock, "Consumer Motivations in Black and White," *Harvard Business Review*, May–June 1961, pp. 89–104; July–Aug. 1961, pp. 110–124.
8. Donald E. Sexton, Jr., "Black Buyer Behavior," *Journal of Marketing*, Oct. 1972, pp. 36–39.
9. Ulf Hannerz, "What Negroes Mean by 'Soul,'" *Trans-action*, July–Aug. 1968, p. 61.
10. Burleigh B. Gardner, "The Black Ghetto Market and Social Change," presented at Northwestern University Graduate School of Management, Fall Management Conference, Nov. 14, 1968, Chicago, Illinois.
11. James Coleman, Elihu Katz, and Herbert Menzel, "The Diffusion of an Innovation among Physicians," *Sociometry*, Dec. 1957, pp. 253–270.
12. Reported in *Chicago Sun-Times*, Nov. 19, 1974.
13. Earl L. Kahn and Lee Rainwater, "The Retail Dealer: Boss or Hired Hand?" Social Research, Inc., unpublished paper.

Suggested Readings

Caplovitz, David, *The Poor Pay More* (New York: The Free Press, 1963).
Coleman, James S., *The Adolescent Society* (New York: The Free Press, 1961).
Daedalus, "The Negro American," *Journal of the American Academy of Arts and Sciences*, Fall 1965.

Frank, Ronald E., William F. Massy, and Yoram Wind, *Market Segmentation* (Englewood Cliffs, N.J.: Prentice-Hall, 1972).

Grossack, Martin M. (ed.), *Understanding Consumer Behavior* (Boston: The Christopher Publishing House, 1964).

Handel, Gerald (ed.), *The Psychosocial Interior of the Family* (Chicago: Aldine, 1967).

Harrington, Michael, *The Other American* (New York: Macmillan, 1962).

Katona, George, *The Powerful Consumer* (New York: McGraw-Hill, 1960).

Kramer, Judith R., and Seymour Leventman, *Children of the Gilded Ghetto* (New Haven: Yale University Press, 1961).

Laumann, Edward C., and James S. House, "Living Room Styles and Social Attributes: The Patterning of Material Artifacts in a Modern Urban Community," *Sociology and Social Research*, Apr. 1970, pp. 321–342.

Lenski, Gerhard, *The Religious Factor* (New York: Doubleday, 1961).

Myers, John G., and Francesco M. Nicosia, "On the Study of Consumer Typologies," *Journal of Marketing Research*, May 1968, pp. 182–193.

Newman, Joseph W., *On Knowing the Consumer* (New York: Wiley, 1966).

Potter, David M., *People of Plenty* (Chicago: University of Chicago Press, 1954).

Seeley, John R., R. Alexander Sim, and E. W. Loosley, *Crestwood Heights: A North American Suburb* (Toronto: University of Toronto Press, 1956).

Strauss, Anselm L., and Lee Rainwater, *The Professional Scientist* (Chicago: Aldine, 1962).

vii

Social
Stratification

In the search for understanding of marketing behavior, one
of the most important and interesting general variables is social
stratification. People in society can be stratified into hierarchies
in terms of such issues as intelligence, income, political power,
physical prowess, beauty, and so forth, and each issue can provide some insight into the marketing behavior of those who are
placed at different levels. Social class is a powerful means of
such stratification. W. Lloyd Warner, a pioneer in the study of social class in America, noted this.

> Studies of social class in the several regions of the United States dem-
> onstrate that it is a major determinant of individual decisions and so-
> cial actions; that every major area of American life is directly and in-
> directly influenced by our class order; and that the major decisions of
> most individuals are partly controlled by it.[1]

Such a determinant seems worth special attention, to see what is
its nature and how its influence radiates in people's marketing
actions.

The social class of a person is basically an expression of *how
he or she participates in the society and how that participation
is evaluated by the other people* in the society. That is, social position is a complex social judgment arrived at by the group about

its members. It is heavily influenced by the place of the family into which one is born, which in turn reflects the power of the occupational activity of the family, its accumulated resources in money, location, housing, and other real and symbolic goods; and the consequent deference these are given. The result is a socio-economic status (SES), a classification that can be quite informative. Robert Havighurst has also commented on the significance of this placement.

> Knowing the SES of a child or youth allows a more accurate prediction of the following than does any other single fact: his intelligence quotient, the educational level he will achieve, the occupational level he will achieve, his attitudes toward work, his age at marriage, the number of children he will have, his sexual behavior, the kind of neurotic behavior he will exhibit if he suffers a neurosis, the number of books he will read during his lifetime.
>
> The SES of an individual will not predict *every one* of these characteristics better than any other fact about him will predict any one of the characteristics; but the SES is a better predictor of this whole array of behaviors and attitudes than is any other one fact.[2]

Simply speaking, the social system hierarchy is seen to have an upper class, a middle class, and a lower class. With more refined study, the classes are often subdivided further, so that each class includes, in turn, an upper and a lower subclass. In a large community, a middle-middle class might be demarcated as well. More distinctions can be made by observing that each class segment has a portion of people who are either upwardly or downwardly mobile out of that group, or who are either overprivileged or underprivileged relative to other members of their group. Any social-class segment might be of interest to marketers, although commercial marketers are commonly most concerned with the upper-middle class, the lower-middle class, and the upper-lower class.

The topic of social class is a provocative one. It intrigues people because they are sensitive to their own place in society and are alert to cues that may help them better discern how they are fitting in, where they are going, and what they might do to entrench or improve their position. The topic is also an exciting one because it awakens anxieties and defenses. Not uncommonly, the idea of social class is resisted because it seems an invidious way to classify and compare people, raising up some and putting down others and implying that they are either doomed by sociology to a fixed place in society, or are having their social strivings made self-conscious and public. Some people deny that a democratic society even has social classes.

At the same time, the concept of social class is widely studied and applied, as all societies seem to have elites and inferior groups of varying degree. It has notable appeal to behavioral scientists where it has been a central subject matter or is used as a methodological tool. The goals of investigators vary greatly. Some seek to understand what societies are really like, others argue for various political, social, or economic theories, and many have in mind learning how to improve or change society.

There are fashions and there are partisans. In one important category community studies seek to delineate the social structures of particular places. Many workers are absorbed in cross-class comparisons, observing how the strata are similar and how they are different. The class structures in various countries are examined for variations in sizes of classes, criteria for position, rates of change, and so forth. Some thinkers try to reserve the word "class" for Marxian analyses of groups in conflict as different from measurements of strata in society.

As mentioned earlier, after a phase in the 1950s in which it was fashionable to talk of the lower class or working class as a vanishing breed, there was a great upsurge of interest in the people below the middle class. This is not a new interest—higher-status people have always had some romantic fascination with those of lower status, one that Chekhov warned against when he said, "There is peasant blood in my veins, and you cannot astonish me with peasant virtues."

The flood of literature on the lower class has something for every taste. One can glean insight into what it is like to teach working-class college students on Staten Island, whether lower-class people are really as criminal as they are reputed to be, or whether this idea is an artifact of statistics and definitions of crimes. In vogue are debates about whether poor people have a valid culture of their own, or whether they really want to be or should be helped or forced to become middle class.

One author argues that part of the working class is being semantically elevated to middle-class status by what he terms the "somewhat hallucinated world of the Census Department," to fit a false version of an affluent white-collar America.[3] Gans analyzes 13 reasons why it is useful to have a lower class, most of them adding up to the idea that it is difficult to be superior without people who are perceived to be inferiors.[4]

STATUS CHARACTERISTICS

The participation and evaluation that locate a person in society are expressed and translated into specific status characteristics. Occupation is the single most evident sign of a person's status. A social position is society's way of showing its regard for what a person does in that society. Consequently, ranking people by their occupations correlates highly with their social placement. Warner found that by adding other indicators, such as source of income, living quarters, and dwelling area, an Index of Status Characteristics could be developed as a convenient measure of social position.[5]

Such an index is a shorthand for the way of life it represents. In the real world, social-class variations are variations in lifestyle. While members of different social-class groups are often not easily distinguished by given behaviors from one another, there are consistent, and sometimes profound, variations that can be viewed as ranging along a continuum or as different patternings using common elements drawn from the core American culture. The influence of social class on marketing behavior can be interpreted by putting together a series of ideas that gain by accumulation a sense of the importance of social class as pervasive. Some generalizations are offered here that sum up findings mainly from various specific studies carried out at Social Research, Inc. over a period of years.*

Values

Underlying the many other differences among social classes as consumer groups is the fact of differences in values. Lower-status

---

*These studies are not reported formally, in the manner of academic studies; rather they are drawn upon illustratively, to show examples of findings in marketing researches of a behavioral nature, done on behalf of organizations out in the marketplace. Because of the usual contemporary confidentiality of such studies, they are drawn mainly from earlier work; they should not be dismissed for that reason but provide incentive for updating by current marketers. In addition, later studies support the stability and typicality of these general findings about the social classes.

people value education less than middle-class people do. This has repercussions in the market in various ways, since many products are consumed as part of gaining an education, as well as depending on having education. Among middle-class people there is a sharper emphasis on morality, respectability, and doing things right. The middle classes believe they can control their destinies and fortunes and achieve successfully, by implementing these values. Lower-status people are more apt to seek immediate gratification, to rely on luck, and to be less willing to risk their security. These are well-known sociological findings.[6] They are mentioned here as a reminder that such broad points of view as these have been repeatedly noted as characteristically varying among social classes. They suggest that social stratification produces different ways of seeing the world, and of consuming, since consuming is ultimately one of the ways in which people implement their values.

One study of femininity[7] indicated that the lower-class woman who feels doomed to the lower end of the economic scale is not likely to feel proud of what she does. There is little to value because life seems dull and unrewarding.[8]

> *I lead a dog's life . . . work. . . . I get up in the morning, cook all day, pick up after four children and a husband, sew. What would you call that — peaches and cream?*
>
> *Dull and boring. I spend most of my time working and have nothing much to show for it.*

The traditional character of the working-class family is being modified, as the women's liberation movement, the new consumer assertiveness, and so forth are having their effects on working-class housewives. Burleigh Gardner notes that these women show increasing self-confidence, a greater sense of competence and worth, and more interest in the outside world.

> This broadening of interests and activities means less time for home and family, and it means decidedly less inclination to make a virtue out of homemaking . . . an increasing focus on . . . freedom to choose the kind of work she wants, without dictation from men or tradition. Freedom from the rearing of many children.[9]

Interpersonal Relations

Another broad factor that influences consumption is the nature of people's interpersonal attitudes. These are, of course, individually ramified in many ways, but some consistencies are visible. Attitudinal differences are seen at the most intimate levels, affecting sexual relations, the use of contraceptives, and the conjugal roles. There are consequences in effectiveness of family planning and preferences in family size. For example, lower-status women who cannot use contraceptive pills are much less likely to use a diaphragm, since its use requires more interpersonal support from the husband than lower-class men are willing to give their wives.[10]

More generally, upper-middle-class women tend to regard their husbands as "companions" and to feel like a peer in money matters. They are likely to demand much of themselves in achievement: to be a good wife, mother, an intellectually stimulating being, home economist, child therapist, and organization woman, and with it all to be a person of composure and competence. As parents, upper-middles need their children to be bright, active, strong, lively, and precocious, and are given to characterizing their babies as "active" and "alert." They look for products that will add to their success, competence, and proficiency as mothers and fathers.

By comparison, lower-middle-class parents are more apt to stress control and conformity and the meeting of values and requirements that relate to cleanliness, politeness, neatness, and order. These parents are most troubled by dirty diapers and the idea of things being messy. Most parents want "good" babies, but lower-middles are particularly likely to want them well-behaved, well-scheduled, and manageable.

Working-class mothers strongly need to enjoy their babies, to get pleasure from them. They will tolerate difficulties with their babies, finding in them self-justification and interpersonal responsiveness. The upper-middle wants her child bright and alert, while the lower-middle hopes for proper behavior, and the working-class woman wants a gratifying possession.[11]

In terms of more general relationships, lower-class women tend to say they dress to please themselves, possibly to justify their bold dress-up urges. Lower-middle-class women place emphasis on what other women think and much less on pleasing themselves. Upper-middle-class women have a broader sense of display and think of their audiences as spread among themselves, husbands, other women, and men in general.[12]

The narrower interpersonal circles of working-class people show themselves in many ways. They make less use of long-distance telephone calls.[13] They have a tendency to relate socially more to relatives than middle-class people do. In taking their vacations, working-class people are distinctly more apt to visit relatives, to stay home, or to have the husband go alone than to follow the middle-class custom of going away from home as a family group.[14]

Self-Perceptions

Consumer behavior reflects the varied self-perceptions or self-images held by individuals and, to some degree, as these are characteristics for members of social class groups. That there are some systematic differences among classes is suggested from various directions. For example, in a study of sanitary protection it was learned that women of lower social status tend to have more sense of taboo about their bodies and less understanding of them.[15] They are prone to think of themselves as having menstrual problems. They are less receptive to the use of tampons, an instance of their slower receptivity to important changes in behavior, their lack of scientific information, and their more traditional ideas and feelings about sexual matters and interpersonal relations.[16]

Compare the ideas and tone of these two women. The first is a girl from an ethnic working-class family:

I am Spanish, you see, and Spanish girls are not made like American girls and are not brought up the same. We would not be able to use anything like that. You see, we are closed up. American girls are opened up at birth, but Spanish girls are not, and we are not opened until we are married and then we go to our husbands and he is the one who opens us.

The second is an upper-middle-class woman who commented on her use of tampons:

I figured if I could accommodate one thing I could accommodate another.

Higher-status people think of themselves as fastidious people. Upper-middle-class women express themselves less urgently when it comes to "needing a deodorant," not believing they smell so bad in the first place, and being oriented to basic hygiene. The self-oriented aspects of grooming, of successful weight control, and of self-esteem are prominent in the reactions of higher-status women, less to the fore among lower-middle-status women, for whom general social motives and self-consciousness tend to seem more pressing. Lower-class women respond more to immediate needs and impulses, thinking in terms of tonight's date and special occasions.[17]

Definitions of men, what a "real man" should be to fit the goals, norms, and values of his social class, reflect many variables, especially those relating to his physical being and his effectiveness in vocational and familial relations. Some relative emphases are discernible among the social classes. Upper-middle-class people tolerate a much more "feminine" conception of a real man. They do not hold to the myth that a real man has to be crudely tough to be effective, but that being clean and well-groomed is part of being a successful person, of demonstrating the kind of narcissism one expects of a higher-status person.

Differences among men are noticeable in their body concepts, sexuality, and the products they find suitable. The narcissism among higher-status men is apparent in their willingness to use cologne, and in wearing stylish variations in underwear. While briefs are commonly worn among all groups, mature lower-status men have some inclination toward the conservative patternings of boxer shorts. High-status men do not seem as motivated to the maintenance of their figures as are their female peers, tending to lose the battle of the bulge more easily than women.

Lower-status men like shirts with sleeves that can be rolled up to display their biceps. The macho urges of some middle-class men are satisfied through ownership of phallic-shaped Pierre Cardin grooming products.

Working-class people see a "real man" as a sturdy guy who can make a decent living. Lower-class men work toward achieving body know-how, physical adeptness, and manual skills, to understand how things work. They want to get along, to get some fun out of life. They expect to work fairly hard and to relax as much as they can, feeling that life uses them up faster than it does higher-status people.[18] A study of age grading among various social classes showed a trend for lower-status people to think of themselves as mature and as old much earlier than do higher-status people.[19]

Daily Life

How do people perceive the total day and how to live it? There are both subtle and gross differences, reflecting occupations, activities, income level, social evaluation, and other factors. Lower-status women are apt to get up earlier in the morning and to feel they can make do with less sleep; in general, working-class people find a problem in needing to get to bed early and wanting to watch late movies on TV. Middle-class housewives are more likely than lower-class women to plan their daily activities with some care, to enjoy trying out new things, to feel a sense of mastery over household chores.

The higher a person's social status, the greater the amount of activity that takes place outside the home and the time spent pursuing expressive activities, such as reading, painting, listening to music, and helping the children with various things. The distribution and use of time shows class trends; for example, the time for the dinner hour varies systematically from class to class. About one-fourth of the lower-lowers in one sample were likely to be at dinner before 5 o'clock, and very few after 7 o'clock, while more than half the upper-middles were still at dinner after 7 o'clock. Also, more time is spent at the dinner table as status rises. Further, the television set is also much more likely to be on during dinner in lower-class homes than in middle-class homes.[20] This behavior is quite stable. In the 1970s it is still characteristic, despite the growth in numbers of TV sets.

These four areas of values, interpersonal relations, self-perceptions, and daily life are broad in character. They reflect the basic facts that groups in our society do different kinds of work, get different types and amounts of financial reward, and are evaluated differently along various dimensions of social esteem and importance to the community. They think of themselves differently, want differently, and behave differently. In relation to more specific marketing areas, these differences find further expression.

Shopping

Social status affects how people feel about where they should shop. The tendencies are for lower-status people to prefer local, face-to-face places where they feel they will get a friendly reception and easy credit if needed. Thus, the same products and brands may be purchased in different channels of distribution by members of different social classes. In the purchase of cosmetics, upper-middle-class women are more apt to shop in department stores than are lower-status women, who are in turn relatively more likely to shop in variety stores. Drugstores seem less status-graded and are equally attractive or suitable to all. Studies of department stores show that there are sharp differences in status reputation, and that consumers tend to sort themselves out in terms of where it is appropriate to shop. This is not an either/or phenomenon—most establishments serve customers of more than one social class. But their proportions differ, as do their purchasing patterns. Upper-middles characteristically go to Sears for certain kinds of goods, proportionately different from the array bought by lower-status customers. Lower-status people often go to Marshall Field's only to buy gifts, and many feel too shy to go there at all. Food chains are similarly selected as varying in status suitability. Taking a close look at some of these patterns, V. Kanti Prasad observed this complexity:

> The study thus suggests that consumers in the higher socioeconomic strata are more likely to exhibit "patronage mix" tendencies, probably preferring to patronize the more conventional department stores and specialty stores for the purchase of products with higher social risk, but favorably predisposed to patronize the discount stores for a vast number of other products that may be characterized as of low social risk.[21]

Thus, the goals, methods, and places of shopping form patterns that distinguish members of the different social classes, in various ways.

Media

The fact that media are approached and used in contrasting (as well as similar) ways among social-class groups is important for an understanding of marketing. At a rather simple level, there are such variations as that lower-status people are less apt to subscribe to newspapers than are middle-class people and more likely to read and subscribe to magazines such as *True Story*. They are more likely to enjoy the comics freely, to embrace television, and to watch late movies. Upper-middle-class tastes with regard to television run more actively to current events and drama. Moving down the social scale, there is a relative rise of interest in soap operas, quiz shows, situation comedy, and variety. Middle-class people worry more about the effect of television on their children than do lower-class people.

The different meanings of media have been explored in many

studies. The media function in varied ways, and each fits differentially into the lives of the social classes. There are (sometimes
sharp) class preferences among the newspapers available in a
community, in evaluating magazines, in selecting television
shows, in listening to the radio, in how newspapers are read, in
receipt and meaning of direct mail, and in general among the total
volume of materials to which people are exposed and to which
they attend in one or another of the media. Higher-status people
see more magazines, read more of the newspaper, and buy more
newspapers. Lower-class people tend to prefer the afternoon paper (where it still exists), while middle-class people tend to prefer the morning paper. These media patterns show some evolution. In the fifties and early sixties, studies of television in 15
major cities showed that upper-middle-class people consistently
preferred NBC, while lower-middles preferred CBS. These preferences were in keeping with the network images and with the
characteristics of the social classes.[22] During the late 1970s, the
situation became greatly fragmented, with more volatility in pursuit of entertainment shows, and much emphasis on the character
of the local news personalities. The social-class generalizations
then need to be made for individual communities.

Advertising

Advertising will be discussed later as a symbolic selling activity. Here it may be noted that the expressly symbolic nature of
advertising is particularly meaningful in aiming it toward the differentiated understandings of members of different groups.
Broadly speaking, upper-middle-class people are the most critical
of advertising, suspicious of its "emotional" appeals and its
claims. They are trained in pursuing subtle meanings and usually
display an attitude of sophisticated superiority to advertising
compared to the more straightforward, literal–minded, and
pragmatic approach of lower-middle-class and upper-lower-class
people.

Not that upper-middle-class people are unresponsive to advertising. They insist on expressing detachment, but they are more
strongly appealed to by sheer difference, by approaches that
seem somewhat individual in tone, that show some wit, that convey elements of sophistication and stylishness, that seem to appeal to "rational" judgment and discriminating taste, that offer the
kinds of objects and symbols that are significant of their "quality"

status and self-expressive aims. Lower-status people are relatively more receptive to advertising that is strongly visual in character, that shows activity, ongoing work and life, impressions of energy, and solutions to practical problems in daily life.[23]

While the points and summary statements offered above would (when elaborated) have interest in themselves, and had interest for various study sponsors in specific instances, they also gain interest for their contribution to a cumulative understanding. They imply that there is a coherence in the marketplace, a social class structure that may start (or end) with variations in income, but which operates more meaningfully than just in terms of amount of money available for spending. The person or family exists in, and is a manifestation of, a milieu that has certain limitations and opportunities. The results have recognizable and usually quite logical consequences, summarized below.

Upper-lower-class people tend to be defined in their total patterning of personality and lifestyle by the fact that society "allots them," so to speak, a manual, physical, body-focused assignment. Being the doers, the handlers, they are expected to act or to behave overtly and to accomplish in ways that emphasize locomotor activity. In law they embody its concrete, physical expression, found in driving cars, pounding on doors, laying on sticks and handcuffs. In commerce they clerk, serve, retail—handling things, making change, wrapping packages. In physical production, they are the mechanics and manipulators, using their hands and muscles with or without skill to produce concrete objects.

Such workers, trained to their world from an early age, become generally restricted in their level of mental function. Their orientation becomes local, concrete, face-to-face, relatively deprived of long-range considerations or broader horizons. Immediate gratifications and readiness to express impulses tend to be observed in these people, since they do not usually perceive meaningful incentives to do otherwise.

Lower-middle-class people characteristically have the cultural assignment of applying known principles to defined problems in an accurate manner. Ideally speaking, they are expected to implement laws, regulations, and systems, to be caretakers and intermediary supervisors. As such, in law they deal with its principles as lawyers and clerks; in commerce they may be bookkeepers and accountants, seeing to it that financial methods are systematically and precisely applied. In production, they are supervisors and engineers, again implementing and using known systems and generalizations about physical processes and structures.

Such workers, trained to their world, become oriented to a functional and pragmatic view, coupled with anxiety about achieving respectability and success through virtuous performance. This gives them a larger perspective than is found in the lower class, one that reinforces the importance of education and of deferring gratifications in favor of long-range goals.

Upper-middle-class people are expected to initiate knowledge, establish objectives and policy, exert judgment, and decide on the methods and procedures to be used. They embody the intellectual, professional, and managerial point of view. In law they are judges, legislators, and highly placed lawyers. In commerce they are managers and controllers, determining the content of the procedures and actions to be carried out by workers of lower status. In a production hierarchy, they may be chiefs, physicists, or other scientists.

Such workers, trained to their world, emphasize executive and creative mental processes, an awareness of more distant horizons, large social events, and concern with individuality and achievement. They use more integrated and varied means of satisfying their aims, feeling free to satisfy impulses frowned on by lower-middle-class people, and able to organize their lives from a point of view beyond the power of lower-class people.

The differences among social classes listed in the earlier series of points that relate to commercial marketing have their roots in the differences suggested in these brief descriptions of the three primary social classes. These differences seem to be major differences, in that they are not simply attributable to variations in income, but are expressions of the profoundly varied forms of experience that become available to members of each social class. Commonalities in human aims and in American experience may obscure the differences, but they seem consistent and persistent in governing approaches to the market.

SUMMARY

1. Social stratification is a powerful tool for understanding variations in behavior in the community.

2. Social-class position is rooted in the value the community places on the activities of the individual, with its consequent def-

erence and economic rewards. It is determined by the participation of the person and how it is evaluated.

3. Status characteristics are found in occupations and in sources of income, and this economic ability is translated into symbols, such as area lived in and type of dwelling.

4. The translation of economic differences into status symbols is part of the development of a social system in which different levels vary in their power and values. The strata gain some self-consciousness expressed in actual conflict among classes, in aspirations to associate with higher groups, and in fears or avoidance of lower groups.

5. Different economic abilities and values and their different ways of life produce variations in marketing behavior along class lines. These variations are not inflexible, and are modified by other social and personal forces. But they suggest the usefulness of social-class analysis as one major approach to market segmentation.

References

1. W. Lloyd Warner et al., *Social Class in America* (New York: Harper Torchbooks, 1960), p. 6.
2. Robert J. Havighurst, "Social Class Perspectives on the Life Cycle," *Human Development*, 1971, pp. 111–112.
3. Andrew Levison, "The Working Class Majority," *The Nation*, Dec. 13, 1971, p. 626.
4. Herbert J. Gans, "The Uses of Poverty: The Poor Pay All," *Social Policy*, July–Aug. 1971, pp. 20–24.
5. Warner's method is explained in Chapter 8 of *Social Class in America*, and has been updated by other workers, most notably in Richard P. Coleman and Bernice L. Neugarten, *Social Status in the City* (San Francisco: Jossey–Bass, 1971).
6. Herbert H. Hyman, "The Value Systems of Different Classes: A Social Psychological Contribution of the Analysis of Stratification," in Reinhard Bendix and Seymour M. Lipset (eds.), *Class, Status and Power* (New York: The Free Press, 1953), pp. 426–442.
7. *Images of Femininity* (Chicago: Social Research, Inc., 1960).
8. Lee Rainwater, Richard P. Coleman, and Gerald Handel, *Workingman's Wife* (New York: Macfadden-Bartell, 1959).
9. Burleigh B. Gardner, "The Emergence of a New Social Force—The Working Class Women" (address), New York, Sept. 25, 1973.
10. Lee Rainwater, *Family Design: Marital Sexuality, Family Planning and Family Limitation* (Chicago: Aldine, 1964).
11. *Babies and Baby Care Products* (Chicago: Social Research, Inc., 1960).

12. *Chicagoland Women and Their Clothing* (Chicago: Social Research, Inc., 1960).
13. *A Socio-Psychological Study of Telephone Users* (Chicago: Social Research, Inc., 1955).
14. *Status of the Working Class in Changing American Society* (Chicago: Social Research, Inc., 1961).
15. *Attitudes Toward Feminine Hygiene* (Chicago: Social Research, Inc., 1957).
16. *Meanings and Motives in the Tampon Market* (Chicago: Social Research, Inc., 1958).
17. *Toothpaste: A Socio-Psychological Study* (Chicago: Social Research, Inc., 1951); *Cleanliness and Personal Attraction* (Chicago: Social Research, Inc., 1955).
18. *Hair Product Preferences* (Chicago: Social Research, Inc., 1951); *Men's Clothing and Tailoring* (Chicago: Social Research, Inc., 1958); *German Men* (Chicago: Social Research, Inc., 1960); *Images of Masculinity* (Chicago: Social Research, Inc., 1961); *Marketing to Men* (Chicago: Social Research, Inc., 1963); S. J. Levy, "The Meanings of Work," *Notes and Essays on Education for Adults*, No. 39 (Boston: The Center for the Study of Liberal Education for Adults, May 1963).
19. B. Neugarten and W. Peterson, "A Study of the American Age-Graded System," *Proceedings of 4th Congress of the International Association of Gerontology*, pp. 497–502, 1957.
20. *Attitudes Toward Television* (Chicago: Social Research, Inc., 1964).
21. V. Kanti Prasad, "Socioeconomic Product Risk and Patronage Preferences of Retail Shoppers," *Journal of Marketing*, July 1975, p. 43.
22. *The Meanings of Newspapers, The Sunday Comics, The Differing Meanings of* search, Inc., 1962); *Newspapers in the Social World of Chicagoans* (Chicago: *Women's Magazines and Television* (Chicago: Social Research, Inc., 1954); *Magazine Readership as Related to Social Class, Age, and Sex* and *Patterns of Radio Listening in the New York Metropolitan Region* (Chicago: Social Research, Inc., 1963); *Attitudes Toward Television in [Various Cities]* (Chicago: Social Research, Inc., several years); I. O. Glick and S. J. Levy, *Living with Television* (Chicago: Aldine, 1962).
23. A *Study of Thematic Coherence in Advertising Approaches* (Chicago: Social Research, Inc., 1961); *The General Nature of Advertising Symbols* (Chicago: Social Research, Inc., 1949).

Suggested Readings

Coleman, Richard P., and Bernice L. Neugarten, *Social Status in the City* (San Francisco: Jossey-Bass, 1971).
Ellis, Dean S., "Speech and Social Status in America," *Social Forces*, March 1967, pp. 48–53.
Kahl, Joseph, *The American Class Structure* (New York: Holt, Rinehart and Winston, 1957).
Levison, Andrew, *The Working Class Majority* (New York: Coward, McCann and Geoghegan, 1974).
Mathews, H. Lee, and John W. Slocum, Jr., "A Rejoinder to 'Social Class or Income?'" *Journal of Marketing*, Jan. 1972, pp. 69–70.
Myers, James H., Robert R. Stanton, and Arne F. Haug, "Correlates of Buying Behavior: Social Class vs. Income," *Journal of Marketing*, Oct. 1971, pp. 74–77.
Slocum, John W., Jr., and H. Lee Mathews, "Social Class and Income as In-

dicators of Consumer Credit Behavior," *Journal of Marketing*, Apr. 1970, pp. 69–74.

Tucker, W. T., *The Social Context of Economic Behavior* (New York: Holt, Rinehart and Winston, 1964).

Walshok, Mary L., "The Emergence of Middle Class Deviant Subcultures," *Social Problems*, Spring 1971, pp. 488–495.

Wolfe, Alan, "Working with the Working Class," *Change Magazine*, Feb. 1972, pp. 48–53.

VIII

The Individual in the Marketplace

Up to this point, the discussion has focused on the importance of group membership as a source of marketing behavior. We can see that broad cultural forces and patterns are sorted out differently by various subgroups in the society, as summed up in Figure 8.

A group's actions may culminate in nothing more than an aggregation or accumulation of things. For example, if each person buys one item, then ten persons buy ten. But social life is often more complex than that. Group members interact with one another and with nonmembers alike, and this turns out to have a kind of multiplicative, rather than additive, effect. Such events as a riot, a run on a bank, a rock band, and a family eating a meal are forms of group life that require analysis of relationships and interactions, and overarching concepts.

At the same time, the way in which individuals act is also a specific, personal result of their sensing and perceiving, their feelings and beliefs, their goals, and how they pursue them. People conform to their culture in personal ways. Psychologically, they are particular kinds of Americans, carpenters, teenagers, or lower-middle-class housewives, with a characteristic temperament, humor, intelligence, and set of personal inclinations. Marketers need to explore the forces at work within the individ-

Figure 8. Group sources of marketing behavior.

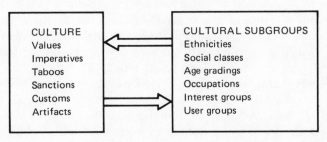

ual in order fully to appreciate behavior in the marketplace, and to appeal to or arouse the personality needs relevant to their specific purpose. This necessity was suggested in the discussion of group behavior in the previous chapters, much of which comes from observing their psychology. Here, the issue is examined directly.

GROUPS VERSUS INDIVIDUALS

In moving from thinking about groups to thinking about individuals, it is helpful to point out some of the differences in these approaches. Not everyone wants to study the psychological aspect of behavior. The fact that various disciplines exist testifies to the different preferences of scientists in finding explanations that suit their inclinations. Anthropologists emphasize the significance of culture in explaining food habits, while biologists focus on bodily needs and cellular processes. These preferences for abstracting do not mean that eating can be reduced either to a cultural or to an osmotic process; the person (being a complex reality) tends to embody concepts or to perform to the satisfaction of both disciplines.

Those who favor one discipline are apt to feel that it is more explanatory, more useful, or perhaps just more interesting than other areas of study. The kinds of problems that dominate an era also make certain kinds of studies seem especially relevant. Demography is in vogue as one of the most important disciplines, even if it is awesome in scope and factual solidity. In a time possessed by the problems of population, race, urban blight, youth, and old age, demography takes on an unusual prominence and glamour. Economists are cited daily as seers or doctors of economic illness beset by the patient's problems.

The study of marketing behavior calls forth its own preferred approaches. There is commonly the wish for practical results, for theories or findings that will increase predictive power fairly immediately. A search for deep understanding or theoretical order often arouses impatience; and microcosmic analyses, which look closely at the very fine details, may seem inadequate for the breadth of basic market phenomena to some people. Group behavior is the focal point, taking in social units and classes. The resulting orientation is toward finding ideas through group discussions, or through studies that account for the greatest variance. There is a tradition of interest in the most common behavior, since modes make large markets.

Sociological generalizations are especially attractive to marketing people, since they correspond to typical marketing concerns. Analyses of roles and occupations have real significance for sellers concerned with housewives, physicians, or purchasing agents as markets; social classes and élites are easily related to concepts of quality markets and influential buyers; studies of ecology or social change help in thinking about market regions and their shifting requirements. Perhaps above all, sociological variables seem readily amenable to measurement and the opportunity for easier measurement is a very attractive offer. This general preference is well summed up by James Carman in a monograph on social class:

> These intercorrelations make cultural class even more important as a basis for market segmentation—more important, in fact, than personality. There are three reasons why this is so. First, the cultural factor subsumes some of the psychological characteristics of individuals so that the persons in the same cultural class should be similar with regard to values, attitudes, motivations, and behavior patterns. [Carman's study shows too many problems in demonstrating this to be the case to take it so for granted.] Second, by definition, psychological characteristics are personal characteristics and, for the purpose of planning promotional strategy in the consumer market, we are not yet at the point where we can consider each consumer as a separate market segment. Third, it is possible to design media schedules directed at one cultural class, but it is not possible to design one that's directed at a particular personality profile.[1]

Carman does not discuss how the planning of promotional strategy and the design of media schedules are to gain their psychological content, which inevitably they must have, that will make them appropriate to the economic or sociological factors he prefers to rely on. The question of how one will know those things needed in order to provide effective information and to plan schedules does remain. Of course, Carman does not mean that such factors should not be studied, but his comment shows that there is a preference exhibited by those who do the studying.

In truth, however, many studies cast doubt on the value of personality study for marketing purposes. The attempts that have been reported seeking to find relationships between consumer action and specific personality variables have not been highly promising. Not uncommonly, a plague is cast on the whole house of psychology. Critics say it is too subjective, lacks an agreed vocabulary, is misled by "Freudian nonsense," and is beset with tools that are sometimes reliable but not demonstrably valid.

In the search for greater security many are driven to denying the relevance of the individual's inner life or the value of using his first-person reports.[2] Sometimes, in despair at making sense out of the bewildering relationships between what people say and what they do, it is tempting to believe that perhaps they are merely animals with a vast capacity for deceptive verbal gibberish. In any event, it is no surprise that John Miner has noted: "It is relatively rare for a school of business to offer course work in marketing taught by a psychologist."[3] But it happens more than it used to.

The kinds of criticism mentioned are rooted in realistic issues and problems that psychological workers must struggle to solve; some are based on ignorance, misconceptions, or inadequate knowledge of the theories or practices involved. From the way marketing people talk about psychology, it is apparent that one of the big problems is that many of them try to use psychology when they do not know it sufficiently.

One young man interested in a career in marketing research said that in a study he had made of human simulation of conflict resolution, "personality did not work." His hypothesis that the more aggressive person would win out in this particular simulation of people arguing was not demonstrated. Asked what did work, he said, "level of aspiration." Now, in some sense this must be an expression of personality. In another study, four variables were being investigated. The first was defined as "venturesomeness" and the fourth was termed "personality." It is difficult to realize how the first can be viewed as separate from the fourth.

By definition, personality always "works." Even though one may find it easier or more useful to think about it in some aggregate fashion (class, culture, life-cycle stage), psychological study is essential to certain kinds of understanding of cultures, social groups, and age levels. Not infrequently, researchers who deny the value of psychological analysis assume it in their discussions or analyses of their groups, thereby sneaking it in the back door, so to speak, and thus perhaps with even less rigor than is applied by those they blame. It is difficult for such people to discuss their data without making some interpretations and analyses in a psychological sense. These interpretations are offered as casual impressions, outside of the study, but they may constitute the most important or influential ideas despite not having been themselves investigated.

THEORIES OF PSYCHOLOGY

Within the field of psychology are numerous different theories. Some are in conflict, while others are compatible but focus on different aspects of human behavior. Psychological theories are generally about how people learn and come to behave as they do, but vary in the units of study and the methods employed. Because marketing behavior is thought about along many dimensions, major psychological approaches are noted. The topics are dealt with in extremely summary fashion. The psychological field and its literature are vast; detailed exploration of it is encouraged.

Learning Theory

Learning theories tend to be concerned with the results gained by providing specific stimuli under given circumstances. The stricter forms of behaviorism[4] are primarily stimulus–response theories that stress objectivity and the role of reinforcement. In this framework of analysis and experimentation, the person is seen as an organism with basic drives and the possibility of elaborating them in secondary ways, with a tendency to link elements of experience through conditioning and through being rewarded for making particular responses. People learn by making responses; if their trials are errors, they are not rewarded. This theory does not concern itself with what goes on in the person's thoughts or feelings.[5]

Much learning is apparently of this kind, and its principles are deliberately applied in many situations, to methods of child rearing, to changing behavior of prisoners, and to working with emotionally troubled patients. Training, via reward and punishment, is an age-old method in human affairs. Systematically applied in its present form, and called behavior modification, it is especially controversial.[6]

Marketing approaches that use this logic fairly directly include the repeating of brand names to build their association with pleasant stimuli such as jingles, television shows, attractive personalities, or perhaps the tasting of samples in supermarkets.

Modified forms of stimulus–response theory take greater account of the subjects' participation in the process — perhaps their initiative, motivation, or selectivity, their ability to perceive the stimuli, or to make a given response.

Perceptual and Cognitive Processes

Investigation of perception is one of the major interests in psychology. The phenomena range from specific technical tasks such as the ability to see complex geometric figures in certain designs, to comparing judgments of weights, to the formation of complex perceptions. Particular impetus was given to the field of perception by the work of the Gestalt psychologists, who studied some interesting phenomena. They stressed the importance of configurations and patterns, the roles of figure and ground, the satisfaction people find in preferring certain perceptions over others, a satisfaction, in one example, that comes to rest on rectangles with a long- to short-side ratio of 1.618:1. Similarly, a figure with interruptions in its depiction will often be perceived as a whole, exemplifying the phenomenon of *closure*. The emphasis on relationships, selection, closure, etc., led to the idea that the perception of a whole is greater than the sum of the parts, and to noting the learning phenomenon termed *insight* in which the individual learns by grasping a relationship that suddenly makes sense rather than by accumulating successful trials.

Gestalt psychology was extended to include concepts of fields and life space, notably in the work of Kurt Lewin, and eventually into how personal and social experiences affect perception. In a famous experiment, Bruner and Goodman demonstrated that coins look larger to poor children than they do to rich children.[7] Another classic study by Muzafer Sherif showed that people's perceptions of the apparent movement of a stationary pinpoint of light were markedly influenced by learning how others perceived the light.[8]

All the visualizations used in marketing make use of perceptual processes — the vertical stripes in dresses that make some women look slim; the designs of packages and advertisements that achieve their effects through color, contrast, composition; the minor shocks to attention from interrupting expected shapes; the rhythm of the Coca-Cola logotype; the surprise of white lettering on black background.

Another related field of study examines the operation of cognitive processes, such as attention, reasoning, development of concepts, memory, and how people solve problems.[9]

Depth Psychologies

A third broad realm of psychology is oriented to the study of human behavior in terms of subjective processes, to encompassing theories of personality, and to the historical genesis of behavior. Usually, such theories of psychology are dynamic, in the sense of postulating active, at times contending, forces within the person, and special attention is given to the emotional significance of experience. While there are sharply divided schools of thought among the workers in this field, there are general tendencies to stress motivation as a determinant of behavior, to prefer to deal with whole persons as the unit of study, and to try to understand experience from the point of view of the subject.

Because depth psychologies focus on motivation and the subjectivity of experience, they stress the *meaning* of events to people, the conscious and unconscious significance of one's body, one's own actions, and of external objects and interpersonal relationships. Experience is interpreted as symbolic — not as merely literal and limited, but carrying some larger reference or more transcendent implication.

Depth psychologies do not deny the force of immediate experience and its power to change one, but they give great weight to the aspects of the person that crystallize early in life and form the enduring part of one's personality and its typical modes of functioning.[10]

The unconscious forces at work are controversial, and many people prefer to deny their existence. Psychoanalytic study tends to focus on the individual's unconscious processes. Carl Jung and Joseph Campbell point to collective universalities in the human unconscious. These "archetypes of the collective unconscious" are fundamental forms and ideas that are pervasive, infusing experience with deeper meanings relating to divinity, masculine and feminine principles, love, death, transformation, and good and evil. The individual uses ordinary objects, enters relationships with other people, and fantasizes about them in order to express the unconscious archetypes through a particular self-hood.

The deeper meanings referred to here do not have to be Freudian stereotypes to be important in affecting marketing behavior. The naming of the Caterpillar Tractor, with its kinesthetic linking of the machine and the crawling insect, Kodak's sentimental evocations of family life, Hamm's amiable vagabond and his burly bear, the common joy in making Xerox reproductions, are varied examples of ways that dynamic, symbolic, emotional processes are put to work in the marketplace.

The Role of the Body

It is a truism that the body is deeply involved in any human activity, but it is also a fact often neglected in marketing analysis. The individual's behavior is the expression of a psychosomatic organism. This means that physiological predispositions, capacities, limitations, and other features provide ways of classifying people, and of interpreting their needs and actions. Typically, one or another organ or tissue system is consistently given greater attention or use as a channel for self-expression. Some people are oriented to the skin, expressing themselves especially through itching, blushing, skin eruptions, or sensuous interests— even seeming to have a special attraction to mosquitoes. Others tend to have a gastrointestinal focus, to go in for stomach upsets, erratic bowel function, poor or voracious appetite. The motor system allows for an emphasis on executive functions, possibly with distinctive orthopedic or muscular involvements or special locomotor interests. Some people are prone to chronic colds or respiratory conspicuousness. Any of the senses may be hyperacute or defective. Of course, people can use their bodies in a highly integrated way without the hierarchy of physiological emphasis being dramatic, or they may move with versatility from one body area to another.

Basic physiological tendencies are complicated by personal and social definitions and relationships. Sensuous yearnings imply a certain egocentricity and a desire for contact and interest in texture. Whether inherent or not, lank straight hair may suggest emotional coolness and red hair a quick temper. There are general social views about people who talk rapidly or slowly, about people's shape, height, weight, skin color, and so forth. These views are worked into the individual's self-concept in some way, being issues each person has to confront.

Marketing study may neglect such ideas, perhaps out of an unrealistic or misplaced delicacy. Sellers of home remedies and personal products are more likely to face up to the issues posed by physical differences. Here and there marketers find it of interest to explore the diverse motivations for use of laxatives, the differential self-concepts affecting motion sickness, and the subtle underpinnings associated with boxer shorts versus briefs.

Individual Differences

There are endless psychological theories and emphases of study, as people work to analyze human behavior, its sources, its components, its development, its abnormality, its treatment, and so forth. Some scholars look for generalizations, others search for differentiations. In the study of individual differences, it is customary to develop means of measuring psychological dimensions of interest, so that assessments can be made of individuals, comparisons with one another or with the norms of groups. The variables, often conceived as traits, may be drawn from any of the areas or theories of psychology. Instruments have been developed for measuring such characteristics as intelligence, interests, values, social functioning, masculinity, introspection, innovativeness, dogmatism, and cognitive style.[11]

The Layman's Eclecticism

Like some psychologists, the lay person tends to be eclectic, finding value in the intuitively plausible parts of each theory, and enjoying occasional revelations that seem strange. Marketing managers usually believe that repetition of a message is useful for some kind of stimulus–response conditioning. They often intensify the stimuli they offer in trying to affect the perceptions of the audience, to make something look good, and they would like to know what bundle of traits their customers are. They are usually more wary of "depth interpretations" of customers, like the behaviorists who consider the inner life of the person a mysterious black box, but they do not doubt that the customers have an inner life, are emotional, motivated, and often irrational. They are likely to be glad to get any information they can that seems related to what they have to do to be an effective marketer, if it is not too complex, expensive, or intangible. These generalizations are, of course, subject to a range of individual differences among managers.

PUTTING IT ALL TOGETHER: THE CONSUMER PUZZLE

What a person learns is distilled from society, from various group memberships, and from private experiences. Cultural expectations become part of individual expectations. People react to their familial participation and to their social awareness, evolving and defining their conformity and their deviation. Whatever one is in these conceptual realms is expressed in daily habits, where it is lived out. Each person's outlook takes something from all available sources to form each individuality. The result is a unique pattern, yet one that shares much with other people.

Individual decision making is this unique pattern in action — the person moving about a life space, observing, organizing, appraising, feeling, and in so doing searching, picking and choosing from what is available. All must consume, because this is how they survive and grow, and all their behavior is some kind of consumer behavior. They work to provide, to make consumer behavior possible.

People can be conceived of as being composed of the objects and services they consume: The products they buy are transmuted into their biological beings, whether food, conditioned air, drugs, or surgery; their psyches process experiences; and their social selves use clothes, houses, cars, and all that forms part of how other people will regard them.

This large and obvious fact has been slighted because psychological theories of personality development tend to be couched in abstractions, to address themselves to needs, traits, phases, stages, and variables. It seems so easy to discuss needs and forget about the human being in operation who has the needs, and how they are specifically gratified. The "needs" abstractions are often manipulated without reference to the practical content that exemplifies them in the real world, where interpersonal conflict so often turns out to be about money (even though, no doubt, the deeper antagonisms are of a different order). Marital conflicts may show up when wives want to buy furniture when their husbands want to buy a car; a brutish husband scorns his wife's purchase of a diaphragm; young love may mean deliveries from a babies' formula service; and infant anality becomes the justification to buy a washer and dryer, a gift of a year's diaper service, or the steady outlay for disposable diapers.

If this is so, a fundamental basis for decision making is the composition of objects and services that a person wants to *be,* as best as one is able to figure that out at the critical junctures. Deciding is not always easy, because the choices available, as well as the dynamics of the psyche, may be too complex for people to make accurate predictions about themselves and the situation. They sometimes buy products that they are uncertain about, soon dislike, or never use.

This uncertainty is not a problem once stable behaviors have been established that are congenial to the self-concept, or when an inexpensive error can be easily dismissed. In other cases, indecision and doubt rule. People cast about among various sources of information, guidance, and permission that will give their fleeting or brooding impressions and associations a sufficiently suitable direction for action. How can consumers discover what is a good buy? They want a consumer "good," but not all goods are equally good to or for one. Decision making has to refer both to characteristics of the products and to interpretations of how they are good for oneself.

Such ruminations make one wonder about the problem of making optimal judgments. What is best for oneself? This is a question to be looked at not from the marketing point of view in some general sense, but from the point of view of the individual—the decision maker. It is clear that psychology has not adequately addressed itself to many related problems, since there is very little psychology of abnormal consumer behavior. The question might be raised, if there were such a discipline what would it be like?

What concept of healthy consumption would be brought to bear? It might be derived from how one's purchasing behavior assisted the economy.

When Americans were counseled to keep buying at one point, a man commented that he would buy a new car to give the economy a lift. He was a serious Republican and may perhaps be believed. On another occasion, President Johnson asked housewives to control prices by not buying expensive foods. It may be that a healthy consumer would be guided by such considerations of what was appropriate for all. In a world of limited resources, Arnold Mitchell of the Stanford Research Institute has referred to Voluntary Simplicity as the style of the future. Perhaps healthy consuming means living within one's income or diligent pursuit of Consumers Union recommendations. Then again, it may be found in the liberation that is expressed in buying unconventional products. Aren't those buyers the free souls who are adapted to their impulses?

Some think that the optimistic and extensive use of credit is a disease, while others see it as a challenge to one's adeptness. Although some attention has been given to some matters of abnormal consumer behavior, such as shoe fetishism, transvestism, alcoholism, and the breakdowns women suffer when redecorating the house, much remains to be done to explain beyond the neurotic consumer to the many varieties of consumer experience, to develop new categories that conceptualize consumer stances. Customarily, simple behavioral categories of nonusers and users have been emphasized because marketers are interested in converting one to the other. But the creative marketer benefits from a richer conception of what consumers are doing.

The Search for Meaning

This brings us to the heart of this thought: the concept that consumer behavior is an expression of the individual's symbol system, a nuanced assertion or a gross statement of the meanings engaged in daily life actions in the marketplace. The buyer and the seller are analogous in this respect, although the seller here is a provider rather than a consumer. Meanings are exchanged. The meaning of purchase and nonpurchase to the seller, and the meaning of all that is offered in terms of the price, the symbolic meaning of the product, the nature of the advertising, and the

channels chosen for distribution—all these elements are seman-
tic, symbolic expressions which may be listened to and utilized
by the potential purchasers.

The Importance of "Trivia"

From this point of view, even matters generally regarded as
minor or trivial can take on importance at decision-making time.
The individual is zeroing in, and for the moment a penny or a
minor object may seem a larger sum or a highly significant object. Krugman has hypothesized that low involvement may be a
significant factor in the kind of learning that occurs "when television bombards us with enough trivia about a product."[12]

But there is a difficulty in judging what is trivial, not only at
the moment of actual involvement, but as between one person
and another, as one's trivia is another's obsession. It is curious to
note how consumers can explain apparently small decisions with
a quality of conviction or involvement that even they might deny
having from a more detached perspective. Here are some casual
examples gleaned from interviews in which women were asked
about deciding to buy something:

> The most recent decision was with some chocolates at a store. I
> thought, will the family get more enjoyment from these chocolates
> than from candy bars? I bought them for purely selfish reasons. I
> crave them, but it was a difficult decision. It was a luxury item, but
> I splurged.

> I like the best quality of everything I buy. I feel that you get what
> you pay for. I'm not satisfied with less than the best. I've tried sev-
> eral times to buy less expensive toilet paper, but I always go back to
> a more expensive one.

A lower-lower-class woman, poor, with no telephone, gave a
little insight into her life:

> Well, about two weeks ago on Friday night, my husband and I went
> in a taxi cab to shop for groceries. We try to buy groceries every two
> weeks. We were out of potatoes—they have been so high that we
> haven't had any. These potatoes' prices were real funny. You could
> get 20 lb for 69¢ and 10 lb for 59¢, so the 20 lb was only 10¢ higher
> and for twice as many too. So we argued and argued about spending
> the extra 10¢, but I finally convinced my husband that it was 10¢
> worth spending because we got another 10 lb of potatoes for the
> dime.

The meanings of the objects and the complex dynamics of the consumer struggling for optimal judgment about dimes, husbands, and cravings for chocolates (or a pink Cadillac) tend to thwart correlation studies, which try to account for given consumer actions with dimensions derived from paper-and-pencil tests of personality variables. With such an approach, one has trouble trying to relate to the life experiences and goals that grow out of, or find expression consistently in, consumer decisions.

Using standard psychological instruments, like the Edwards Personality Inventory or the Allport-Vernon Study of Values, sometimes provides significant results. Studies have achieved good results, but many show spotty, low positive correlation. Dominance and gregariousness are traits that seem to do fairly well, which suggests that vigorous, outgoing people who are up and doing tend to buy the things that are of common interest or the innovations that are likely to be.

Not enough spade work has been done, not enough studies that try to develop richly textured thinking about consumers before hastening to try on the standard variables of paper-and-pencil tests. Not enough is known about the dynamics of consumer functioning, of the ways in which being a consumer is a way of being a person. The store of concepts and variables that have been teased out is as yet so meager as to have barely begun. Much study is needed at all levels to explain fully how customers process their physical, social, and cultural circumstances through their psyches in deciding how to allocate their resources of time, energy, attention, reasoning, emotion, desire—and finally money—in both short-range and long-range terms, to develop, sustain, modify, and elaborate the meanings that matter to them.

Market Style as Lifestyle

The pattern formed by a person's market actions, as a kind of seller or buyer, creates a lifestyle: a large complex symbol in motion. It is composed of subsymbols; it utilizes a characteristic pattern of life space; and it acts systematically to process objects and events in accordance with these values.

All people seek to assert something about themselves and this—or some central set of recurring motifs—is identifiable as the summary fashion of their wrestling with existence. They observe one another's lifestyles, even if only fragments and part-motifs are captured. We can think of people in categorical terms derived from their customary behavior, emotional tone, and expressed wishes, as being donors and recipients to their special forms of taking and giving. So the person oriented to display may take attention and admiration from us, the ambitious leader wants us to obey, the careless driver may want to share an accident with us.

As they show us themselves, order us about, or collide with us, they bring their lifestyles to our attention. We discover something about the content of their personalities and the special fashion or form they give to it. Thus, perhaps this driver apologizes profusely, as perhaps he always does when he hurts others. This leader keeps insisting it is all for the good of others, and this exhibitionist does it by putting on striking clothes rather than removing them.

In expressing their values, in describing the kinds of roles they play in life and how they think those roles should be fulfilled, people reveal both real and ideal lifestyles. In one marketing study in Montana, life was described as slow-paced, with the people geared to the rigors and virtues of frontier life, where it is cold and demanding, where the skills and rewards of hunting and fishing loom large, where men are rugged, touched with the nobility of the natural man and superior to the wan, tender Eastern city man. A man's lifestyle is generally conceived as one of good fellowship, whether with a gun, a rod, or a drink. This may sound like parody, but respondents' comments show the reality of these views as some of the men describe the people and lifestyle of Montana.

> The men here are real good, you can trust them. Most of them are outdoor men; they have to be or else they wouldn't live here. Most of them are honest.
>
> The men here are true Westerners; big, tough, and rugged.
>
> Men are men here, and they are manly. Somewhat more honest and less sharp dealing than in the more civilized parts of the country.
>
> It's wonderful here. It's God's country. I like the frontier atmosphere. Life is casual and leisurely here, no frantic big city pace.

This contrasts with the kinds of lifestyle men in metropolitan environments offer to sum up who they are. Here are found the familiar tunes of urban-suburbanites, where men are first husbands and fathers, and run to the ragged, rather than the rugged.

The men here are very nice, a well-educated group of men who have many outside interests and are very congenial. They're home-loving and conscientious.

Most of my neighbors are young families and pretty well child-oriented. The men are typical suburbanites, very much concerned with crab grass and PTA. They all work hard and bring home brief cases.

To grasp these lifestyles and the way in which they are exemplified in the lives of men, women, and children requires an orientation to configurations, patterns of ideas, feelings, fantasies, and actions. It is necessary to sense the person at work, to feel the peculiar flavor with which he or she invests the work or draws from it joy, irritation, monotony, impatience, anticipation, anxiety about today or tomorrow, comfort, competence, pride, and a restless urge to succeed visibly or to reach 5 o'clock. To explore this large, complex symbol in motion that is a grand lifestyle is to seek to define a self-concept, to describe the central set of beliefs about self and what is aspired to, that provide consistency (or unpredictability) to what is done. Information about such self-concepts may come from various directions. Two students writing class autobiographies hinted at the contrasting sense of focus they felt about what they sought to achieve in life. One summed up that he wanted to live in accordance with "intelligence, truth, and justice," while the other said his approach boiled down to "thrift, security, and cleanliness." Presumably, the former young man represents a better potential market for books, while the latter might be appealed to in soap ads and commercials.

Such self-definitions are useful in perceiving the coherence of behavior in homemakers who relentlessly pursue antiseptic cleanliness, in children accomplishing characteristically in school, as well as in doting or dismal fathers. This idea of "naturally" following our personal bent (often accompanied by the feeling, "doesn't everyone?") is the core personal symbol. Once we understand this about a person, we can begin to trace the intricate pattern of actions to see how it affects the handling of money, choice of clothes, food preferences, interest in shopping, cooking, giving gifts, and home workshopping. Then it is possible to see how the persisting needs of one person to bend people to comply can make a top-notch salesperson, or where the urge to resist produces an obdurate purchasing agent.

The thought should not be too narrowly conceived. The frustrating difficulty in understanding human behavior is the individual's potential variety in the capacity for diverse and inconsistent motives and behavior. Unimotivational theories are apparently doomed, or become uninteresting because of their vacuity. It won't suffice to prepare a simple list of needs, aims, or benefits if the goal is to develop a subtle, rich alertness and sensitivity to marketing behavior. Dynamic interplay is its fascination and its challenge.

LIFESTYLE IS MADE UP OF SUBSYMBOLS

If the lifestyle of a person or a group does have some general symbolic character, it becomes apparent that the objects and activities used to play out this general symbolic meaning and to embody it may be viewed as subsymbols. The clothes-horse needs clothes, the bookworm needs books, and the cliff dweller needs cliffs.

Housing has a meaning that varies with who is to live in it. Kurt Back noted that in Puerto Rico a public housing project could be regarded as a custodial institution or as a technique for upward mobility, making the most progressive and the most dependent families inclined toward the project. Families that fall between these extremes tend to prefer to stay in private housing, even though it may be physically inferior.[13]

Apartment living versus living in a house provides a contrast in the meanings of subsymbols. Apartment dwellers who are not familially oriented, who use housing that exemplifies the exciting values or urban life, like the freer kind of life it represents.

I like living in apartments. The thing I like best about it is the convenience of having everything taken care of.

Apartment life is very relaxing — no fires to tend to, sidewalks to shovel, and no painting. More time for enjoyment.

Those with a greater yearning to belong and to share in a feeling of some social responsibility see apartments as a stopgap that falls short of true participation in life.

The only advantage to apartment living is that it is a stopgap until you can buy a house.

There is very little opportunity for a sense of community life in an apartment.

A complication for understanding marketing problems comes about in the multiple meanings of objects and communications. The same person may see several meanings and different people may see different meanings. A picture of a skier shows a man standing on two sticks. This may signify a pleasant sport, a dangerous sport, an expensive pastime, new ways of leisure in America, superior social status at an elegant resort, and the competitiveness of the Olympics, conceivably a cause of perspiration in a deodorant advertisement.

Examples could be multiplied to show how people behave in accordance with their own view of themselves and how they want to do things that fit this view. This extends into interesting realms of action and nonaction. A study of why women do not visit physicians for examination as often as they should to detect cancer showed that one reason was a reluctance to change underwear habits. For example, many felt they had to iron a brassiere in order to seem like the kind of women the doctor is presumably accustomed to examining. More importantly and to the point, women did not want to explore the possibility of having cervical cancer. Many believe it is a venereal disease and would reveal their sexual practices. Similarly, even a modern man with a skin problem has uneasy thoughts about what it hints about his sex life and the kinds of products he should buy to cope.

The use of subsymbols affects all who go to market, not merely buyers of consumer goods looking for "status symbols." For example, institutional food buyers show the pervasive effects of how buyers define themselves, their institutions, and their customers, to give their food purchasing its special flavor and meaning. Dietitians and home economists, pursuing their professional roles, tend to emphasize nutritional values and balanced menus. Buyers oriented to cooking or to the clientele of an establishment devoted to the arts thought in terms of the palate and visual esthetics. More business-oriented managers made money a foremost consideration in the style of planning they showed. These were occupational lifestyles, each reflecting a typical symbolic configuration that had developed. The subsymbols of place, titles, preferred suppliers, utensils, and foods, all played roles in sustaining the larger significance these people sought to convey.

It is easiest to see objects being employed symbolically where the goal is to display and where visibility is high, since these can be quite elaborate. In displaying dress and furniture when "company is coming," for example, the importance of having audiences intensifies the presentation of lifestyle. Nevertheless, one's lifestyle is always operative, even if privately at a different level. It is hard to believe that there is ever a time when no one is looking—there is always God. And even if standards are relaxed to the point where people scratch their behinds, wear their socks a second day, or read faster than comprehension can keep up, such lapses are also part of themselves. They support the purchase of subsymbolic products that make up the covert lifestyles that let one sneak a secret drink, chew gum in private, or consume pornography or more television than one likes to admit.

A CHARACTERISTIC PATTERN OF LIFE SPACE

An interesting aspect of symbolism is the significance of life space. As people express their lifestyles, they move through their environment, perceiving it and using it in their own special ways. Individuals vary in their yearnings for space: some love roomy old houses, while others prefer restricted, efficient space. Higher-status people have a larger world view. They look and move toward more distant horizons. They are among that classic 20 percent of the population who do 80 percent of the living, using airplanes and long-distance telephones in sharply disproportionate degree. Lower-status people are apt to use even their own city in narrower fashion. Some never go downtown or leave the neighborhood.

Michael Balint[14] has devoted a book to exploring the psychological consequences of basic interest in *things* versus basic interest in the *spaces* between things. He believes that people have fundamental orientations that lead them either to emphasize clinging to objects or to emphasize moving between objects. The latter orientation is characteristic in the thrill-seeking of skiing and roller coasting, whereas clinging to objects turns *ocnophils* (as Balint calls them) toward stability and security. A study of mobile home dwellers highlighted this contrast with cases of women who bewept the fact that their less root-minded husbands did not provide homes with entrenched foundations and enough space to accumulate more objects.

Such concerns can be extended into assessments of how people organize objects in the space available. Are they orderly and precise, or do they want things to look lived in? People and companies may be judged for their lifestyle according to the way they use space, ranging from Japanese austerity to Victorian clutter. A clear desk can mean efficiency and high status or a figurehead who lets others do the work. A desk piled high may be interpreted as sloppy, comfortable, the home of a drudge or a procrastinator, or it may be seen as belonging to a hard worker who likes everything right at hand: "I have it right here."

Modern architectural design is struggling with whether to "waste space" by leaving open areas or to allot everyone a tight cubicle. Should an office building be like a hospital or like an atrium? Will the public think better of the corporation if the street level is built like an expensive garden plaza instead of having convenient and profitable shops flush to the sidewalk? In Chicago, the Hancock Center Plaza seems dreary compared to the thriving beauty of the First National Bank Plaza.

PROCESSING OBJECTS AND EVENTS

What are the practical implications of this view of lifestyle that stresses its symbolic character? It emphasizes the fact that buyers see objects and events in the real world as having certain potentialities. These potentialities are scanned, screened, and processed for their symbolic suitability, not only because the products can provide some specific results, but because they become incorporated into the lifestyle of the person. This does not mean all product choices are razor's edge decisions between the real-me and the not-me, with a nod to the fake-me. But still, what do they all add up to?

From a marketing point of view—one that might startle traditionalists—a consumer's personality can be seen as the peculiar total of the products he or she consumes. Shown a picture of a young man in an advertisement, one respondent deduced the following:

> *He's a bachelor. His left hand is showing, and it has no ring on it. He lives in one of those modern high-rise apartments, and the rooms are brightly colored. He has modern, expensive furniture, but not Danish modern. He buys his clothes at Brooks Brothers. He owns a good hi-fi. He skis. He has a sail boat. He eats Limburger or any other prestige cheese with his beer. He likes and cooks a lot of steak and he would have filet mignon for company. His liquor cabinet contains Jack Daniel's, Beefeater gin, and a good scotch.*

Through his lifestyle does she know him.

Think of a woman who uses Crosse & Blackwell soups, subscribes to *Gourmet* magazine, has live lobster flown in from Maine to Chicago to serve guests, drives a Renault, does not shave under her arms, and sends out Christmas cards with two names on the return address to show she shares an apartment with a single man. The pattern suggests a value system engaged in choosing things from the marketplace that add up to a lifestyle quite different from that of the housewife who uses Campbell's soups, reads *Family Circle* for ideas on how to furnish a play-room, stretches meatloaf with oatmeal twice a week, rides in her husband's Dodge, and scrubs the kitchen floor three times a week.

By studying these configurations of lifestyle, by observing how people put together those ways of living they think appropriate for a 40-year-old surgeon on the make, a prosperous factory fore-man in a working-class suburb, a woman who feels she leads a dog's life and likes to "go out and eat," or a woman who feels she is "not a raving beauty, but is attractive to men," one can learn how they use products most meaningfully for themselves.

Much work is needed to study consumer lifestyles, to create a taxonomy of lifestyles to help marketers think more system-atically about different kinds of people, and to build a theory that illuminates the dynamic process by which people turn their primitive needs into nuanced and elaborated sets of discrimina-tions among the objects in the marketplace. So often this process seems to fall between the meshes of the research net. It laughs at the clinical items or general traits in personality inventories or the stodginess of questionnaires that fail to take account of the ludicrous, shy, quicksilver, or perverse elements of lifestyle.

Marketers do not just sell isolated items that can be interpreted as symbols. What they sell are potential pieces of a larger sym-bol—the consumer's lifestyle. Marketing is a process of providing customers with parts of an evolving mosaic from which they, as artists of their own lifestyles, can pick and choose to develop the composition that for the time may seem best. Marketers who think about their product in this way will seek to understand its potential settings and relationships to other parts of consumer lifestyles, thereby increasing the number of ways of fitting into them.

This logic works most readily when applied to consumers whose lifestyles are centered around finding the right neighbor-hood in which to live, the suitable house, the right school for the children, the right clothes, the latest "ideal" diet, and so on, in an effort to yield to, conform to, or assert one's position in life, one's aspirations, one's special qualities.

But other kinds of customers are also exhibiting a lifestyle. Wherever any buyers are located in the marketing system (retail buyers, purchasing agents, wholesalers, manufacturers' representatives) they too express their typical orientations. They have their pattern for manner of negotiations, preparation of proposals, quality standards, preferred suppliers, and reputation for the way they do business. Some organizations use buying committees, while others prefer individuals to take the responsibility. Some have policies requiring that three proposals be solicited from competing suppliers. Others stick with certain suppliers. Each way is usually rationalized in terms of efficiency, economy, control, and other values, which are complicated by such elements of lifestyle as secret payments, favoritism, lip service, going through the motions, and other means of covertly thwarting them.

STUDYING LIFESTYLES

The fullest manner of studying lifestyles is through the use of case studies. Each person in the sample is examined for the pattern characteristic of that individual, and the various motives, goals, values, conflicts, and typical means of resolving them are put together.

Because it is not always feasible or economic for practical marketing purposes to study each individual so thoroughly, compromises and shortcuts are used. For example, one method that seeks to summarize patterns of lifestyles or to provide a psychographic (as contrasted to a demographic) profile of marketing groups is the inventory of activities, interests, and opinions developed by William Wells and his associates. The instrument (AIO) includes 300 items that the subject responds to with agreement or disagreement, like: "I usually read the sports page in the daily paper," "I love to cook," "I like a party where there is lots of music and talk."

Various studies showed that users of given products shared clusters of such items, helping illuminate what kinds of people those users are within the boundaries of what the cluster of items seems to say about them. Compared to nonusers, users of eye makeup showed greater agreement: "I often try the latest hairdos when they change," "I would like to spend a year in London or

Paris," "I am interested in spices and seasonings," and "I really do believe that blondes have more fun."[15]

The use of certain products is often accompanied by the use of other products. Therefore, one means of suggesting the lifestyle of consumers is to observe what products seem to go together. The eye makeup users also used a lot of other cosmetics, were above-average smokers, and used more gasoline and long distance telephoning. With this logic in mind, Alpert and Gatty studied behavioral lifestyles of 5,424 men by analyzing their use patterns of 80 items of products and services. They drew out 25 factors as The Hard Drinker, The Car-Conscious Man, The Candy Consumer, The Well-Groomed Man, and so on. In the next step they used these factors to compare beer drinkers with non-beer-drinkers and Beer Brand Y drinkers with Beer Brand W drinkers. Beer Drinkers were more like Hard Drinkers than like Soft Drinkers or like Liquor and Wine Connoisseurs; and Brand Y drinkers were Outdoorsmen, and Hard Drinkers more so than Brand W drinkers who were more like the Cosmopolitan Traveler and the Dress-Conscious Man.[16]

There are numerous other possibilities ranging from the full case study with its great detail and consequent great reliance on the interpretive skill of the marketer who works with it to the lifestyle pattern that correlates or factors specific product behaviors.

As a practical substitute for an extended personal history, the so-called depth interview is used: one- to two-hour conversations with appropriate subjects on the topic of interest, with enough openness and flexibility to permit a lot of individual, subjective information to emerge. The value of this method over the inventory and correlational methods is that fresh categories and patterns relevant to the specific marketing topic have a chance to be expressed, whereas standard instruments predetermine the categories, and new combinations are limited to them. A shortcut version of this approach is the focus group interview. This method is handy and convenient, since it is a quick discussion with a relevant group. But it is much abused and is often only a sloppy substitute for adequate research.

SITUATIONAL ANALYSIS

Another way of focusing on consumer behavior is to place great weight on *the situation* in which the behavior occurs. This method was suggested in 1963 by Boyd and Levy who recommended the value of thinking about consumption systems, referring to "the way a purchaser of a product performs the total task of whatever he or she is trying to accomplish when using the product—not baking a cake, but preparing a meal; not installing a transmission, but building an automobile."[17] Three layers of analysis are noted:

Looking beyond purchase behavior to use behavior.

Deliberately studying the "total" consumption system for the sake of additional insights.

Analyzing the consumption system in the further detail of the many interrelated subsystems resulting from different kinds of people making different use of the same product or the same use of different products.

By making the close, detailed observations necessary to analyze a person involved in a consumption system, one is pressed to think about not only what the person is doing, but why. What are his or her thoughts and feelings and how does the product fit in with other objects and actions that are part of the process of doing the laundry, gardening, or whatever?

In a discussion of situational segmentation, Tauber illustrates the way partisans exclude other approaches in order to exalt their own.

Yoell . . . , in a devastating attack on psychographics and other consumer typologies, suggests that life situations, not life styles, are the key to universal behavior. He questions whether product choice, e.g., carry-home food, is due to hedonism, impotence, a venturesome style of life, or just because a woman is too tired to cook.[18]

A rich theory of marketing behavior is necessarily more eclectic than that, and has room both for hedonists and for people who are too tired to cook at the time. The point is to know when it is more relevant to think about hedonism and when about fatigue. Tauber goes on reasonably to stress the importance of environmental factors, indicating that "situational segmentation *begins* with the assumption that people are basically the same but have different needs when in differing situations. . . . A second assumption is that many people will have similar needs when they find themselves in similar situations."[19]

The situational approach is an affirmation of the Gestalt, or Lewinian, approach to psychology. It is useful for new product development because it opens up discussion of potential alternatives to what people are currently doing in given situations. The situation needs attention as an analytic variable because behavior occurs in particular environment contexts and is affected by them. In addition, the situational environment is something that the marketing manager is often in a position to create or alter, and experiment with.

SUMMARY

1. When people behave, they are performing a marketing action because they either present something for others to receive and consume, or they receive and use something. This behavior is the culmination of many forces. It may be interpreted for its historical development, its genesis at an earlier point in time, for the degree to which it reflects or proceeds from the many sources of behavior that have been discussed.

2. It isn't enough to explain behavioral variations with simple categorizations. If girls wash dishes and boys do not, the variation between two washing groups is "accounted for" by the sex difference (or perhaps the variation between the two sex groups is accounted for by the washing difference), but is that the end of the explanation? Obviously, many more questions can be raised about the sources of the behavior—questions about the culture, about the social groups involved, the family, how important dishwashing is, problems, the feelings of the participants, and what they do in the dishwashing situation. Such questions are important if there are such marketing goals as introducing new products, changing the way dishes are washed, changing who does the washing, eliminating dishwashing, communicating about dishwashing, shifting cost/benefit relationships, and so on.

3. Marketing behavior is made up of the actions, internal and external, of individuals. Thus it is basically a psychological matter.

4. Psychological theories help in understanding marketing behavior, by seeking to explain its sources. Different approaches explain at different levels or with interest in different behaviors. Behaviorism stresses conditioning and reinforcement via the association of stimuli and responses, in producing learning. Field psychologies examine perceptual processes and how people organize their experience. Depth psychologies look to the individual's history and the role of symbols, the force of emotions and motives in producing behavior.

5. All approaches are used pragmatically by marketing managers, as basic rationales for decision making.

6. The individual (and market segments, in the aggregate) organizes a Lifestyle. It is a complex symbol, meaningful to each person and to the others in the environment. It expresses a current way of life, and is powered by abilities, achievements, possibilities, aspirations, and conflicts. The factors listed in Figure 8 may be extended to show their interaction with the individuals who make up the cultural subgroups, as shown in Figure 9.

Figure 9. Marketing behavior as a complex outcome of many factors.

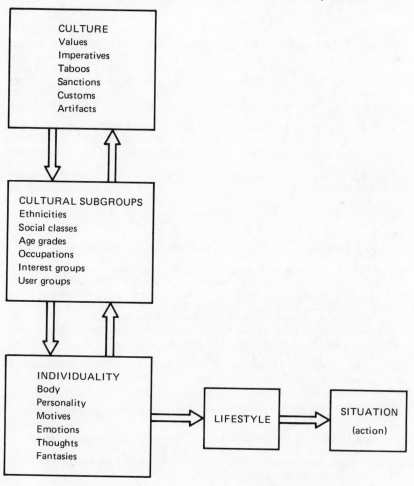

Marketing behavior is a complex manifestation of the pattern called the lifestyle. It is derived from the manner in which over time the culture is manifest through, and affected by, its subgroups and further complexly processed through the people who make up those groups. The lifestyle is the way in which people act out their own membership patterns, expressing their bodies, the enduring qualities called personality, and their thoughts as these are pressed toward, and evoked by, current situations.

References

1. James M. Carman, "The Application of Social Class in Marketing Segmentation," *IBER Special Publications* (Berkeley: University of California, 1965), pp. 63–64.
2. Eugene J. Webb, Donald T. Campbell, Richard D. Schwartz, and Lee Sechrest, *Unobtrusive Measures: Nonreactive Research in the Social Sciences* (New York: Rand McNally, 1966).
3. John B. Miner, "Psychologists in Marketing Education," *Journal of Marketing*, Jan. 1966, p. 9.
4. B. F. Skinner, *About Behaviorism* (New York: Alfred A. Knopf, 1974).
5. David A. Lieberman (ed.), *Learning and the Control of Behavior: Some Principles, Theories, and Applications of Classical and Operant Conditioning* (New York: Holt, Rinehart and Winston, 1974).
6. Edwin J. Thomas (ed.), *Behavior Modification Procedure: A Sourcebook* (Chicago: Aldine, 1974).
7. J. S. Bruner and C. C. Goodman, "Value and Need as Organizing Factors in Perception," *Journal of Abnormal and Social Psychology*, 1947, pp. 33–34.
8. Muzafer Sherif, *The Psychology of Social Norms* (New York: Harper & Row, 1936).
9. Michael I. Posner, *Cognition: An Introduction* (Glenview, Ill.: Scott, Foresman, 1974).
10. Gardner Lindzey, Calvin S. Hall, and Martin Manosevitz (eds.), *Theories of Personality: Primary Sources and Research* (New York: Wiley, 1973).
11. Leona E. Tyler, *The Psychology of Human Differences* (Englewood Cliffs, N.J.: Prentice-Hall, 1965); H. A. Witkin, R. B. Dyk, H. F. Faterson, D. R. Goodenough, and S. A. Karp, *Psychological Differentiation* (Potomac, Md: Lawrence Erlbaum Associates, 1974); Irving L. Janis, George F. Mahl, Jerome Kagan, and Robert R. Holt, *Personality: Dynamics, Development, and Assessment* (New York: Harcourt, Brace, Jovanovich, 1974).
12. Herbert E. Krugman, "The Impact of Television Advertising: Learning without Involvement," *The Public Opinion Quarterly*, Fall 1965, p. 353.
13. Kurt W. Back, *Slums, Projects, and People* (Durham, N.C.: Duke University Press, 1962).
14. Michael Balint, *Thrills and Regressions* (New York: International University Press, 1959).
15. William D. Wells and Douglas J. Tigert, "Activities, Interests and Opinions," *Journal of Advertising Research*, Aug. 1971, pp. 27–35.
16. Lewis Alpert and Ronald Gatty, "Product Positioning by Behavioral Life-Styles," *Journal of Marketing*, Apr. 1969, pp. 65–69.

17. **Harper W. Boyd, Jr.,** and **Sidney J. Levy,** "New Dimension in Consumer Analysis," *Harvard Business Review,* Nov.–Dec. 1963, p. 130.
18. **Edward M. Tauber,** "Situational Segmentation," *Food Product Development Magazine,* July–Aug. 1974, p. 12.
19. Ibid., p. 12.

Suggested Readings

Anastasi, A., *Fields of Applied Psychology* (New York: McGraw-Hill, 1964).

Arndt, William B., Jr., *Theories of Personality* (New York: Macmillan, 1974).

Bandura, A., and R. H. Walters, *Social Learning and Personality* (New York: Holt, Rinehart, and Winston, 1963).

Bower, G. H., and E. R. Hilgard, *Theories of Learning,* 4th ed. (Englewood Cliffs, N.J.: Prentice-Hall, 1974).

Britt, Steuart H., *Consumer Behavior and the Behavioral Sciences* (New York: Wiley, 1966).

Bruner, J. S., J. Goodnow, and G. Austin, *A Study of Thinking* (New York: Science Editions, 1962).

Cox, Donald F., *Risk Taking and Information Handling in Consumer Behavior* (Boston: Harvard University Press, 1967).

Erikson, E. H., *Identity and the Life Cycle* (New York: International Universities Press, 1959).

Feldman, S. (ed.), *Cognitive Consistency: Motivational Antecedents and Behavioral Consequences* (New York: Academic Press, 1966).

Howard, J., *Marketing: Executive and Buyer Behavior* (New York: Columbia University Press, 1963).

Kassarjian, Harold H., "Personality and Consumer Behavior: A Review," *Journal of Marketing Research,* Nov. 1971, pp. 409–418.

Katona, G., *The Powerful Consumer* (New York: McGraw-Hill, 1960).

Lessig, V. Parker, *Personal Characteristics and Consumer Buying Behavior* (Pullman, Wash.: Washington State University, 1971).

Manis, Jerome, and Bernard Meltzer, *Symbolic Interaction* (Boston: Allyn & Bacon, 1967).

Rokeach, Milton, *The Nature of Human Values* (New York: The Free Press, 1973).

Sommers, M. S., and J. B. Kernan (eds.), *Explorations in Consumer Behavior* (Austin: Bureau of Business Research, 1968).

Spiegel, John P., and Pavel Machotka, *Messages of the Body* (New York: The Free Press, 1974).

Tucker, W. T., *Foundations for a Theory of Consumer Behavior* (New York: Holt, Rinehart, and Winston, 1967).

ix

The Sellers' Meanings

As with the buyers, the actions of sellers grow out of their psychologies, group memberships, and cultural influences. They, too, have their lifestyles. These lifestyles are what sellers express in the marketing dialogue. When buyers are exposed to a component of the seller's lifestyle, they interpret what it means to them, working in two directions. They reason toward the seller, making inferences about what the piece of information received tells them about the total (company, brand) and they reason toward themselves, interpreting how they should act in terms of their own lifestyle.

This chapter explores in closer detail some of the things that marketers do that carry their messages to the segmented subgroups in the marketplace. Although it has been customary to act as though messages are supposed to be transmitted through sales pitches and advertising, there is growing awareness that all the things an organization does can add to the public's understanding about it.

For example, if a company fails to hire minorities, parts of the black or Latino markets will interpret that fact and not buy. This example highlights the marketing aspect of the company's personnel policies and refers to the personnel manager's marketing task. In another case, an insurance company was thought likely to be very conservative because it was located in the Midwest, when that was all that people elsewhere knew about it. The elegance of an annual report suggested to recipients that the company was prosperous and sold high-quality merchandise, although the figures in the report showed losses.

OBJECTIVES AND ACTIONS

Seen from the point of view of the marketing managers who sell, how are they to govern the marketing process? Guiding their decisions is a hierarchy of policies, objectives, and goals. The broadest aims are often taken for granted and may range from such vague views as "increasing shareholders' wealth" to "getting along as best we can in a tough market." Often, companies do not clearly define their policies and objectives.[1] They proceed on the basis of unwritten policies, and objectives they think are understood, commonly in the belief that this permits greater flexibility and more rapid adaptation to changing circumstances. This situation comes about partly because of the difficulty of formulating objectives that are practically useful and specific that can be fairly predictably achieved, partly because of familiar "custom and usage," or inertia, and partly because of a belief in the inevitable need to rely on the judgment of managers.

The history and structure of an organization tend to produce characteristic kinds of objectives. They are inherent in the nature of the industry, the organization, and the kind of people who are responsible for it, who establish its traditions, and who are constrained by legal mandate. Boyd and Levy discuss some of the sources of typical broad objectives:

Focus on material resources.

Concern with fabricated objects.

Major interest in events and activities, requiring certain kinds of products or services.

Emphasis on kind of person whose needs are to be met.

Catering to specific physical parts of a person.

Examination of wants and needs, and seeking to adapt to them.[2]

Within these broad frameworks, the organization asserts its posture, being perhaps an aggressive innovator, a shrewd follower, a backward-looking aging plant, or a make-do outfit. Managers responsible for marketing and promotional decisions might operate in an environment that wants them to forge ahead and show initiative. Possibly they are told this, but in practice they are thwarted and denied sufficient funds—the way Congress sometimes passes programs but fails to appropriate the money to support them.

Some organizations are cautious and parsimonious or expect managers to prove their judgment with research. Some expect managers to be ethical, while others expect them to make money no matter what. Most of such complex, subtle, intangible situations ultimately affect promotion, in the sense that what the organization *is* works its way into its actions, which tell us about its nature and thereby impress the market in some distinctive way.

The audience comes to recognize in a general way that the particular company is public-spirited, the particular hospital is not service-oriented, and the government agency is less bureaucratic than usual. A simple notion of the marketing concept with its stress on customer satisfaction overlooks the force of the groups on the providers' side of the dialogue. They cannot and will not merely defer to the customer, since they have their own values, goals, and personalities.

Effective managers recognize that all the actions emanating from the organization are communications, and have in mind a general conception of what they want to say. If the overall message is about a high-quality, customer-oriented company, they will not want to use advertising themes, media, or salespeople (or even lobby displays, landscaping, and stationery in the home office, if they have any voice about these things) that do not support this image.

Given these organizational foci and interests, some specific plans are then developed. They are necessitated by such circumstances as annual reviews, the appointment of a new manager, a new advertising agency, new laws, or a perceived change in the status of a company or of one of its products resulting from any of the forces in the marketplace (such as economic changes, competitors, and fashion shifts). Fundamentally, this means that at intervals one person responds to the challenge of the current position, or of some necessity in it, determined to initiate fresh thinking and action. This goes on parallel to the maintenance activities already in process, and may take place either under routine circumstances or at a time of crisis.

The particular objectives are infinitely varied, given the many

kinds of organizations, personnel, and problems involved. However, they are generally expected to include (1) a time period (six
months, one year, three years), (2) an arena in which certain aims
are to be accomplished (among dealers, consumers, patients, citizens, advertising, point of purchase), and (3) an estimate of the
benefit to be achieved (in sales volume, size of vote, profit, kind
and degree of attitude change). Such objectives are usually directed toward producing growth in some market response, but
the problems and plans vary according to the aim, whether
it is to keep response levels increasing to greater heights, to ar-
rest and reverse a declining pattern, or to inaugurate acceptance
of a new idea, activity, or product. The demarketing situation has
its own characteristics, as discussed by Kotler and Levy.[3]

THE PROBLEM OF MAINTAINING OR INCREASING RESPONSE

When a product, service, or brand is doing well, and the objective is to maintain and build, the emotional outlook is normally
one of animation, expansion, and optimism, often underlain with
anxiety and uncertainty about keeping up and making the arduous efforts that even small increments may require. People
may joke about not really knowing what they are doing right, and
worry lest a fickle market suddenly abandon them, or that others
in the organization are being smug and complacent. Well-en-
trenched politicians worry about efforts being undermined by
overconfidence. Commonly, it no longer seems adequate to do
the customary things that are making the public aware of the
product and its merits. The manager may feel that most people
already know about it and that special means are needed to stimulate further growth. Various avenues are available for accomplishing this objective.

One approach is through intensified pressure on the sales
force, distribution system, or customers. Incentive programs are
one way of urging these groups to respond. Special sales, contests, impulse displays, and coupons tend to come across as being
extraneous to the product. They imply that the merits of the
product are familiar, but that some special favor is being offered
to encourage greater use of it. A state may decide to run a lottery
to obtain more revenue, thus adding a kind of voluntary tax.

A second approach that is often suggested involves concern
with the image of the organization or brand. If the manager be-

lieves that the customers' impressions and knowledge need refreshment or redirection, he or she may reappraise the organization's advertising policies as the quickest and most vigorous means of accomplishing this aim. Any attempt to modify the brand imagery may take boldness and nerve in a positive situation. But some managers believe that if they wait until the need becomes apparent through sales softening, it will be too late to recapture the initiative. Occasionally, in the desire for a new advertising approach, and even in the face of the ongoing competence of the present advertising agency, the company may hire a new one.

In general, the aim is to communicate that the product or service has use, qualities, and significance not previously associated with it. Arm and Hammer baking soda built its market vigorously by promoting varied household uses, especially refrigerator deodorizing. Seven-Up is an example of a brand that offered itself in a new light, using new imagery. Its campaigns emphasizing the themes of "wet and wild" and the "Uncola" reshaped any previous digestive associations, and implied a lively youthfulness and a stronger competitiveness with cola drinks. A hospital held an open house to show it was a pleasant place as well as an efficient treatment center.

A third approach seeks to find and develop special market segments. Couponing may gain leads for salespeople or for dealers. Special salespeople may act as missionaries to explore novel product views in potentially new buying units. Advertising may be directed toward the arousal of new forces among customer groups. Canteen Corporation ran a series of simple, dramatic advertisements offering institutional food service as a new management tool. The media used were those read by upper management, and the appeal was aimed directly at high-level concerns rather than the nuts and bolts of inplant feeding. The result was an unusual influx of inquiries on company presidents' letterheads. It was clear that Canteen had strengthened its position in the buying situation by invoking the influence of an important market segment. A city may run a festival or a fair to build excitement about it in the minds of tourists and inject pride in the local inhabitants. Two cities that come to mind are Chicago and New York, where ethnic motifs provide the focus.

Most of the activity aimed at maintaining and increasing market interest requires an orientation to refinement of marketing understanding. This means a search for intensification and variation of meanings and exploration of interstices, nooks, and crannies in the market in order to elaborate one's place in it. In its earnest effort to serve in every corner of the market, the *Miami Herald*, already very widely read in its area, once commissioned a study of nonreaders of newspapers, a segment in the market that is both minute and peculiar, although perhaps not as strange as it used to be.

THE PROBLEM OF DECLINING RESPONSE

With increasing sales, the problem is both not to rock the boat and to keep doing interesting and stimulating things that say, "Yes, we are still 'with it.'" With declining response, the situation is very different. The human mood is apt to be depressed and anxious. The manager feels threatened, relations among the promotional groups are probably strained and irritable, perhaps touched (or even giddy) with gallows humor. Unless the reason for the decline is truly obvious, there is a preoccupation with diagnosing the trouble, while various kinds of flailing around may go on. Blame is apt to be cast in all the marketing directions: internally, for an inferior product or foolish mistakes; at the sales force for inadequate effort; at dealers for indifference; at the advertising agency for lack of creativity; and even at customers for their stupidity. (For example, an advertising man wrote in the margin of a marketing research report, alongside a critical comment by a consumer, "Dummy!" probably in double resentment at the consumer and at his own failure to communicate well enough.)

This situation creates dilemmas. Everyone who would like to be helpful has a suggestion. Presumably marketing research would be useful to assist in determining the kind of problems to be solved. But because of the worsening financial picture, research budgets are often cut instead. An organization may avoid this particular problem by an ongoing research program with regular soundings that give early indications of trouble and some of its sources. In any event, formal research, more casual kinds of inquiry, or even just hashing it out may lead to some diagnosis, and then to activities aimed to cure it.

If the general economic situation seems at fault, intense price activity may occur, replete with deals, coupons, and rebates, in sometimes rather desperate efforts to stimulate the market. Promotion is expected to carry the burden, especially when the product-development people seem stymied for ideas, when price competition does not appear effective or possible, when a competitor has hit upon a dramatic appeal and is wooing away customers, and when historical trends seem to be turning the market away despite the established values of the product.

The Quaker Oats Company faced a situation of this kind as a result of the long-term decline in the per-capita consumption of wheat flour and a concomitant weakening of the pancake mix market. Its Aunt Jemima brand had been advertised in keeping with the values of an earlier time when emphasis on hot, filling, nutritional, economical food for hard-working people formed a strong appeal. A study by Social Research, Inc. pointed out the changing attitudes that made this appeal less attractive. The advertising agency, J. Walter Thompson Company, formulated new objectives, turning away from the Southern plantation breakfast, to present the brand with these new aims:

> To project Aunt Jemima as a modern, up-to-date brand, adapted to meet the needs and desires of today's housewife.
>
> To make an especially forceful appeal to younger families where consumption of pancakes is greatest.
>
> To make pancakes seems easier, more fun, more interesting to serve. To get pancakes served more often in more different meals.[4]

These and other actions (pancake houses, a new shaker method of preparation) produced some revival of interest in pancakes. Such revivals may be temporary, or may not occur, since perhaps the basic process of decline is inevitable or cannot be solved in time or at all by promotion. Despite frantic efforts, some brands fade to a small brand share or die: Fitch shampoo, Ipana toothpaste, Packard cars, the *Saturday Evening Post*. Schick electric shavers were once outstanding sellers in their fields, but were unable to withstand competition or social change.

THE PROBLEM OF NEW PRODUCTS

The promotion of a new product is an especially challenging problem because so much seems to depend on what is communicated about it to establish its initial desirability. While it is hard to verify the high percentage of failures, it is apparent that many products or services do not succeed. This is a troublesome area of judgment. The effort put into developing a new product and the eagerness to have it succeed produce strong partisan feelings in the company. The skeptics are thought to exaggerate the product's shortcomings or to be timid. Those who developed it are pleased with themselves and press to go ahead. Research may be done at different stages to develop and evaluate the concept of the product and the forms it might take to express the concept more meaningfully or to try out customer reactions. These various steps provide information for what to say in sales literature and in advertising.

The promotional goal is to bring about a certain kind of learning. Its parts include getting people to know about the product, and to know it well enough and in a way that makes it attractive and desirable. The special opportunity here lies in the fact that the new product comes more or less fresh to the customer, and there is a chance to affect how it will be perceived prior to any experience with it.

Initial communications may be addressed to a special segment of the market in order to gain entry under auspices that will speak well for the product. Coricidin was prescribed by physicians before it became an over-the-counter pharmaceutical. Dial soap was introduced by four-color ads of relatively high-status families to avoid the cheap, lower-status deodorant-soap definition that characterized Lifebuoy at that time. There is a steady search in marketing study to define and locate innovators — those who will be most receptive to anything new. While innovativeness is evidently a general trait, it is also evident that no one innovates equally in all areas. Managers have to find their own most susceptible audiences.

THE SELLER'S GESTALT = THE BRAND IMAGE

In seeking to solve the ongoing problems of introducing something to the market, sustaining or building it, or rescuing it, the seller's actions produce a certain configuration or gestalt. Managers examine the lifestyles (and their components) of actual or wished-for buyers, and interpret what they mean, reasoning both toward the buyers and toward the implications for further actions. The pattern of the seller's actions, the lifestyle of the product, service, organization, or brand, and its positioning among the alternatives available, is perceived by the audience as having a certain character, which is generally termed the brand image. In some instances, the configuration at issue may be the corporate image or the industry image.

Since all the seller's actions, like the buyer's, are communications that contribute symbolically to create the brand image, it may then be said that the overall task of marketing managers is to relate all the symbols they can control to the general aim of the organization, and to the aim of their product responsibility. Marketers need to study what specific means are available to them and what they will accomplish by using them. Analysis and interpretation are needed if they are to know whether it is plausible for them to claim that their brand connotes youthfulness, durability, or sociability; whether to reinforce the recollection of the name or to build in new associations; whether sales force or television is needed to demonstrate the product; even whether they can lead or must follow.

In doing whatever they do, marketers are contributing something to the final configuration, which determines how the market views them. All their specific subactions en route to the larger goals carry their own meanings and interact with the others. The adept manager thinks about the goodness of fit as well as the pragmatic value of each action. The accumulation of symbolic meanings produces more intense understanding.

For example, the complex of symbols offered by the American Oil Company coheres in such a way as to create an overall message that defines it as a most reliable American middle-class gasoline brand (despite the problems of the energy crisis and the oil industry, in general). It is one that brings across product, service, and cleanliness in a patriotic and remarkably harmonious way. It is red, white, and blue, it assists the traveler (as you travel, ask us), it rhymes (advice, sir) with de-icer; its commercials show that it returns lost dogs and dolls, has amiable station managers; and as might be expected (but still to one's gratified surprise), it invents the alliterative final filter to show imaginative and minute attention to customer needs.

To understand the process whereby the marketing manager produces such results, it will help to explore, in greater detail, the concept of the brand image, and the symbols used to work toward one's aims.

WHAT IS A BRAND IMAGE?

Brand image has become an important concept in the worlds of marketing, advertising, and research. It is much talked of and much examined. This idea was introduced by Gardner and Levy in a 1955 *Harvard Business Review* article,[5] and has since flourished. It provides a way of thinking and talking about the presentation of brands and products as they are received by any public. Because it is useful and reflects long-felt realities, the brand-image idea moved quickly into trade terminology, has found general use in the larger society, and has gained partisans and critics, including those who "knew it all the time."

The inevitable by-products of such speedy and general acceptance are oversimplifications, extreme and distorted definitions, and the use of catch phrases rather than optimal awareness of the concept's spread and meaning. One of the main tendencies, for example, has been to identify brand image with advertising that emphasizes visual material. Another misconception limits the creation or development of brand images to the subtleties of soft sell, and some people equate brand image with motivational research.

Artwork is clearly tremendously important in its contribution to a brand image, but so are words (and total format, product, history, price, media, and packaging). Soft sell produces certain qualities in the public's thinking about a brand, but so does hard sell, and in some cases the advertising aim may be best fulfilled by one or by the other.

What, then, is a brand image? What is the value of the concept? How can it be used helpfully in communicating about products and brands? A brand image is a constellation of pictures and ideas in people's minds that sums up their knowledge of the brand and their main attitudes toward it. It is a summary that allows them to act toward it and with it without thinking too laboriously or extensively about it. The notion of imagery reminds that action in the marketplace is based on impressions and interpretations that people derive from their experience of a broader sort than that which narrowly relates to the objects they buy or sell. They cannot learn all the facts available, and they cannot keep in mind all those they do learn. In addition there are various influences pressing them to have one opinion or another about the product, service, or company at issue. The image is a distillation of all these facts and influences, reduced to manageable proportions.

Drawn from many sources, then, brands (whether products, organizations, people, etc.) have a kind of identity made up of central conceptions and impressions to which the audience responds. The image includes such ideas as these:

1. *Knowlege about technical matters* helps people define a brand. For example, the image of Volkswagen might include the fact that it has four cylinders; or the image of Jell-O may say it is high in protein.

2. *Awareness of other product characteristics* that are somewhat less objective, but that seem like facts, is part of imagery. Here might be included the idea that a certain fabric will survive laundering, that Falk gears are well made, or that a certain movie is very funny.

3. *Beliefs about the value of the object* come to be part of its image. For example, the conviction that a Rolls-Royce is worth the cost, that Budweiser is indeed a premium beer, that Pepsi-Cola has a lot to give — such ideas become bound up in the image of those brands.

4. *Judgments about the suitability of the brand* are influences added to the image. Brands come to acquire a greater sense of appropriateness for some kinds of people than for others. It is part of the image, then, that it is thought to be a cigarette mainly smoked by men, a beverage preferred by teenagers, a food too spicy for average American tastes.

As these points suggest, imagery is a mixture of notions and deductions, based on many things. It is fundamentally subjective, a fact that troubles those who believe marketing decisions should be made only on "hard facts," that is, in accordance with their ideas about what is rational or economically sound. The harder fact is, however, that people live by their images and these are governed by their individual experiences, their values, and how they interpret what comes across to them, as earlier chapters have discussed. At times, the imagery is indeed partly illusion, for example, the belief that some product is highly nutritious when it is not, that a carrot will contribute significantly to improved vision, that a particular automobile make is near-perfect in quality or that another offers the unusual degree of "functional" transportation believed to be the case. Other images are debatable: Will a sports car enhance one's sexuality and youthfulness? Will ownership of a particular appliance brand imply a higher status level or a more attractive lifestyle? No, say some, a deodorant or toothpaste will not make one more alluring to the opposite sex; on the other hand, say others, bad breath and dingy teeth are realities that are offensive and of little help in social relations, as the advertisements imply.

The idea of imagery is not restricted (as often criticized) to mean only those aspects of products or communications that are misleading or which try to make things seem more attractive or valuable than they "really" are. It also refers to any inferences drawn about qualities that seem well grounded, for example, the image of diamonds as hard and durable, of prices as rising, of refrigerators as noisy, of candy as sweet, of tires as safer than they used to be, or Mercedes-Benz cars as socially impressive.

A brand image can vary a great deal in its complexity, just as it may vary in its stability, its closeness, and its relevance to its audience. It may be summarized in a single thought ("Oh, that cheap one"), or in much more complicated beliefs. It is normally a group of impressions reflecting the kind of thing at issue, the consumers' notions of what "things like that" ought to be, plus all the modifications in ideas and emotions produced by particular communications.

The brand-image concept serves many purposes. Initially, it has the vitalizing effect of producing a shift in how one thinks about products and brand and the means of presenting them to the public. Attention moves from an overly narrow focus on technical concerns, important and central as they may be, to thinking about how one's product and brand are a symbol to be interpreted for consumers' and audiences' reactions and behaviors. New kinds of information are then sought in research, and new perceptions become available to marketing people. The basic goals may remain the same, but a new content becomes available for thinking and talking about them. Marketers give more attention to what kinds of imagery goals they want and to how to achieve them.

Many problems are involved in working toward the right imagery goals. Often, managers do not realize how a given action will affect the imagery about their brand or their company. For instance, an emphasis on stylishness or an upgrading of quality may unexpectedly modify either the customers' views of a product's value or desirability or their feelings about a company's suitability to their habits, tastes, and identities. Managers may not know how to bring about the imagery they want to present, what precise ideas to offer, the context in which these are appropriately dealt with, and the channels of communication that will best accomplish this objective. Their imagery goals may have conflicting elements.

An example of how an image might come about inadvertently would be that of a high-status store that runs frequent sales without realizing that its merchandise may come to be regarded as inferior in quality. When a brand creates imagery that boasts of its popularity, there may be difficulty in trying to suggest that it is also a brand with an intimate character. Brands that seem large tend to seem impersonal.

It can be seen that a marketing action is both a short-run effort and an investment in the long-run reputation of the brand. If the short-run decisions are made without reference to the long-run implications, as is commonly the case under competitive pressures and the varied demands of dealers, advertising agencies, and package designers, the results may be haphazard and confused. Over time, the brand image is not well oriented to its market segments, or it turns out to be an image quite different from what the seller has in mind. Managers cannot control the action of competitors whose innovations may have negative effects on their own brands.

IMAGES AND SYMBOLISM

It was pointed out earlier that thinking in terms of symbols is something that people do naturally, and that a person's lifestyle may be seen as a complex symbol in itself, moving through time, choosing among the component symbols of the marketplace to create and revise that lifestyle. The symbols of the marketplace are the images that people perceive there. Therefore, it seems useful to develop further the discussion of symbols initiated in Chapter IV on the way to examining in some detail the symbols managers use in their marketing actions, as in Schramm's words they try to "employ signs that refer to experience common to source and destination."

An image is an interpretation, a set of inferences and reactions. It is a symbol because it is not the object itself, but refers to it and stands for it. In addition to the physical reality of the product, brand, and organization, the image includes its meanings — the beliefs, attitudes, and feelings that have come to be attached to it. These meanings are learned or stimulated by the component experiences people have with the product, and these components are particular symbols. For example, part of the "real" experience of riding in a convertible is the wind blowing one's hair. This experience becomes symbolic of the convertible, a component that holds such meanings as freedom, youthfulness, and irresponsibility. As a rider, one feels a release from conventional restraints, and watchers see the riders visibly showing (probably flaunting) their disorderly hair. Another reality is the increasing rarity of convertibles, as well as the inferences people make from that.

Even human experiences which start out presumably being direct, basic, or in some sense nonsymbolic promptly acquire symbolic meanings. Beyond the earliest days of infancy, it is hard to imagine an object, sound, or motion that "just happens" without being related to or referring to other things, events, or feelings. Milk and how it is offered comes to represent how Mother feels toward the baby and how the baby interprets the Mother. The crib soon means being secure or restrained. The tones of voice mean one is good or bad. It is difficult to believe that thunder and lightning are not expressions of the wish to frighten, that rain is not someone's tears or God's interest in a harmonious agriculture.

This kind of early symbolism takes on a deep, built-in character, getting so taken for granted that it is hardly regarded as symbolic. People assume that their clenched fist is *being* angry, paying little attention to the fact that it is also *symbolizing* anger, perhaps only reminding about the possibility of a blow. People soon learn to show the symbols of intentions when the actual intentions are absent or are the opposite, as in a treacherous handshake or raised palm of peace, as in the seductive adornments and movements of a frigid woman or the macho pretensions of a Don Juan.

THE MARKETING MANAGER'S SYMBOLS

Brand imagery is usually strongly attributed to or blamed on advertising; and undoubtedly advertising can and does play a major part in creating it. But, as has been noted, meaning in the marketing dialogue comes from many directions. All the elements of the marketing mix have symbolic values. They are potential messages and components of the brand image. They may not be used or be available to the audience. Most organizations' offices or plants play little role in the public's awareness of them, but many do have a distinct impact such as Lever House in New York, the Sears Tower in Chicago, and other prominent buildings.

The Meaning of the Product. At the heart of the brand image is the meaning of the product. Usually, the central impression of a brand image is compounded out of the essential nature of the product. The essential nature of the product suggests what kind of thing it is, what intrinsic functions it serves. Most people evaluate brands in terms of how well they match the ideal conception of what the product ought to be: in polling studies, the first and most agreed upon answer to "Why do you use X?" is some comment to the effect that "It does what X's are supposed to do." If X is a soap, it washes; if it is dog food, it feeds the dog; if it's an auto, it moves people from place to place in the way automobiles do. A brand has the most desirable image among its users when it is seen as a valid and true product for its functions.

But such validity and rationality are not enough. The world of functions ranges far from the manufacturer's most basic design. Cars contribute to social status as well as to transport; shampoo permits carefree soapsuds dawdling as well as cleaning hair; filter cigarettes show one's refinement as well as reducing tars. The extent to which a given brand supports and communicates various secondary and tertiary functions is important to its brand image, and is of course crucial when there are competing products that all perform the desired basic function. When, on point after important point, the fit between the idealized product and the particular brand is good, the brand image is generally perceived as very good, and likely to appeal to major market segments. When a brand most notably embodies the product (historically or in specific features), it becomes generic in character. Examples are Kleenex, Kotex, Coca-Cola, Xerox, and Blue Cross.

This logic does not mean that there is only one best brand image for each product area, although very often one brand does dominate the market. The possibility for various desirable brand images arises in any given product field because brands can have many intrinsic qualities, and buyers are not homogeneous groups. Lifestyles differ and seek to incorporate the brand images that seem suited to them, therefore preferring, for example, Scott tissues, Modess sanitary napkins, RC Cola, A. B. Dick copiers, and Prudential health insurance.

To the most intrinsic qualities of the product both senders and receivers add other functions, desired qualities, and motives.

These may override the technical merits of products—for example, the most popular beers are those which not only fit an adequate conception of "beerness," but also fit into certain contemporary values and trends in esthetic taste and socializing patterns. In this respect, there are different values in different product areas. A "coffeeish" coffee generally does better in the marketplace than a "beery" beer!

The understanding of any given brand image involves close study and analysis, covering many dimensions of the product's existence. Commonly, techniques of multidimensional scaling and perceptual mapping are used in efforts to determine what attributes are important for a product area and how these attributes are perceived to be distributed among the brands of that product.[6] Figure 10 illustrates physicians' perceptions of some ethical drug brands.

Brand 6 is a hypothetical ideal brand. The other five are real brands. The physicians involved in this study were asked to compare brands for their similarity and dissimilarity. The labeling of the axes was achieved "by analyzing other data collected during the study and by relying on the advice of knowledgeable people in the pharmaceuticals industry." In other instances, the variables are derived in different ways, and the approaches may gen-

Figure 10. Perceptual space of brands of ethical pharmaceuticals.

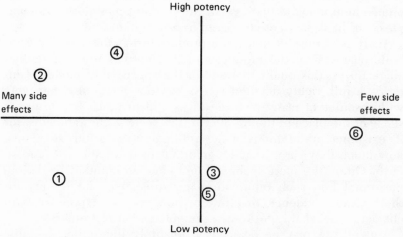

SOURCE: Lester A. Neidell, "The Use of Nonmetric Multidimensional Scaling in Marketing Analysis," *Journal of Marketing,* Oct. 1969, pp. 37-43.

erate several maps that show the numerous possible relationships of the brands. Methods of this kind have the advantage of drawing out and measuring specific product dimensions. But they also often have the effect of oversimplifying complex situations, and may make no room for the less tangible forces that are at work in the perception of the brands, making the physicians seem more rational and professional than they actually are in their perceptions of pharmaceuticals and company sources. For example, why Brand 1 — so far from ideal — is prescribed at all is not explained.

In studying and explaining buying behavior by scaling and ordinary surveying methods, marketers concentrate on three main foci: (1) product attributes and functions, (2) conventional motives, and (3) buyer characteristics. Product attributes include size, color, durability, taste, and performance usually taken per se rather than for their implications. Motives are readily conventionalized into such categories as convenience, economy, pride of ownership, and style.

Buyer characteristics are usually demographic categories, and may sometimes include personality traits or some associated attitudes as discussed in Chapter VIII. These approaches tend to be piecemeal and thus do not provide the integrated analysis that may be gained from searching for the "core dynamisms" that distinguish a product area. Good taste is a common variable, but it does not help much to explain the particular qualities and appeals of peanut butter compared to cigarettes. Nor does convenience help much to distinguish the relevant motive–action complexes of bank services compared to frozen foods.

Analysis of the dynamics of a product brings together the symbolic character of the product and the motives relevant to that character. At this qualitative end of the spectrum of modes of inquiry, a full, richly detailed study provides marketing managers with a source of many possible ideas and insights. It can give a sense of the place of the product in the society, the rationales for its existence in the minds of the public and its various segments, how much they care, what is important to them about it, and so forth. Often, the more technical and concrete-minded marketing personnel find such information too subjective and literary for their tastes, evidence that information, too, is a product with characteristics that repel some segments and attract others.

Appendix A may be taken as a leisurely digression that discusses the nature of symbolism in greater detail. Appendix B includes a series of examples of product areas interpreted briefly but sufficiently to highlight the difference between such explorations and the kind of information provided in Figure 10.

Figure 11. Sources of sellers' meanings.

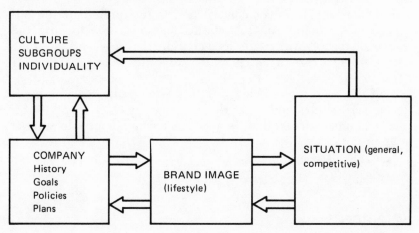

Figure 11 summarizes the sources of the sellers' meanings that originate (like the buyers' meanings) in the culture, its subgroups, and individuals, finding particular expression in a given company and its policies. The marketing manager acts in relation to these and in response to the environment, both generally and competitively. A central symbol—the product—is put forth as a major component of the brand image. The meaning of this central symbol is modified by all the other image components discussed in Chapter IX and summarized later in Figure 13.

SUMMARY

1. The behavior of the marketing manager—and the marketing behavior of all the managers in the organization—carries information and significance to the various publics (customers, consumers, suppliers, employees), and thus comprises the sellers' meanings. All the actions of the members of the organization contribute to the ultimate meaning that the brand (product, company, industry) will have for its audiences.

2. These actions derive from the objectives of the organization.

Ideally, they cohere to produce an integrated assertion of the nature of what the organization has to offer. In practice, there will be varying degrees of confusion, ambiguity, suboptimization, clarity, or force as managers are insightful or not, and as they struggle with the various emotional situations created by growth, shrinking, innovation, and other factors.

3. The result, however constructed, is interpreted by the audience of customers (buyers, clients, patients, etc.) to form the Image of the offering, with its variations by segments, as they reason from its core meanings to its suitability or unsuitability for themselves.

4. At the heart of the image are the basic meanings of the product or service that tell what the offering symbolizes and mobilizes in human affairs, that deeply affect whether people want it at all or not.

References

1. *Formulating the Company's Marketing Policies* (New York: National Industrial Conference Board, 1968).
2. **Harper W. Boyd, Jr.,** and **Sidney J. Levy,** "What Kind of Corporate Objectives?" *Journal of Marketing,* Oct. 1966, p. 54.
3. **Philip Kotler** and **Sidney J. Levy,** "Demarketing, Yes, Demarketing," *Harvard Business Review,* Nov.–Dec. 1971, pp. 74–80.
4. "The Quaker Oats Company," in Harper W. Boyd, Jr., Vernon Fryburger, and Ralph L. Westfall (eds.), *Cases in Advertising Management* (New York: McGraw-Hill, 1964), pp. 203–207.
5. **Burleigh B. Gardner** and **Sidney J. Levy,** "The Product and the Brand," *Harvard Business Review,* Mar.–Apr. 1955, pp. 33–39.
6. **Richard M. Johnson,** "Market Segmentation—A Strategic Management Tool," *Journal of Marketing Research,* Feb. 1971, pp. 13–18.
7. **Lester A. Neidell,** "The Use of Nonmetric Multidimensional Scaling in Marketing Analysis," *Journal of Marketing,* Oct. 1969, p. 41.

Suggested Readings

Becker, Ernest, *The Birth and Death of Meaning* (New York: The Free Press, 1962).
Bonime, Walter, *The Clinical Use of Dreams* (New York: Basic Books, 1962).
Boulding, Kenneth, *The Image* (Ann Arbor: University of Michigan Press, 1963).
Brown, Roger, *Words and Things* (New York: The Free Press, 1959).

Dichter, Ernest, *Handbook of Consumer Motivations* (New York: McGraw-Hill, 1964).

Edelman, Murray, *Politics as Symbolic Action* (New York: Academic Press, 1971).

Firth, Raymond, *Symbols* (Ithaca, N.Y.: Cornell University Press, 1973).

Forgus, R. H., *Perception: The Basic Process in Cognitive Development* (New York: McGraw-Hill, 1966).

Grigson, Geoffrey, and Charles Gibbs-Smith (eds.), *Ideas and Things* (Englewood Cliffs, N.J.: Prentice-Hall, 1957).

Hall, Edward T., *The Silent Language* (New York: Doubleday, 1959).

Henry, W. E., *The Analysis of Fantasy* (New York: Wiley, 1956).

Jung, Carl, *Collected Works* (Princeton, N.J.: Princeton University Press, 1968).

Murray, Henry A. (ed.), *Myth and Mythmaking* (New York: George Braziller, 1960).

Myers, John G., *Consumer Image and Attitude* (Berkeley, Calif.: Institute of Business and Economic Research, 1968).

Neumann, Erich, *The Great Mother* (New York: Pantheon, 1955).

Stone, Gregory P. (ed.), *Games, Sport and Power* (New Brunswick, N.J.: Transaction Books, 1972).

Werner, H., and B. Kaplan, *Symbol Formation* (New York: Wiley, 1963).

Wolfenstein, Martha, *Children's Humor* (New York: The Free Press, 1954).

Zaltman, Gerald, *Marketing: Contributions from the Behavioral Sciences* (New York: Harcourt, Brace, Jovanovich, 1965).

X

Image Components

The product is the core symbol. Each marketing manager has to choose how it will be presented. There are, of course, constraints in the ongoing situation, as traditions of the society, the industry, and the company commonly dictate much of what is to be done. The manager may come to a company that customarily uses a large, widely dispersed, decentralized sales force or to a small company that operates out of the central office, which may enjoy, or be averse to, the idea of public relations, and have either a large or small advertising budget. When gratifying results have been obtained in the past, the tendency is to persist. Thus, Hallmark is known for its television specials, Rexall for its $1 sales, and Procter & Gamble for its aggressive use of several approaches — in the retail store, stepped-up consumer incentives, and large television advertising expenditures (over $100 million a year).

Some marketing science developments seek to assist the promotor by providing decision-making models. These may depend on equations or curves that express relationships among promotional costs, sales, and profits. They may use operations research manipulations, simulations of consumer behavior, projections of test-market experiments, and other techniques. Most of these methods are still relatively young, with individual success stories here and there, and very slow growth toward results that can be readily applied to new situations. Most companies do not use them. The greatest and most widespread reliance is still on qualitative judgment and preferences, and the interaction of pressures from within and without the organization.

A typical instance is shown by a company that sets out to develop a stronger competitive position with an improved office machine. The marketing manager decides to add three new salespeople who will concentrate on selling the innovation, and to develop a special training program for the existing salespeople to give them the know-how to contribute to the effort against the more entrenched competitors. This seems reasonable to top managers, who are happy with their new machine, but are uncertain about how well it will sell. Inspired by the innovation, however, the advertising agency prepares a bold campaign, and with a strong, exciting presentation persuades the company president to approve a $500,000 advertising campaign. Since this is about five times the normal budget, the increase is a breakthrough for advertising, one that the president proudly marvels about socially: "The next thing I knew, those guys talked me into a half-million-dollar ad budget." The hiring of additional salespeople is deferred.

The logic that prevailed in this example basically argued that "pushing" the product through the proper channels by launching a greater personal selling effort would make too small a dent in the market when up against the impressive, giant names already dominating the field. The advertising effort was seen as a forceful means of announcing the intention of the company to become a serious contender, with an entry worth public boasting. This logic says something about the character of the forms of promotion. Despite overlaps, each form expresses the company in a particularly dynamic way.

Whether they stick to tradition or work against its constraints, marketing managers have at their disposal a vast array of symbolic means to modify a given product into the particular version that constitutes each brand. These symbolic components are discussed in this chapter as forms of promotion, with certain ones highlighted for their special interest.

In considering the many factors that make up a brand image, it is customary to focus on those which appear most important—the product itself, its price, and its promotion. Much has been written about product development and evaluation, pricing problems, and many aspects of advertising. By far the greatest percentage of this material is essentially technical in nature, oriented toward teaching procedures, economic analysis, or explanations of industrial tradition. Although there is some attempt to encourage thinking about such elements as psychological pricing techniques, ad hoc analyses of why certain marketing approaches have succeeded or failed, and package designs, extended analysis of the complexities of people's actions and of the significance to consumers of what the sellers do is often left to trade press and newspaper articles. Many studies are carried out by companies doing marketing research on such matters, but these are not generally reported in the marketing literature.

Among the neglected topics of formal study are the meanings of brand names, as well as of logotypes and logograms, the psychosocial significance of channels of distribution and sales outlets, the clothing worn by sellers' representatives, the role of tags on appliances, consumer incentives, business cards, showroom literature, and so on, through the numerous tools used by managers to express their brand imagery. This discussion inquires, in turn, into the meanings people attribute to such traditional promotional elements as advertising and personal selling, and the symbolic implications of some of the neglected elements of the marketing mix.

THE DISTINCTIVE QUALITIES OF ADVERTISING

Most discussions of the force of advertising and how it works center on the achievement of advertising goals through "educational value and sales stimulus,"[1] by providing information that affects the demand for the product. Other explanations include these:

> Advertising adds a new value to the existing values of the product.[2]
>
> Advertising is a contribution to the complex symbol which is the brand image — as part of the long-term investment in the reputation of the brand.[3]
>
> The function of advertising is to help to organize and modify the *basic* perceptual processes of the consumer, so that he or she is guided toward *seeing* and *feeling* a product in a given predictable way.[4]

While true of advertising, these qualities do not distinguish it from the general category of promotional activities, all of which are capable of teaching, adding value, building brand imagery, and affecting the way consumers see and feel about a product. Advertising possesses features that produce results that differ from those of other forms of promotion, which include at least four major aspects: public presentation, pervasiveness, amplified expressiveness, and impersonality.

Public Presentation

Advertising operates differently from personal selling in that it is not restricted to a more-or-less private, two-person conversation. The recipients of the advertising message see it in public places or recognize it as being sent out to anyone who is there to see the billboard, receive the radio or television waves, or buy the magazines and newspapers. Through advertising, the seller implies that what is being promoted is purportedly a standardized product and that there are many similar copies available, all of which probably meet legal requirements. As a public announcement it appears "democratic," rather than exclusive, and has the reassuring effect of presumably excluding no one who can afford to buy.

The viewer, reader, or listener is aware of a shared audience, that other people are getting the same message. A kind of communal spirit is appealed to, so that the act of buying becomes not one of idiosyncrasy, but one that is "legitimated" in the marketplace by the action of countless others. Closely related to this invocation is the idea that the purchase will be a socially informative one because other people will know what it means to buy or use that brand.

Pervasiveness

The prevalence of advertising and the repetitive effect of a specific message in different media provide frequent opportunity to learn it and to compare the appeals of competitive brands and alternative products. The consumer is given ample time to mull over the possibilities without rushing to a decision. The pervasiveness of the campaign suggests considerable success, popularity, and again, relative lack of exclusiveness.

Amplified Expressiveness

All promotions have something to say, but an advertisement can amplify its expressiveness. Its pride and boastfulness can be extreme. People have come to expect that of advertising. An ad can take advantage of the whole ingenious repertoire of visual, auditory, and other sensory techniques to present music, art, typography, movement, odor, variations in size, and so forth. Thus, it is possible for advertising to put people off by being too intense, too loud, or exaggerated, or for it to be dramatically impressive and absorbing. The "selling" intention of an ad may be diluted (or enhanced) by its frequent entertainment value and by the intrinsic pleasure many people find in its colorful and animated character.

Impersonality

Advertising lacks personal aspects, despite the fact that it does show people and often seeks to direct its personalized appeals. By virtue of its public, pervasive, and expressive attributes, no ad can come across with the personal touch of a first-hand human interaction. How can it be attuned to the individual nuances in the audience's reactions and adapt to them at the right moment?

This impersonality has two interesting results. First, the self-interest of the promoter of the product—no matter how great—seems less urgent and less obvious than that of face-to-face selling. The audience's awareness of the medium itself and the feelings of self-interest it has are in the background and are referred to an impersonal corporation.

Second, balancing this relatively muted sense of self-interest is a muted obligation in the "promotee." The person perceiving the advertisement is relieved of having to feel obligated to buy the product. The company has no way of knowing who is receiving the advertisement at a given moment (one supposes), nor how much pleasure is being gained from it, and no doubt the company can get other customers to react out of the many people who see the advertising. The widespread dissemination of an advertisement, as well as the large volume of different ads, reduces the pressure of individually felt obligation.

In sum, the distinctive qualities of advertising contribute both to its effectiveness and to people's ability to resist it. They can certainly learn from and appreciate the message, but they needn't feel compelled to follow all its dictates. The extent to which these qualities of advertising are emphasized is also informative, in terms of inferences people make. The more lively and widespread the advertising, the lower status it is apt to take on; on the other hand, if it isn't vividly expressive, it tends to appear austere and oriented to appeal to a higher-status or a more mature group.

CRITICISMS OF ADVERTISING

The prevalence and visibility of advertising make it easy to criticize, and criticism is readily elicited. Stimulated by the tenor of remarks and attitudes in the media, as well as by the activity of various leaders in the consumer movement and organizations inside and outside the federal government, the public engages in much faultfinding with advertising. Furthermore, everyone has private pet peeves—commercials that are annoying and advertisements that fall short of some standard.

Attacks on advertising have been launched in many quarters. A major study was reported in 1968 by Raymond A. Bauer and Stephen A. Greyser.[5] E. B. Weiss summed up several frequently expressed complaints about:

Excessive advertising as an invasion of privacy—as exemplified by the deluge of radio and television commercials and by some publications in which the reader must hunt to find the lean editorial contents.

Advertising that encourages the "wrong" type of consumption—consumption for social status, the junk culture.

Advertising pressures that reduce broadcast entertainment (TV) to the lowest common denominator.

Advertising that overemphasizes the gross material pleasures of life.

Excessive competition in advertising expenditures, with the bill paid by the public.

Advertising that unduly influences (and misleads) children.

Advertising that features nonexistent "exclusive" features for identical products.

Advertising that promotes poor, harmful, even dangerous products.

Advertising that contributes to our environmental problems.

Corporate image advertising that salutes the corporation as the great benefactor of humankind; irresponsible social responsibility advertising.

Advertising that contains a modicum of information.[6]

People may grumble audibly about advertising and its intrusion into programs or reading materials, or they may respond negatively in surveys—many even claim distinction by purporting to pay no attention to advertising. But it is also apparent that much attention is paid to advertising, that readers, viewers, and listeners are known to accept and enjoy it. When they aren't making protests, consumers praise (even bemusedly recite) advertisements as entertaining and as essential to learning and gaining reassurance about products and specific brands. Less self-consciously, and at times denied, advertising is one of the means people use to keep up with what is going on in their world. Most notably, ads mark holidays and other special occasions, add new language or jargon to daily conversation, create jokes, and so forth. Thus, attitudes toward advertising campaigns vary on several levels.

ADVERTISEMENTS AS SYMBOLS

Marketing research projects often are carried out to explore the effect of specific advertisements on their audiences, testing whether the intended messages are being appropriately decoded by the desired market segment. Commonly, such inquiries focus on whether the specific claims made in the advertisement are understood, believed, remembered, and positively evaluated. Sometimes the exploration of reactions is subtler, aimed at determining what the components of the advertisement—color, forms, illustrations, particular words, format—suggest in themselves, or add up to overall. Examined this way, the advertisement is analyzed not so much as an explicit communication with a manifest message, but as a complex symbol that creates some net effect, and which contributes both overtly and covertly to the brand image. The following examples illustrate these implications.

AN AUNT JEMIMA PANCAKE AD

Two children are shown happily rousing their father from bed with "Horray! It's Aunt Jemima Day!" The general content is that of a vital, vigorous, interacting family hungry for good pancakes as part of the gleeful way they enjoy each other.

The bedroom scene suggests intimacy and body warmth (enriched by the golden blanket and the other warm tones of the ad). The pillow indicates the lively, playful, aggressive atmosphere of father and children at a time like this. The atmosphere is intensely interpersonal, closely familial, and rewarding.

The symbolic effect for the brand: a pancake to fill the appetites and needs of young growing families in gratifying ways. To a housewife, it offers the product as a festive, celebratory means of gaining pleasant response from her children and her man. It can have the interesting effect of arousing a fantasy of the pancakes being made in the kitchen.

A CONTINENTAL AIRLINES AD

A woman and a man are being served afterdinner liqueurs on the Continental Golden Jet, getting Jet-Europe treatment within the United States. The impression is of upper-class gratification and of sophisticated people.

The idea is conveyed by the transatlantic snobbism, the woman's purple outfit, the emphasis on being served exotic liqueurs. The fact of flight is not even alluded to, making the plane like a home, restaurant, or nightclub. The atmosphere is one of relaxation, security, a cultured playing with the minor choices of leisure-class beverages. It is a fling through space and time while moving toward more serious executive goals.

The symbolic effect for the brand: a carrier for people of the world, people of means, who understand, appreciate, and know how to behave with liqueurs, service, and fine food. It suggests an airline that is luxurious, capacious, perhaps too fancy, indulgent, and costly for ordinary people, but an attractive dream all the same.

INDUSTRIAL ADVERTISING

Brand images and symbolism in advertising tend to be linked more readily to consumer advertising than to industrial advertising. People often work under the assumption that industrial advertising requires only the presentation of facts, that hardheaded purchasing agents and industrial buyers are not susceptible to other kinds of imagery.

In the academic setting, industrial marketing is seen as a discipline that is part and parcel of marketing in general. In the abstract, whatever principles of marketing are propounded generally show no distinction between industrial and consumer marketing, since both involve such basic functions as buying, selling, financing, storing, product design, channels, pricing, and communicating. As a result, many curricula do not offer courses in industrial marketing, cases dealing with industrial marketing problems are less frequently developed, and industrial advertising attracts less attention as a special activity.

In the business world, the realities of specialization make themselves felt. Patterns of marketing are established. Some advertising agencies devote their efforts entirely toward industrial accounts. Industrial advertising conferences are held. There are media and promotional activities the general public never hears about. Still, what marketing research exists in this area is somewhat restricted. The nature of industrial marketing remains in the background.

There are also other reasons for this situation. Overworked notions serve to lock ideas into the same general patterns. Two of the main clichés run along these lines:

1. *Industrial marketing is primarily a matter of personal selling:* Here the focus has to be on the problems of salesmanship and sales management, which means the interesting and "glamorous" communications areas aren't much considered. This sets up a special tension in advertiser–agency relationships. Advertisers show a strong awareness and orientation to the distribution system not appreciated by many agency personnel.

2. *Buying within industry is an impersonal matter:* This idea puts aside any motivating considerations other than price, delivery, performance, and service. In other words, buyers' gut reactions are governed by specifications, value analysis, and other technical dictates. They are wooed by symbols of rationality, of decision making, supposedly unaffected by human feelings that get in the way of economic sense.

The obvious contradiction and complication suggested by these patterns have to do with the juxtaposition of personal selling and impersonal buying. Partly responsible are the artificial distinctions, which fade in actuality. A good salesperson is usually quite aware of the personality of the specific buyer in addition to the formal requirements that constrain the purchase. He or she may recognize, and perhaps take account of, the buyer's reaction to fun, friendship, praise, corruption, and sympathy.[7] More typically, the industrial buyer (subject to what is apt to be the serious critical judgment of work associates and superiors) is diligently supplied with impersonal, rational information about the product and its service-oriented elements, with less regard for the direct human aspects of reactions. Those human aspects that do come across about purchasing agents tend to be the wary, skeptical, stubborn ones they often use to protect themselves in the buying situation.

Another familiar source of complicated reactions in the industrial marketing area is *multiple influence:* The penurious eye of the financial-minded, the strivings of engineers for quality and efficiency, the customer appeal that helps the salespeople, and the effective coordination sought by management may not add up to the same purchase. The marketing approach has to communicate and integrate the needs within organizations.

PERSONAL SELLING

More has been written about personal selling, its problems, its personnel, and how to do it than on just about any other subject in the business literature. It ranges from instruction on making presentations, handling objections, and closing the sale, to recruiting, selecting, testing, training, compensating, evaluating, even firing. Seminars, conferences, and institutes abound in which sales force training and management are discussed and practiced.[8]

At the same time, academic exploration of the topic has fallen by the wayside. Among the more than 200 articles appearing in the 1973–1974 volumes of the *Journal of Marketing* and the *Journal of Marketing Research,* only eight dealt with personal selling problems—this, despite the fact that in 1970 alone about $32 billion was spent on the activity of personal selling, compared to about $21 billion on advertising.[9]

Selling is a human endeavor that apparently requires constant instruction to build, sustain, and improve the sales forces in the country. Selling situations range from fast, simple order-taking to extended, complex cultivation of relationships. The sales personnel needs range from variety store clerks to salespeople who close deals costing millions of dollars. Analysis of all such varied situations would include an infinite number of topics. For the sake of a behavioral perspective of this area of promotion, to suggest some general insight, a few salient points will be noted. These are drawn from the basic ideas that are at issue when salespersons and potential customers come together: personal confrontation, cultivation, and required response.

Personal Confrontation

At the heart of personal selling is the confrontation of two people, one of whom wishes to bring about assent to a purchase, while the other person may or may not want to cooperate. The distinctive feature of this promotional activity is that it is alive and immediate, with chances for interaction. Whether it occurs briefly in passing, or includes many meetings over time, the two people can size up each other, make their overtures, use the "fronts" they regard as appropriate, and make mutual adjustments to their respective communication strategies.[10]

Face-to-face confrontation permits a closeness of knowledge, a chance to observe details, settings, and individuality. Interest in and by the customer, if expressed, can focus closely and make its intensity felt. This interest is expected on both sides, accounting for the frequent frustration when the seller or the buyer fails to show it. The confrontation also stirs alertness and sensitivity to what the other person intends, and if the relationship is more than passing, these intentions are explored.

Cultivation

Exploring the relationship, the salesperson and the customer can cultivate it and cause it to grow. All kinds of human relationships may go on, including great friendliness and affection, matter-of-factness, coolness, or hostility. One can almost live with this seller and come together to play golf, go to the theater, eat at restaurants, and at times, to be realistic, develop even greater intimacy. The interpersonal aspects of the face-to-face selling situation are so alive and so strong in their potentialities that they commonly arouse great feeling. A salesman is someone who is vividly evaluated for the kind of guy he is, and how he goes at his job. A saleswoman may be admired for her special understanding.

The salesperson thus has a particular chance to give personal meaning to what is being sold, to surround it with a unique glow of personality. One may sell well because the customers want to

be personally pleasant, to do a favor, or even because they dislike the seller in such a way that they want to do combat and buy
when they lose.

Commonly, at the heart of the cultivation is a recognition that
salespeople are in a deferential position. They may show this by
humor, or studied casualness and detached hovering, as ways of
marked obsequiousness, flattery, brightness of attention and good
wooing the customer. They want the customer to yield and may
plead or push hard, as they interpret the necessity. Usually, they
communicate some degree of urgency and self-interest that is a
motive apart from or in addition to that of the company being
represented. The chance for personal gain is an element in the
situation. It may be interpreted as a greater force for the sale, or
it may be cause for mistrust by implying the salesperson will do
anything to make a sale—exaggerate, misrepresent, bribe, make
false promises. Because personal selling is so often defined by
these two features—the need to coerce, cajole, or force, and the
suspicion of salespeople's ethics—it is a calling in general social
disrepute, a fact with which each individual has to come to terms
by the way he or she contributes to it or overcomes it.[11]

Required Response

When a customer becomes involved in such a personal interaction, the situation may be casual, as in many retail-store situations. But even there, and especially in the more complicated
fields of insurance, brokers, furniture, office supply, and industrial selling of all kinds, the selling situation makes demands on
the shopper for some emotional involvement and response. To be
helped by a clerk, to be shown merchandise, to hear advice from
service personnel, to listen to a lengthy sales pitch, sets up a
two-way process, fostering a feeling of obligation to do something
in return. Obviously, this may be no more than a "thank you"
(and often enough not even that), but the felt necessity to respond is one of the things that gives personal selling an advantage over an advertisement.

The closeness of relationship possible between salespeople
and buyers is illustrated by the common dependence of clothing
customers on certain salespeople who somehow "know how to fit
me," or who seem to have similar taste; and the tendency for
those who buy insurance to buy from agents who are physically

like themselves, or to believe that the agents share the buyer's social, religious, or political views (even when they actually do not).[12]

Among the analyses of personal selling or its role in the marketing mix, a few are of special interest. John Udell examines the market strategies of a large number of successful products. He suggests a theoretical approach for determining the relative importance of product efforts and sales efforts in marketing programs. He stresses sales management and personal selling as evaluated by 485 manufacturers to be the most important competitive activities, especially for industrial goods, but also for consumer durables and consumer nondurables.[13]

Henry L. Tosi sums up the theoretical elements that influence the dyadic (face-to-face) interaction of sellers and buyers, providing an example that explores the relationships between successful selling and the expectations of the participants, based on research on wholesale drug salesmen and retail pharmacists. His findings suggest that there is no simple relationship between what the participants expect and the salesman's success, although whether there were many or few suppliers seemed to be important for people's judgments.[14]

Using another approach, Theodore Levitt reports a simulation study in which sales presentations of different kinds are made to various groups. Inferences are drawn concerning the relationships among a company's reputation, the activity of its salesperson, and its advertising as these elements are affected by the degree of risk in the situation, the quality of the sales presentation, and the reputation of the company. It thus has the merit of being an integrated way of thinking about the components of promotional behavior, recognizing that people make complex judgments about the value of various promotional forces, taking into account whether the risky situation requires reassurance from the reputation of the company or whether the salesperson can be trusted.[15]

The needs of salespeople that may affect their performance have received some attention. Donnelly and Ivancevich reported a study that suggested the salesperson's job interest, satisfaction, and inclination not to leave the job are correlated significantly with role clarity, the extent to which required information is communicated and understood. While this might seem generally true of people, the sales personnel studied showed this relationship more than did a comparison group of production supervisors.[16] Along similar lines, Marvin Jolson concluded that highly structured canned sales presentations may, in some respects, be a more effective tool for the encyclopedia salesperson than the flexible customer-specific presentation. For some kinds of selling, the ambiguity of the sales situation is too great or requires excessive adaptability, leading to these advantages in canned clarity and preparation. From the imagery point of view, the use of the canned presentation did not seem to lose vitality as is often feared, the audience finding it exciting and not very impersonal. However, the customer-specific approach seemed to lead to greater understanding of the product and less sense of pressure.[17]

A study of marketing behavior that is old, but relatively unique and of enduring value in its content, was reported in 1955 by George F. F. Lombard. He analyzes in great detail the behavior of a group of sales clerks in relation to one another, to executives, and to customers. He discusses the importance of sensitivity to and awareness of one's own and of other people's values for satisfaction of both sellers and buyers—a familiar emphasis nowadays, but worth repeated stress.[18]

CONSUMER INCENTIVES

Among the wide array of methods available for stimulating sales, for fostering special involvements with brands, are the miscellany of promotions called incentives. These encompass any more or less temporary advantage offered some marketing personnel beyond the usual encouragements provided by the product itself, its price, and other ongoing means of presentation. Rewards to the sales force for making efforts to compete or to reach quotas, gifts to suppliers, the exchange of expense account courtesies, and so forth, are common phenomena, as are the coupons, premiums, cents-off, stamps, sweepstakes, contests, and games frequently used to appeal to consumers, especially during recessionary periods when the need for incentives seems greater, or whenever competition becomes intense.

These devices may be termed consumer incentive promotids (CIPs), *promotids* a term coined to refer to any promotional element. The use of CIPs has not been analyzed much for its contribution to brand imagery. Usually the problem is thought about in a practical, economic way: What will the incentive program do for awareness, inquiries, sales? and the more the better. A study sponsored by J. Walter Thompson Company sought to examine CIPs more closely, focusing on the kinds of use women homemakers make of them, how they evaluate them, and the kinds of symbolic contribution they make to brand imagery. Some of the findings are summarized as follows.

CIPs are fun. Women generally enjoy the liveliness of competition in the marketplace represented by incentives. They perceive incentives as bids for their interest, product trial and use, with a variety of opportunities to participate or not. Although most people assume that the consumer pays for it all in the end, that "there is no free lunch," incentives nevertheless often have the atmosphere of a gift, and reward those who join in compared to those who do not. Their perception of the source is an important part of their evaluation of the worth of the offer.

CIPs may have negative implications. There is some struggle with the less appealing meanings of consumer incentives. Their use may be ordinary, but they still suggest that some problem leads to their use. Perhaps the company is not doing well, is losing out competitively. The product may be of lesser quality or is getting outdated. Perhaps it is overstocked and not the freshest. Frequently women reason the product is overpriced, and that they would prefer a better price to begin with rather than an incentive reduction. There are also complaints that CIPs interfere with the kind of judgment that should be exercised about the product itself rather than the appeal of the deal.

Positive inferences are made, too. Overriding the negative meanings are thoughts that an unusual opportunity is available and that a strong marketer is being vigorous in the marketplace. Depending on the nature of the CIP, the company may seem generous and friendly, out to appeal to a broad market, to keep in the swim.

As a familiar part of the market, consumer incentives are a challenge to the customer to use them intelligently. Some women disdain them, but most feel it is foolish not to take advantage of them, especially when economic pressures make it seem imperative to buy carefully. At the same time, there are so many being offered simultaneously that it is not possible to use them all. The various incentive techniques have different characteristics and values, differentiated meanings and appeals.

When *samples* arrive they seem like gifts. They are usually not solicited by the consumer, they are free, and they may bring something new and surprising into the home. Women like to try out new products. The samples arrive sporadically, one is surprised to open the front door and find this gift hanging there, or to get it through the mail. The no-strings-attached sample suggests confidence, integrity, and performance. Women tend to think of this as a not very coercive type of incentive. They are free to make their own decisions about the brand and the product gained with no expenditure of money, red tape, or special effort.

Samples seem an expensive form of promotion, feasible only for major companies that have confidence in the performance and quality of their new products and the integrity to allow consumers the chance to prove for themselves that the product claims are valid.

Coupons are a widely used CIP. Major sources are mailings, magazines, newspapers, and in-stores (bulletin boards, point of purchase displays, on or in packages). Mailings seem like an event. Attention is focused on the envelope and its thick contents, and the colorfulness and range of the assortment are attractive. Women like to receive mailings for varied products. The mix satisfies curiosity, and provides a quick shopping expedition into several product areas, and the greater likelihood of something useful. Even higher-status women, who usually state the clichés about junk mail, can show some intrigue with specifically useful coupons.

> *I usually just throw the envelope in the trash. Just more junk mail. I might open it and thumb through it but it would probably end up in the trash. Well, it is springtime and I could use this one for Windex, and we do use Ultra Brite part of the time. The kids are always looking for ways to have their pictures developed cheaper.*

Newspaper coupons seem practical, close at hand, a regular way to accumulate savings via coupons. They also seem dull, arduous and time consuming to organize and utilize, suggesting the most penny-pinching attitude and stress on economic limitations. Newspaper coupons are most heavily used by working-class women; many higher-status women think it beneath their dignity and a waste of time to cut up the newspaper for coupons.

Reactions to *coupons provided in packages* are somewhat complicated. The general emotional tone is a bit begrudging, with women tending to say coupons in packages are allright, and not otherwise showing much enthusiasm. The incentive seems generally somewhat mild in getting attention and motivating toward action. The main underlying issue aroused by a coupon in a package (that usually means cents off on the next purchase of the product) is that the reward has been deferred, making one wonder, why not now?

Women who approve of this type of incentive do so on pragmatic grounds. They recognize the intention of the method and accept it as useful. There is some charm in buried treasure, and it may mean an opportunity to repurchase a quality brand one might not otherwise buy so frequently. The reward focuses the attention of the user on what might be especially good about the product, highlighting rationales for buying it again. The regular user receives encouragement to persist.

Critics of the incentive method regard in-package coupons as a nuisance. They complain irritably that the coupons are always at the bottom of the package, that something which doesn't belong in the package causes messing and spilling if the product is powdered or granulated, perhaps resulting in a dusty or torn coupon. Coping with the coupon at the moment one is trying to use the product may be a distracting interference, either mechanically when the coupon hampers the flow or removal of the product, or psychologically when one is oriented toward the activities of cooking rather than shopping.

The variety of appeals of CIPs, and their range of meanings, can be shown by comparing sweepstakes with contests and premiums. *Sweepstakes* are simple, and with contests, relatively exciting. But the excitement is mainly a quick flare-up of interest, a fast entry by signing one's name, and unless one wins something, a rapid dismissal. The value to the brand image seems minor, and since most entrants win nothing, it turns out to be a form of low-level teasing and frustration.

Contests get fewer entrants than sweepstakes and make a distinctive appeal to those who enjoy the involvement of the required task. The participation is itself gratifying, arousing pride in the craft or intellectual potentiality of the contest challenge. *Premiums* are like samples in the pleasure of their tangibility, whether a small doodad of a gift in a Cracker Jack package or something bought with a box-top discount. The existence of premiums as a way of getting things that one desires but would not normally buy gives them the lure and image of a found opportunity.

THE IMPORTANCE OF NAMES

If all words are important symbols serving the many complex functions of language, names are intensifications of this general process. A name serves to integrate and focus identifying attributes of an object, to make a *proper* noun of a person, place, or thing. It is then specific, not a common noun. The attributes are "one's own," not generally shared.

In an ordinary, rational way, names come after the fact of the attributes, being labels to indicate their presence, Main Street being the main street, Mr. Shoemaker a man who makes shoes, and Hills Brothers Coffee, the coffee sold by those particular brothers. The process of naming becomes more intriguing when the meanings elaborate, as when the planet Mars, being reddish, is given the name of the war god and is imbued with some of his attributes.

The emotional and magical processes of naming are engaged when the name is given as a means of wishfully investing the object with some desired qualities (naming a child Felix or Joyce to encourage happiness, or Theodore to enhance his relationship with God), and when names come to have various mysterious powers. Many people explicitly believe that to name something is to gain power over it, to subdue it, to gain a share in its power. Certain names are believed to determine the destiny of the person, whether in some deep mystical sense or in the everyday way that a name is one of the causes of the reactions the bearer of it receives.

Names gain their meaning from many directions—from graphics, phonetics, similes, analogies, and so forth. The historic, social, and personal significance of names affects the owner of the name, positively or negatively, and alter with the vogue. Percival, Clarence, and Elmer have tended to become emasculated, seeming prissy or doltish, yielding to the more recent fashions for Michael, Richard, Steven, and Bruce. The earlier feminine preference for names such as Fanny, Hepzibah, and Emma is often replaced by Leslie, Beverly, and Jennifer. Cassius Clay became Mohammed Ali. Mary and John and their variants endure, and the fashion tides wash back and forth with respect to Biblical names, Anglo-Saxon names, French names.

Similarly, among brands, naming is taken as a powerful tool, one important enough to warrant spending an alleged $100 million to change a famous petroleum name to Exxon, and imprint it widely. In recent years, hundreds of companies changed their names to conform to some more contemporary set of attributes or aspirations. Here are some of the motives that have been offered, or that seem apparent:

For brevity's sake

To recognize expanded operations

To identify with a popular brand name of the firm

To escape from adverse publicity

To make identification easier for the public

For legal reasons

Especially pronounced among the many changes is the increase in the use of initials (for example, EMI, DCL, PSP, DRG, IAC, IPM, MEI, TFI, TMA, TEC, VCA, VLN, AID, AMF, AFCOA, BBI, and CMI). The reasons are logical, but the results, and often the regrets, suggest that these companies may have more difficulty becoming widely known in their new guises, compared to the earlier distinction of IBM and RCA. Another general trend among these new names is the movement away from *Company* toward *Corporation* and *Industries.* In many cases the names given up were family names or names that described a specific product function, as shown in these examples.

OLD NAME	NEW NAME
Aerodyne Machinery Corp.	General Resources Corp.
American Sugar Co.	Amstar Corp.
Allen Aircraft Radio, Inc.	AAR Corp.
Reeves Industries	RSC Industries
Official Films, Inc.	Official Industries, Inc.
John's Bargain Stores	Stratton Group, Ltd.

Occasionally, a company name change surprises by moving away from greater impersonality, as in the instance of Plastic Dynamics Corp., which became Jerry's Inc., or from generality as with the Cantor (H&W) Enterprises Inc. which became Leisure & Learning, Inc.

As new products and brands arise, naming them becomes part of the marketing task, as the name can be an influential part of the imagery. Lippincott & Margulies, Inc., a firm of industrial designers active in the field of brand naming, urge objective analysis to replace casual inspiration. The analysis may require formal study of the kind of imagery associated with the product, its benefits, its users, and of the alternative names generated by the various customary means — suggestions from all involved, consultation with experts, letter and syllable combinations from the computer. The experts may be from a company like Lippincott & Margulies, from the creative staff of an advertising agency, from a poet such as Marianne Moore whose many suggestions were bypassed in the naming of the Edsel, or from marketing researchers studying the relative appeals of Pet Ranch versus Puppy Palace.

Ultimately, however, a choice must be made, based on the judgment of the marketing manager(s). Table 3 lists attempts by Lippincott and Margulies to provide an objective framework, as well as to illustrate the subjective content that inevitably appears when some specific famous names are evaluated. To the criteria of audio appeal, visual appeal, image, equity, and overall rating used in the table might be added the other elements of analysis being developed throughout the discussion in this volume: What personality or psychological arousal is likely, with what consequences for which groups in the society?

The significance of the brand name is recognized in its legal status. Not only do some names seem inherently superior to others, but they also become valuable through their total marketing activity over time. They are then proud possessions used to ward off trespassers. The great names struggle against generic use, to keep Kleenex, Coke, Frigidaire, Xerox from being used to refer to all such products. The issue is highlighted when two brand names raise the possibility of confusion or deception. Sidney A. Diamond, an attorney, cites a typical instance where the court had the problem of judging between two similar names.

> Assuming the customer is familiar with "Tornado" as a brand name for electrical equipment of various types, will he think that "Vornado" electrical appliances are products of the same manufacturer? Do the two trademarks so resemble one another in appearance, sound or meaning that, taking into account the similarity of the merchandise, there is no reasonable likelihood of confusion.[19]

The struggle with such meanings is complex, since three judges voted against Vornado and two dissented. Diamond notes that marketing executives sometimes find it difficult to believe that lawyers and judges who deal with trademarks are concerned with consumer psychology.

> Perhaps the most significant point in the Vornado case was made by one of the dissenting judges in the course of his detailed discussion of

Table 3. Product name-rating chart:

Name	Audio Appeal	Visual Appeal
BRECK	Excellent, incisive, sharp. Uses hard, crisp consonants.	Good, distinctive, short. Interesting letter configuration.
LIFE SAVERS	Good. Two short, pithy words. Repetition of f and s sounds makes it esthetically pleasing, memorable.	Excellent. Variety of letter forms is particularly good for graphic treatment.
SCHLITZ	Poor. Unpleasant sounding to the American ear. Difficult to pronounce.	Fair. The sequence of letter forms is unfortunate, poses a problem for effective graphic treatment. The word is too "busy."
DENTYNE	Excellent. Effectively combines crisp and soft sounds.	Excellent. Pattern of letter shapes provides opportunities for interesting graphic treatment.
THUNDERBIRD	Excellent. Rhythmic, almost poetic. Note the effective use of assonance and alliteration.	Good. Overall configuration is interesting, although the name is somewhat long.
COCA-COLA	Excellent. A smooth, rolling name.	Good, since three of the four letters in each word are identical; however, care must be used in the graphic treatment.
PEPPERIDGE FARM	Good, but too long. First part nicely combines alliteration and crispness.	Good. Length is a problem, but fortunately the distinctive element is the longer part.

Seven famous names analyzed*

Image	Equity	Overall Rating
Poor. Totally unsuitable for a cosmetic product.	Intrinsically, only fair, but because so well known, overall equity is high.	Poor—but only in the abstract. Actually, Breck's top-flight advertising and packaging has turned this name into a real asset.
Superior. Distinctively and effectively relates to the physical form of the product.	Obviously priceless.	Superior. This may be the greatest of American product names. It is ideal in that it connotes both the appeal and the appearance of the product.
Fair. German-beer association is good, as is the family-name endorsement. But the word is vulgar in its connotation, suggests cheapness.	Good. Customer familiarity and usage have overcome the poor associations attached to this name.	Fair. This name poses a puzzling problem. Should it be altered in some fashion, or has tradition established it too securely in the consumer lexicon?
Excellent. Is immediately associated with dental health.	Excellent, both because of its inherent qualities and its long-established consumer familiarity.	Excellent. One of the best of the early-coined brand names.
Superior. Ideally suited for a quality sports car. Indian association (god-power-flight) is particularly apt.	Excellent. Inherent potentialities are so good that within a few years this name has become an integral part of the consumer vocabulary.	Superior. Probably the best automobile name since World War II.
Excellent. Is associated with pleasant relaxation, flavor.	Excellent. Well worth the many legal battles to secure this valuable name. Intrinsic equity, however, is not good, since the name is too easily imitated.	Excellent. Still the best of the soft-drink names.
Excellent. A genuine, natural name, which summons up a picture of quality, home-baked goods.	Excellent, this name could and probably will have many imitators, but no invented facsimile could match.	Excellent. Only the length prevents this from being a great name. Question: Should the "farm" be dropped?

*From *Design Sense 24* (New York: Lippincott & Margulies, Inc., undated).

consumer psychology. "Trademarks are psychological," he wrote, but he noted that the record of the case did not include any tests on the "psychological impact" of "Vornado."[20]

TRADEMARKS, LOGOTYPES, AND LOGOGRAMS

The issue raised above with regard to names can be enlarged to the general issue of the brand name in relation to its method of presentation. The symbolic nature of what the marketing manager puts forth in the marketing dialogue was long ago recognized as fundamental. In a remarkable statement that in 1942 anticipated the insight that began to flourish in the 1950s, Supreme Court Justice Felix Frankfurter wrote this:

> If it is true that we live by symbols, it is no less true that we purchase goods by them. A trademark is a merchandising short-cut which induces a purchaser to select what he wants, or what he has been led to believe he wants. The owner of a mark exploits this human propensity by making every effort to impregnate the atmosphere of the market with the drawing power of a congenial symbol. Whatever the means employed, the aim is the same — to convey through the mark, in the minds of potential customers, the desirability of the commodity upon which it appears. Once this is attained, the trademark owner has something of value.
>
> The creation of a market through an established symbol implies that people float on a psychological current engendered by the various advertising devices which give a trademark its potency.
>
> The protection of trademarks is the law's recognition of the psychological function of symbols.[21]

"Advertising devices" are not the only means by which trademark potency is gained, as the whole marketing mix is at work, but this statement supports the attention and money given by some managers to seemingly minor details of presentation. Modern graphic technology permits such flexibility in the design of logotypes and logograms — the various symbols of identity by which names are presented on products, advertisements, packages, buildings, and stationery. Great pressure to change the designs of identifying symbols comes from the passage of time and the changing outlook of both manager and publics.

Gradually or suddenly, people become aware that a symbol seems unsuitable or less appropriate than it was, that it is somehow out of step with the times. The implication is that symbols

carry acquired and transient meanings as well as basic or enduring connotations. It is the interplay of these that results in the effectiveness of given symbols at a point in time. RCA changed its
logo from a dog listening to a phonograph, Quaker Oats changed
the drawing of its Quaker man, Mobil's flying horse faded into
the background, the ARCO lettering supplanted the Sinclair lettering and dinosaur, and the Cities Service pale green clover
yielded to the Citgo red pyramid.

All such instances raise the problem of judging the nature of a
specific design, what about it is contemporary, what is not, and
how it fits into corporate objectives. The basic means are the visual elements, line, form, and color, and their application to let-
ters, words, and objects. Useful avenues to analysis include eval-
uations of the era for its prevalent esthetic — the kinds of artwork,
movies, dress, and personal display that seem widespread in appeal.

Regardless of one's own market segment, the general current
scene is the orienting context, so that the market group of immediate interest can then be judged as generally leading, deviant,
conventional, or lagging. Within this framework, the circle, tri-
angle, perspective, and thickness or thinness of line, with their
various senses of unity, stability, vista, strength, and delicacy and
the relevance of specific objects, such as crowns, umbrellas, eyes,
and rabbits, may be interpreted. Their meanings draw on the
qualities of those objects plus from the particular way they are
used in their brand versions (Hallmark, Travelers, CBS, and
Playboy). This analytic complex is summed up in Figure 12.

THE SPECIAL CHARACTER OF INDUSTRIAL FILMS

Among the many facets of self-expression available to an organization, the film is an interesting one. Often overlooked as a part
of the marketing repertoire, it can serve a useful function. Industrial films are of several kinds: documentaries, public service,
training, and the like, often made available to associations,
schools, clubs, and companies. Each film has its own specific aim
and significance, as suggested by the following summary ap-
praisal culled from a research report about a film by the American Dairy Association shown to groups of teenage girls.

In summary, this film seems a useful one to show to groups of teenage
girls. It is an arresting communication which arouses ideas about life

Figure 12. Model for analyzing visual symbols.

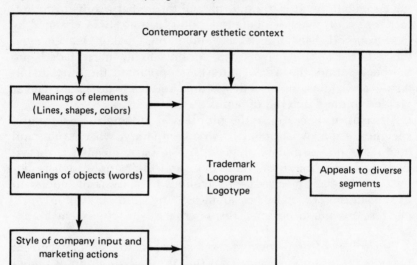

goals and feminine attractiveness via physical fitness based on sports participation and proper diet. Compared to other health films girls have seen in health classes, this one is very appealing—dramatically interesting and personally meaningful.

Industrial films, while undoubtedly very diverse, and often designed to be entertaining and moral, have a basic documentary and instructive character. A fundamental goal is to make people think about some problem and, if possible, how to solve it. The factual and "rational" aspects are prominent. Despite other appeals built into industrial films, audiences distinguish them as aimed primarily to instruct and inform. This makes them potentially subject to a variety of special problems.

They are almost destined to seem dull and repetitive, easily too long.

They tend to seem boring by showing ordinary people doing very ordinary things.

They are especially appealing to upper-middle-class people who recognize their value. Lower-status people may feel intimidated or wary.

Their audiences are often not well defined. This is a general problem of adult education.

The purpose of the sponsor is apt to be ambiguous or suspect. Commercially sponsored education easily becomes "propaganda."

Industrial films, despite their brevity, are likely to give more information than people want or can assimilate about the topic.

At the same time, people are prone to criticize them as being over-simplified or superficial.

Industrial films often ask for changed minds from *some* audience and therefore meet with resistance and defensiveness rather than receptivity and accord.

They easily fall into narrations or declamatory speeches that are self-conscious or self-righteous.

These are some of the more-or-less "natural" consequences of trying to make adults think. In practice, probably no single industrial film gets all the criticisms listed, and some are very successful in avoiding most of them. Also, industrial films have certain advantages which work in directions contrary to points on this list. Some of these advantages are:

Industrial films are realistic, and realism has its own rewards.

They *do* teach, and when people are able to learn, they feel edified and enlarged.

They give people a sense of having "inside information," since the films deal with special topics and are not generally distributed.

They lead people to take a fresh look at familiar environments.

They widen people's horizons.

They lead people to marvel at truth being "stranger then fiction."

Regardless of criticisms and suspicions, they usually reflect well on a judicious sponsor.

Above all, and most crucial, industrial films make demands on the audience to participate, because they are rather obviously out to teach and get the audience to do something.

This last point is perhaps the fundamental justification of the industrial film, and probably the best criterion of how successful a given film is. Unlike the fantasies of television and the motion picture theater, the business film tends to make people think directly about themselves. They may do this uncomfortably or defensively, but the net effect is to arouse self-evaluation and healthy judgments about one's own personality and occupational, social, or financial circumstances. Because the films are talking about and showing real things, real events, and real possibilities, there is a push to reassess one's own possibilities, and to move toward new actions.

Industrial films tend to reinstate the schoolroom. Symbolically, they represent pedagogical authorities trying to give adults some medicine that's good for them, often somewhat sugar-coated with humor, music, color, and animation.

THE MEANING OF TAGS

At another point in the spectrum of marketing communications is the tag. The tag is a card, folder, or leaflet attached to such products as an appliance, article of clothing, or a toy. As minor and casual as these tags may seem, they may be quite influential in affecting actions at point of purchase.

Shoppers have very definite expectations about tags. In talking to women shoppers about tags, it quickly becomes apparent that they have definite ideas *where* they expect to find them—in which kind of store and on which particular kinds of products. They look for certain kinds of information and are helped to evaluate the brand.

Reputable stores carry merchandise that has a manufacturer's tag. Most women interviewed in a private survey are convinced that the best and most reputable stores carry merchandise bearing manufacturers' tags. This idea seems to be true for all types of products, whether they are appliances, furniture, clothing, or other household goods. To the question, "How would you describe a store that puts tags on the appliances they sell?" the following are typical responses.

> I'd say it's usually a store with good quality merchandise and they want to stand behind what they sell.

> I like to shop there. You like to know what you're buying. Without question, it would be a more reputable store.

> Good store, high quality.

For the more thoughtful and analytical upper-middle-class women, the question as to what the store is like that carried mostly tagged brand merchandise causes some confusion. For them, the tagged merchandise suggests that the manufacturer is reputable, but that this is not necessarily true of the store.

Very-high-fashion shops may not use tags at all. Discount houses are cited as examples of stores that are perhaps not entirely reputable or always fully trustworthy, with their practices of fluctuating discounts and price cutting. But most of these stores do carry many brand items that carry merchandise tags. The reaction of the women is that if they buy tagged brand items it is perfectly all right to buy at a store that is not as reputable as a large department store. The fact that the brand is presented with a manufacturer's tag and possibly a guarantee can be more important than the nature of the store.

> The stores that put tags on the appliances they sell? You mean the manufacturers' tags — well, the stores are usually the ones that handle the most advertised and best backed-up kinds of appliances.

> I thought the manufacturer puts the tags on and when they do that they're definitely a responsible company respectful of the customer. It doesn't necessarily imply anything about the store, I don't think. The discount houses have them on many of the items they sell, and if you buy a brand item with a tag on it, you're perfectly safe in buying it there. We've bought a lot of things at Polk Brothers. They do have good discounts, but unless I knew exactly what brand I was buying and got all the instructions and the guarantee information with it, I would not buy there.

These are the general implications carried by tags:

1. *Tags are reassuring* and provide the shopper with a sense of security. Tags on the products, as "proof" of the brand and the reputation or the manufacturer, reassure customers that they are safe in buying this particular product. Tags give the consumer a sense of security by implying that he or she is doing the right thing and making the right decision.

2. *The information on tags* is thought to be objective and factual. In most cases, women seem to believe the information about the product that is presented on the tag. It is viewed as factual and objective, not intended as a means of convincing the customer to buy this particular item over another, in the sense that advertising is. When customers are afraid of aggressiveness and pressuring from the salesperson, they often say they prefer to "sell themselves." That is, they will read the information about the different products presented in the tags and then, using this objective authority, make their decision accordingly.

3. *Tags are for home reference.* Women refer back to the tag when information is needed on how to care for the item (cleaning in the case of appliances, washing and ironing as opposed to dry cleaning in the case of clothing). They also refer back to tags in an emergency situation when something breaks or goes wrong.

While most of the comments about tags are pragmatic in character and tone, other symbolic implications are strong, reflecting well on the manufacturer's integrity and interest in the customers.

RELATING TO SPECIAL PUBLICS

Opinions and attitudes about products, brands, services, and companies are shaped by many forces and can be affected by public relations. A common idea about public relations is that it stimulates *publicity* about the company, its products, and its people. This is one function of this marketing specialty. Its aim is to help develop news and impressions that reflect favorably on the image of the corporation. Such public relations materials are thought to be especially effective in determining the views of publics because they are so often items of information that show up in news and feature columns. newscasts, and in other apparently impartial forms.

As the public relations activity has grown, it has taken on many areas beyond issuing news releases, dealing with complaints, or trying to counteract other unfavorable events that may occur. Public relations personnel concern themselves with the various publics of organizations, such as stockholders, employees, financial analysts, and government officials, as well as any relevant groups among the general public. PR people assist in holding meetings and conferences and in preparing services materials of many kinds.

As suggested earlier, some of the activities of marketers carry negative implications for their imagery. It is one of those damned-if-you-do-damned-if-you-don't situations: To gain the benefits of advertising, a company bears the onus of "doing" advertising. Similarly, and perhaps to a greater extent, the mere *fact* of using public relations counsel is enough to bring about cynical snickers — as if good relations with the public should come about naturally, spontaneously, and sincerely, rather than through planning, deliberation, and prepared announcements.

THE SYMBOLISM OF RETAIL OUTLETS

All the means of distribution — the channels, the transportation, the outlets — may differ in their technical characteristics, such as size, ability to handle given kinds of merchandise, cost, and kind of personnel. Therefore, choices among them depend on grounds of necessity. Planes are faster than trains, and hardware stores don't usually sell food.

Each decision involving the distribution system has its own set of sociological and psychological ramifications. For example, whether to ship by rail or by air freight is not only a function of a need for speed, but may allow the prestige and the glamour associated with flight to justify the greater cost. The customer who learns that the merchandise was actually *flown in* from California or Florida has images aroused by the means of transportation (as well as the state names), which differ from those elicited by the image of the product being *trucked from* those places — a fact not likely to be mentioned in ads. Emery Air Freight found that users of their service got positive feedback from their customers, who were impressed with the idea that the shipper cared enough to send the goods by air.

Similarly, it makes a difference to customers to find the product in one kind of retail outlet than in another. Further image distinctions are made among the same kinds of stores. For example, cosmetics may be bought in department stores, drugstores, variety stores, discount houses, and supermarkets. The type of outlet is geared toward different market segments, even for the same brand of cosmetic. Many women of status wouldn't think of buying cosmetics in variety stores, whereas lots of lower-class women refuse to buy them in department stores. Then, among department stores, there are higher-status and lower-status stores. Whether for cosmetics or anything else, many high-status women will shop at Marshall Field's but not at Goldblatt's; and conversely, many lower-status women will shop at Goldblatt's, but not at Field's.

Of course, the imagery of stores is not so narrow or inflexible that no overlap occurs. But the spectrum of distinctions is definitely present and becomes more pronounced when extended to include expensive specialty shops with exclusive clientele and stores in slum neighborhoods where middle-class people will not venture.

In a study of the imagery of drugstores, some of the complex associations surrounding the outlet were interpreted. From discussion with consumers, a set of "paradoxes" was noted, which shows sources both of richness in the conception of a drugstore, and also of some conflict and mixed feeling about what drugstores were like and how they have changed[22]:

PARADOXES OF THE DRUGSTORE

It is highly public	It deals with secret problems, has a private, "bathroom" quality.
It provides treats and items of self-indulgence	It is an austere necessity in providing medications.
It is commercial.	It is professional.
It is close, familiar, defines the "old neighborhood."	It is a place of change, where much is new and different.
It is a sociable, pleasurable place.	It is more efficient, larger, self-serviced.
It has an interpersonal atmosphere.	It is more impersonal.

The subject of the drugstore was examined in several ways, among them a comparison with other kinds of retail outlets. The sample was small, but the results, although not definitive, were interesting in suggesting how experience with different types of stores leads to quite different feelings about knowing them and about what may be expected of them (Table 4).[23] Rather intriguing was the dramatically poor view of furniture stores, reflecting people's low level of contact in coming to know them, compared to food stores and drugstores, and the uncertainty and insecurity that result. Since this study, perhaps the situation has been improved by the new merchandising techniques adopted by many furniture outlets.

THE ENDLESS STREAM OF SYMBOLS

It should be apparent by this point that symbolic analysis of any element of marketing activity—not merely what it is, but what it connotes—can be made by the marketing manager who wants to raise the question. The means by which the answer is reached are as varied as thought and research ingenuity will allow. There is no prescription for this kind of analysis, and it may be as casual and superficial as the feeling that a grocery store seems a friendly place or as "deep" as the idea that a haircut is an aggressive, emasculating act that can be transformed into a loving, titillating experience.

The latter notions are more difficult to elicit from consumers in surveys and may therefore be more difficult, or impossible, to

Table 4. Attributes of five retail outlets.

Comments	Food Store	Hardware Store	Drug Store	Clothing Store	Furniture Store	Don't Know
Fun to shop there.	21%	23%	8%	32%	12%	4%
People always hanging around.	20	6	61	6	4	3
Gives serious attention to customers.	10	6	27	24	32	1
Really know their business there.	21	17	33	11	16	2
I know the owner.	28	17	36	10	9	0
Their profit margin is out of line.	15	6	18	13	43	5
Usually have what I want.	58	14	16	11	0	1
I don't feel at ease there.	3	15	6	21	26	29
It's hard to judge the merchandise.	4	14	11	16	50	5

N = 218. All figures expressed in percent.
SOURCE: *The American Drug Store: A Qualitative Study of Its Image, Use, and Function* (New York: National Wholesale Druggists Association, 1958), p. 9.

prove, especially to the satisfaction of a behavioristically oriented audience. But enlightened marketers can believe that people have erotic sensations when being groomed by others, even if most usually will not admit it. Also, that dirt motorcyclists enjoy getting themselves dirty. There are clues to marketing action in knowing that flight attendants' uniforms say something seductive about the airline, in contrast to the message of the registered nurse who attended passengers when airlines were more symbolic of the danger of illness than they are now. Bankers' traditional garb spoke of their gray eminence (and still does in the august baronial reaches of upper management), although the Harris Trust and Savings Bank for more practical purposes became the Harris Bank, on its way to presenting The Money Store, perhaps eventually to wind up as Stan's Bank, as symbols change to meet the changing times.

In these ways, the marketing dialogue continues. Managers observe the symbols being projected in the behavior of their customers and try to understand what language they have available in the marketing repertoire of communications — whether product, channels, names, coupons, clothing, media, salespeople, and other possibilities too numerous to illustrate here.

Figure 13 takes account of the discussion in this chapter to extend the situation diagramed in Chapter IX. It shows that the central summary symbol, the brand image, is the consequence of the intentional inputs from the company plus the projective expression of the total complex of symbols used in making it and offering it to its publics.

Figure 13. Image components of sellers' meanings.

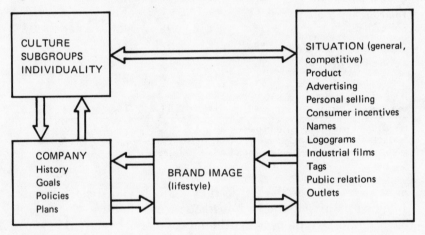

SUMMARY

1. As managers work to create, sustain, or recreate the brand images for which they have responsibility, they do so by calling upon the innumerable means of implementing marketing goals.

2. Added to the symbolism of the product are the choice of media, the design of packaging, the pricing policy, the styles of salespeople, the business cards, the letterhead, the furniture in the waiting room, the voice at the switchboard, the shipping cartons, the advertising themes, the logo, the name, and so on, all providing chances to express the nature of the company and its offerings. The managers choose where their emphasis will go, as Revlon chose advertising, and Avon chose personal selling (in addition to TV advertising).

3. Examination of the symbolism of these many means of communicating with customers enables managers to exercise imagination, to develop nuanced distinctions about their brands.

References

1. **Arno H. Johnson,** "The Growing Importance of Advertising in Our American Economy," in C. H. Sandage and Vernon Fryburger (eds.), *The Role of Advertising* (Homewood, Ill.: Richard D. Irwin, 1960), p. 61.
2. **Martin Mayer,** *Madison Avenue, USA* (New York: Harper & Row, 1958), p. 310.
3. **Burleigh B. Gardner** and **Sidney J. Levy,** "The Product and the Brand," *Harvard Business Review,* Mar.–Apr. 1955, p. 39.
4. **Irving S. White,** "The Functions of Advertising in Our Culture," *Journal of Marketing,* July 1959, p. 8.
5. **Raymond A. Bauer** and **Stephen A. Greyser,** *Advertising in America: The Consumer View* (Boston: Harvard University, 1968).
6. **E. B. Weiss,** "Where Are Today's Ad Rebels?" *Advertising Age,* Dec. 7, 1970, p. 52.
7. "Every Salesperson a Psychologist," *Sales and Marketing Management,* Feb. 6, 1968, pp. 34–36.
8. **John M. Rathmell** (ed.), *A Bibliography on Personal Selling* (Chicago: American Marketing Association, 1966).
9. **Richard P. Bagozzi,** *A Behavioral Model for the Selection of Salesmen,* dissertation (Evanston, Ill.: Northwestern University, 1975).
10. **Erving Goffman,** *The Presentation of Self in Everyday Life* (New York: Doubleday-Anchor, 1959).
11. **John L. Mason,** "The Low Prestige of Personal Selling," *Journal of Marketing,* Oct. 1965.
12. **Franklin B. Evans,** "Selling as a Dyadic Relationship: A New Approach," *American Behavioral Scientist,* May 1963, p. 79.
13. **John G. Udell,** "The Perceived Importance of the Elements of Strategy," *Journal of Marketing,* Jan. 1968, pp. 34–40.
14. **Henry L. Tosi,** "The Effects of Expectation Levels and Role Consensus on the Buyer-Seller Dyad," *Journal of Business,* Oct. 1966, pp. 516–529.
15. **Theodore Levitt,** "Communications and Industrial Selling," *Journal of Marketing,* Apr. 1967, pp. 15–21.
16. **James H. Donnelly, Jr.** and **John M. Ivancevich,** "Role Clarity and the Salesman," *Journal of Marketing,* Jan. 1975, pp. 71–74.
17. **Marvin A. Jolson,** "The Underestimated Potential of the Canned Sales Presentation," *Journal of Marketing,* Jan. 1975, pp. 75–78.
18. **George F. F. Lombard,** *Behavior in a Selling Group* (Boston: Harvard University, 1955).
19. **Sidney A. Diamond,** "The Psychology of Trademarks," *Advertising Age,* Mar. 4, 1968, p. 56.
20. Ibid., p. 56.
21. From Supreme Court decision in Mishawaka Rubber case, May 4, 1942, quoted by Daphne Leeds, "Confusion and Consumer Psychology," *Journal of the Patent Office Society,* Dec. 1955, p. 894.

22. *The American Drug Store: A Qualitative Study of Its Image, Use, and Function* (New York: National Wholesale Druggists Association, 1958), p. 10.
23. Ibid., p. 9.

References

Asam, Edward H., and **Louis P. Bucklin,** "Nutrition Labeling for Canned Goods: A Study of Consumer Response," *Journal of Marketing,* Apr. 1973, pp. 32–37.

Backman, Jules, *Advertising and Competition* (New York: New York University Press, 1967).

Bauer, Raymond A., and **Stephen A. Greyser,** *Advertising in America: The Consumer View* (Boston: Harvard University, 1968).

Bearden, James H., *Personal Selling: Behavioral Science Readings and Cases* (New York: John Wiley & Sons, 1967).

Boyd, Harper, and **Sidney J. Levy,** *Promotion: A Behavioral View* (Englewood Cliffs, N.J.: Prentice-Hall, 1967).

Bursk, Edward, and **John F. Chapman,** *Modern Marketing Strategy* (Cambridge, Mass.: Harvard University Press, 1964).

Dreyfuss, Henry, *Symbol Source Book* (New York: McGraw-Hill, 1973).

Engel, James, Hugh G. Wales, and **Martin R. Warshaw,** *Promotional Strategy* (Homewood, Ill.: Irwin, 1967).

Ferber, Robert, and **Hugh G. Wales,** *The Effectiveness of Pharmaceutical Promotion* (Urbana: University of Illinois, 1958).

Fox, Harold W., *The Economics of Trading Stamps* (Washington, D.C.: Public Affairs Press, 1968).

Houston, Michael J., The Effect of Unit-pricing on Choices of Brand and Size in Economic Shopping," *Journal of Marketing,* July 1972, pp. 51–54.

Huggins, W. H., and **Doris R. Entwisle,** *Iconic Communication: An Annotated Bibliography* (Baltimore, Md.: Johns Hopkins University Press, 1974).

Hurwood, David, and **Earl L. Bailey,** *Advertising, Sales Promotion, and Public Relations—Organizational Alternatives* (New York: National Industrial Conference Board, 1968).

Mauss, Marcel, *The Gift* (Glencoe, Ill.: The Free Press, 1954).

Meredith, George, *Effective Merchandising with Premiums* (New York: McGraw-Hill, 1962).

Rathmell, John M. (ed.), *A Bibliography on Personal Selling* (Chicago: American Marketing Association, 1966).

Sandage, C. H., and **Vernon Fryburger,** *The Role of Advertising* (Homewood, Ill.: Irwin, 1960).

xi

The Past and the Future

This chapter brings the discussion of marketing behavior to a close. The subject is a vast one and has inevitably moved along several different avenues. The central purpose has been to relate the perspectives of buyers and sellers by suggesting ways of thinking about the situations of each. Each group has its own aim and sources of behavior, which are connected by the offering and receiving of symbols. The basic themes asserted are these: First, marketing is a process of exchange that requires analysis of both sides in order to understand the providers and the receivers. Second, the exchange is a communication process in that the things being transferred (objects, money, actions, attention, feelings) are not merely things in themselves, but are symbols open to the perceptions and interpretations of the participants. As signs, they have meaning; that is, they are represented in the mind by thoughts, pictures, and relations to other objects, and they arouse certain attitudes and feelings about them and their sources.

Finally, the meanings assigned to these signs and symbols approach universality in some cases,[1] but for the most part they are interpreted in terms of the social and psychological context in which they appear. Thus, it is necessary to explore the sources of meaning in the individual's personality, in group memberships and cultural matrix, as well as in features of the product or service.

The text has suggested some ways of pursuing the exploration, not as much through specific research techniques as through encouragement to think both analytically and imaginatively in terms of the general model of buyer–seller exchange. The complex, multidimensional, qualitative model has been approached from various points of view to express the interacting whole.

The manager is commonly forced to confront these issues as a result of external pressure: to think about the package because of a new competitive package, to change the price because of new materials costs, to search for new market segments because sales volume is declining. Managers also decide to initiate change for internal reasons—fear that the advertising is becoming boring, feelings of expansiveness about broadening their current line, an urge to travel. Such factors lead them to call on customers in San Francisco or to do marketing research in New Orleans.

INTEGRATIVE THINKING

All the bits and pieces may be interwoven, but that is not always apparent. The general framework for thinking about marketing interaction takes up many components that might inform the manager—the role of culture in governing the meanings of its constituent objects and activities, the challenge of infinite segmentation, the psychological dynamics at the subjective core of human actions, and the symbolic implications of the endless means at the disposal of managers. In all of this there is some hazard of getting lost in the details. A closing chapter might suitably emphasize the importance of thinking integratively. This can be done in two ways: (1) by illustrating the importance of guiding concepts in the creation of brand imagery, and (2) by applying the overall logic to observing the idea of marketing behavior as a product in the history of marketing.

Integrating the Brand Image

Often, the brand image, corporate image, or industry image seems the consequence of one main element, and no doubt some inputs are more important than others. The nature of the product usually sets some basic limits to the ideas people will accept about it. The steady devotion to quality in engineering traditionally attributed to Chrysler illustrates the force of one central idea.

The distinction of names such as Kodak and Xerox and the charm of the Morton salt girl with the umbrella are three more examples of such outstanding elements. But they should not obscure the fact that such elements are not sufficient in themselves. The total configuration must be taken into account, and even if the other elements are in the background, it is important that they be there too. The image is a resultant, a distillation, or concentration of experience. Those brand images that come about through consistent adherence to themes appropriate to the offering and suited to the segment of receivers are the most successful. A consumer may respond positively even if there is conflict in his or her thinking about the elements of the brand image. Drawn to the alluring image of the Cutlass automobile, one consumer was overheard in conversation:

Tom, how do you like your new Cutlass?

Oh, it's pretty good; the usual shit from Detroit, but it's pretty good.

Other images are either confusing in the imagery they foster or are clear but less relevant or compelling to the audience being sought. When imagery inputs are not well integrated, individual elements may be effective in themselves, but may not be fitting to the guiding concept.

The advertising manager of a major printing company worked with his advertising agency to develop a new advertising campaign: Their idea consisted of a series of animal pictures illustrating that their competitors were as slow as snails, that their own shop was available at night like the night owl, and so forth. Research showed that customers and potential customers understood the idea and enjoyed it. When presented to management for approval, the campaign was sharply criticized by a senior salesman as amusing and pointed, but nevertheless petty, trivial, and demeaning to the company. He felt it was incompatible with the dignity of the company and with his serious relationships with customers, which involved contracts for millions of dollars.

The point can of course be argued, as it was by the advertising manager, who thought the dignity of the company too heavy anyway. But the debate indicated the need for greater consensus about the company's self-concept and about how to resolve the fit between the imagery coming across in the advertising and the way the organization was being represented by the salesman.

The coherence of brand imagery need not be ridiculously tight, but it at least requires the recognition that the audience interprets each element against the others. This means an awareness, as another instance, that a price is not just a price, but a number that will be judged for value and worth by how it fits the source and what else is known about it. Such appraisals underlie the willingness of consumers to pay more for commodities under one name rather than another. The desire for this coherence in imagery is so strong that consumers will often insist that a well-known brand is superior, regardless of the generic character of the product. Bayer aspirin and Domino sugar are examples.

Most modern marketing people are knowledgeable about brand images, but often restrict the meaning of the concept. In the fullest sense, the brand image refers to the complex of perceptions of the brand, including the inferences about suitability made by customers and attributed to them by sellers. Brand images are what people think the brands are, and an extended discussion of any brand brings out the many interactive components of its image.

Like any generalizations, brand or corporate images are more difficult to define as the number of elements grows. For example, Jell-O gelatin and Maxwell House coffee offer a simpler basis for focusing ideas about them than do diversified corporations, such as GTE Service Corporation or Avco. The images held by different market segments will necessarily select from the patterns of ideas that are available. The general public will think of Procter & Gamble mainly in connection with soap and detergents, whereas members of the financial community will also be judging the corporation for its suitability as an investment. Other groups will be more or less aware of other facets of the company. Almost all will think of it as large and successful.

The dynamics of imagery formation are such that immediate experience may play a large or small role in affecting the final outcome. For example, U.S. citizens may describe favorable experiences with government personnel, but still go on to generalize that government personnel are inefficient.[2] This idea is perceived as a guiding concept. The phenomenon seems notable enough to suggest that the American public clearly wants to perceive its government as inefficient, this being equated with a safe, democratic political style. Again, the process is interactive. Managers can only affect it from the selling side, doing just so much, and they are confronted with the difficult challenge of weighing the effect of specific actions upon the general outcome.

The basic integrative principle consists of fixing on a significant guiding concept, or set of concepts, that will act as a source of direction to all those involved in implementing the marketing program, whether that of buyers or sellers. A guiding concept is the idea of an umbrella, a definition of the kind of brand (company, person,) all the marketing actions are designed to communicate.

A family might decide on a Lifestyle policy of severe economy, for example. This purpose would guide members in their actions, and those actions would inform other people and influence the developing image of the family. A government agency might decide to convey an image of warmth, helpfulness, and effectiveness to compensate for its inevitable inefficiency. United Airlines asserts that it will be guided by friendliness, and Marshall Field said, "Give the lady what she wants." The guiding policy may not be formulated, but it is acted out consistently so that one company comes to be known as cutthroat, another as easy to do business with, another as innovative, and another as shrewd.

This consistent acting out of the guiding concept seems relatively simple if one simply "will not be undersold," or if returns are guaranteed accepted without question. The personnel are motivated to see to it. It becomes more problematic when symbols have to be chosen to fit in with advertising, package design, selection of colors, building locations, dress codes, conferences, and so forth, through the endless possibilities of imaginatively communicating the image.

Sometimes one message says one thing and another says something quite different. A classic example was the advertising claim by Camel cigarettes that the cigarettes were mild. Although told this repeatedly, consumers tended to believe that Camels were among the strongest cigarettes, because of their association with the camel on the package, the idea of the hot, dry desert, and other elements. It was probably preferable for the advertisements not to say the cigarettes were strong, but to suggest this tempering element of mildness.

Brand images are subtle configurations, and useful effects may come about through the use of contrasts, variations, and other surprises that act as interesting overtones to the fundamental guiding concept. A washcloth in the detergent package every time helps build a brand image of lesser quality, as a coupon with every package of Raleigh cigarettes probably did also. But an occasional premium or coupon can be a grace note or pleasant fillip for a well-established brand.

Brand images are the varied forms of a product or service. They will vary with respect to how they are perceived to present the core satisfactions or ideal variables sought by customers. Some of the variables are of a general nature. Any object or organization might usefully seek to be friendly or economically rational. Other ideas are more intrinsic to the product: taste and nutrition are especially relevant to foods, durability to fabrics, beauty to flowers, and so on (and the choice may be to be bitter-tasting, fragile, or ugly). Often less obvious are such ideal variables as social status, age, gender, time orientation, civility, and control, and the ways in which the specific promotids chosen to communicate the guiding concepts refer to these variables.

> Some of the important dimensions in the automotive and oil products area are power, refinement, lower-classness, danger, etc., or ideas derived from these. In some way or other communications will refer to these ideas; and the central problem of any brand is how to present itself optimally in the way it employs them. Some need to be played up, others down, or modified in subtle ways. In the 1970s the issues of social responsibility and energy crisis came to the fore with fresh force as ideal variables.

Whether set by a deliberate written policy or by the management's prevailing tone (say, Mr. Woodruff's concern with truth mentioned at the outset of this book, or perhaps a genial, venial, or venal president), its particular character ultimately filters through to the audience who are interpreting it and assessing its relevance to their lifestyles. Seen in its essence, a transaction anywhere in the marketing system is the interaction of the brand image and lifestyle.

PAST AND FUTURE OF MARKETING BEHAVIOR

It is a curious fact that the subject of marketing behavior did not become a lively issue for intensive and extensive study until the middle of the twentieth century. Actually, before the early 1900s there were no marketing courses, marketing textbooks, or directors of marketing. This seems odd, considering that marketing had of course always gone on, from the beginning of exchange activity, perhaps in the Garden of Eden. Some retrospection highlights the reasons for this neglect of the topic. One observes a progress of shifting emphasis in a natural history of the evolution of marketing thinking, with an interweaving of changing activities and the different concepts they embody, as follows.

Production

Initially, it is natural to focus on producing the goods necessary for survival, subsistence. The earliest energies go into extracting food from the soil, minerals from the mines, timber from the forest, fish from the water, and into the arduousness of hand crafting products. The elements of marketing are all present in the marketplaces and bazaars, the Phoenician merchants, the hawking of peddlers, the haggling over prices, the buyers and sellers interacting everywhere. But the integration of a discipline did not exist, given the relative stress on producing and the readiness of the population to absorb the little it could afford.

Human energies then yearned for the technologies that emerged with the growth of physical science. The heroes were the scientists and engineers, the inventors who made possible the Industrial Revolution that conquered the production problems (even if they were also hated and feared and their machines sabotaged with wooden shoes).

Transportation

A basic part of the technology required early on, as soon as there were any goods to work with, was the means of transport. The idea of marketing germinated, as people thought about how to carry their production to some market or to some customer. It is hardly "marketing thought," as so much is taken for granted. Nevertheless, when textbooks came to be written, the earliest ones started to define marketing with "the movement of goods" at the heart of the definition.

When production and transportation are the focus of concern, as was historically necessary and as occurs in many places and companies at the present time, the situation is referred to as *production oriented*. Management tends to be preoccupied with technical problems of manufacturing and delivery. The market is likely to be perceived vaguely, as relatively monolithic and undifferentiated.

Distribution

Such a production and transportation orientation largely prevailed until the beginning of the twentieth century, when the technologies of production and transportation reflected the achievements of the Industrial Revolution and mass production. The needs for new thinking, for transporting goods in terms of more complex allocations, for getting orders to facilitate production planning, for achieving the absorption of the volume that was possible — all this brought about the distribution revolution.[3] The American salesman became a new folk hero of sorts, both loved and despised, but exalted for his ability in the art of selling. The definition of marketing grows from the emphasis on the movement of goods to include the "transfer of ownership," which is effected by the salesperson. The sales ability that could sell anything, from the Brooklyn Bridge and gold bricks, to iceboxes to Eskimos, came to the fore, expressing the ever-enlarging network of transactions between sellers and buyers. The production orientation had added to it the selling orientation. Although it later became fashionable to sneer at the production and selling orientations, as if they merely reflected indifference to customers, they were skillful adaptations to the environment of the times, reflecting the drive and know-how that distinguished the American experience.

Consumption

World War II may be taken as a watershed period in the development of marketing. The technologies of production and transportation were tremendously developed. When the war ended, the country's industrial ability was geared up, business capital and consumer savings were at high levels, and consumers were eager to make up for the rationing and deprivation of goods. The situation was a dynamic one, and the Consumption Revolution was vigorously under way.

Competition

Equipped with the production facilities and looking for opportunities, old companies turned to new product areas and new companies entered familiar fields. More and more alternatives became available to consumers. In olden days customers walked into the traditional general store and found an array of commodities in bulk—a sack of coffee beans, a barrel of pickles, a wheel of cheese—with little opportunity for choice. As the goods began to be branded and to arrive with distinguishing names and packages, competition grew, alternatives proliferated, and the dramatic variable of choice entered the picture.

The availability of choices teaches people to be fickle. If other products have merit, as they probably do, why stay with this one? The desire for novelty is kept alive and stimulated by the continuous introduction of new products. The dress has been worn to too many parties and a new one is needed; one wants to try a new restaurant, visit a different country, find out "what's new?"

Segmentation

Of course, fickleness is partially offset by peoples' wishes for the familiar, the habitual, the convenient; and by devotion to the choices that seem most apt to one's self-concept and preferred lifestyle. Awareness of the many bases for market segmentation grew as it was recognized that the market was heterogeneous in more than the customary divisions by geography, income, age, and other demographic variables. The many ways of seeking satisfaction are part of the content of this book.

Innovation

A kind of snowballing occurred as managers strived to keep up with the burgeoning and complementary phenomena of competition and segmentation. The process fed on itself, so that the more people responded to novelty, the more they were segmented psychologically and sociologically. As they switched from segment to segment, the more urgently managers felt the need to innovate. Companies became organized to accomplish this with corporate development units, research and development, and new venture teams. The concept of product life cycle arose to assist in recognizing when products have matured and declined so that they may be phased out or repositioned. Pride was expressed in how many products that did not exist five or ten years ago could now be found in the stores.

Communication

With a segmented mass market, the necessity for fresh means of communication became apparent. The communications industry developed its technology along with that of production and transportation. Added to the face-to-face communication of salesmanship, the role of advertising and the contribution of the mass media came to dominate. Often entrusted at first to sales managers, the handling of advertising rapidly grew to a separate function. It required specialists in communications, people who understand printing, radio, television, mailing, and the nature of communicating through such nonpersonal means.

Investigation

Given the new postwar situation, the period of 1945–1960[4] was one of particular ferment in the kinds of questions that managers asked. Some were wondering why their long-time customers began to turn to alternatives. The question of why people behaved as they did had not come much to mind when managers were busy with the problems of producing and transporting. Managers also began to think that innovations, whether new products or improvements on old ones, should sensibly start with research on consumers' attitudes and needs. If consumers are given freedom of choice through alternatives and discretionary income, it is too risky to put forth products without first learning what might be appealing to some given segment of the market. What differential communication themes are needed to woo these segments? Added to technical product-oriented research was a great interest in marketing research. Added to the gathering of demographically oriented statistics was investigation into qualitative, behaviorally oriented problems.

The developments described as highlighted in the period after World War II have continued to the present time. They are characterized as being marketing oriented, rather than production or selling oriented. The emphasis on understanding the consumer as a fundamental starting point for marketing management came to be known as *the marketing concept*. It implied a fresh philosophy, a larger point of view, and the need for new personnel and new organization to manage the marketing functions. The impact on companies was not, and is not, always pleasant when management tries to shift to this marketing-dominated outlook. The engineers, financial people, and other managers wonder who these marketers are and "who sent for *them*?" Recently, in one bank that is trying to become more marketing oriented, an operations manager was heard to disparage the new marketing person hired by saying, "I think he's just supposed to pick out our stuffed animal premiums."

Regulation

The marketing concept is not the end of the story, which will continue to evolve into an uncertain future. As the marketing managers and much of industry shifted away from the robber baron approach of "the public be damned" to the seemingly more virtuous one of meeting the needs of customers, fresh problems arose. Rather like biting the hands that fed them, the middle-class critics found the affluent society offensive. The young criticized its gross materialism, and the leadership of Kenneth Galbraith, Vance Packard, and Ralph Nader gave voice to various socioeconomic ills. It became fashionable to protest the sense of excess, of unneeded goods, and of being swamped by commercial messages. The desire for information and truth as means of finding one's way pressed for government involvement, so that regulation became a more omnipresent factor. The lawyers' role has become so prominent that, rather ironically, marketers came to protest the intrusion of the legal department, wondering as the engineers did: Who sent for *them*?

Conservation

Part of the protest movement generally known as consumerism is an attempt to give consumers a countervailing power to cope with business, government, and labor. It found expression in concern over pollution of the environment. With the energy crisis, a broad anxiety about natural resources came into being. Although the population at large tends to go along, often seeming relatively indifferent to the need and pleas for cooperation, there is widespread recognition of the problem. Many are not sure of the reality of the problem, or merely hope that greater minds will solve it.

As the need for conservation continues to grow, it will become increasingly powerful as a force, pressing against all participants in the marketplace and at all levels, changing the nature of society, differentially affecting various social groups and market segments, and stirring psychological dynamics and physical reactions. The need for managers to think about marketing behavior will remain.

References

1. Johanna Kraut-Tabin, A Psychological Study of the Universality of Interpretation of Symbols, unpublished dissertation (Chicago: University of Chicago, 1948).
2. Sidney J. Levy, "The Public Image of Government Agencies," Public Administration Review, Mar. 1963, pp. 25–29.
3. Walter Hoving, The Distribution Revolution (New York: Ives Washburn, 1960).
4. Two articles of particular significance in detailing the developments are by J. B. McKitterick, "What Is the Marketing Management Concept?" in Frank M. Bass (ed.), The Frontiers of Marketing Thought and Science (Chicago: American Marketing Association, 1957), pp. 71–82; and by Robert J. Keith, "The Marketing Revolution," Journal of Marketing, Jan. 1960, pp. 35–38.

Appendix A

The Nature
of Symbols

The study of the nature and formation of symbols goes on in various specialized fields as workers examine how symbolization comes about and develops and its relations to language, thinking, social relations, pathology, art, and so forth. Such ramified study attests to the importance of the topic, but is often highly abstract and technical, not easily accessible to lay readers in those fields.

There are also the difficulties of professional controversies over different theories, definitions, and interpretations. It is clearly hazardous to deal simply with such a topic, but nonexperts should be able to gain some understanding without becoming embroiled in the technicalities of monoremes, syncretic fusions, dystaxia, and the like, or arguing the nuances of signs, signals, protosymbols, true symbols, and exemplificatory representations. Any approach to the nature of symbolizing is difficult enough to begin with. This chapter does it rather generally, without getting entangled in terminology. The necessity is suggested by Werner and Kaplan:

> Thus man, destined to conquer the world through knowing, starts out with confusion, disorientation, and chaos, which he struggles to overcome. This struggle is a never-ceasing process, continuing throughout life: man's objects are always touched with a coefficient of indeterminancy and, as long as he is open to new environments and ex-

periences, they are constantly in a world of becoming rather than in a world of being. Now it is our contention that in order to build up a truly human universe, that is, a world that is known rather than merely reacted to, man requires a new tool—an instrumentality that is suited for, and enables the realization of, those operations constituting the activity of knowing. This instrumentality is the *symbol*.

Symbols can be formed for, and employed in, the cognitive construction of the human world because they are not merely things on the same level as other existents; they are, rather, entities which subserve a novel and unique function, the function of *representation*."[1]

1. *Symbolizing Economizes*. A basic function of symbolizing is to economize. Telling about an elephant playing a piano is a saving compared to carrying around such a phenomenon. By raising an eyebrow (*super cilia*), a brief physical movement becomes a complex symbolic expression (superciliousness), and a wealth of energy is conserved. A wink speaks volumes with a minor motoric output. Not only does a picture speak 10,000 words, but the 10,000 words are also economical symbols that can capture centuries of history.

2. *Symbolizing Elaborates*. The mind is not merely stingy; thinking is more than a mechanism for condensing experience. It also includes playful, elaborating interests; the imaginative restoration of lost objects; and numerous ways of enriching experiences. Seen from this point of view, symbolizing is a technique for achieving an enlargement of life by investing events with nuance, implication, and subtle reference. The raised eyebrow conserves energy, but it may also complicate interpersonal relations considerably if its subtle implication offends another person. Similarly, a wink may save energy in expressing an idea, but its implications may lead to greater personal rewards.

3. *Symbolizing Is Expressive*. The need to symbolize is an expressive need, a way of projecting oneself. It goes on inside, but there is also the wish to let it out. It gratifies the urge to take the "stuff" of inner life and to organize it into an outward form that says, "This is how I feel, what I think about things, how I judge and evaluate what my senses have brought to me." At first, this outward expressiveness is spontaneous, not designed to inform other people. The gleefully gurgling baby thereby gives vent to and shows a state of contentment and happy surplus energies. But very soon, probably sooner than people realize, this outward show of feelings becomes communicative. The adult whistling happily or moping stormily when alone is not only being ex-

pressive, but may also be trying to communicate to someone, even though the someone is present only in imagination.

4. *Symbols Communicate.* Once it is discovered that other people do respond to gurgling, crying, whistling, and moping, and that they will labor to elicit a smile, run at a cry, and comfort a mope, everyone seizes on the great weapon of communication. Symbolizing may become synonymous with communicating. The ability to influence others, for better or worse, is felt as a tremendous source of power. Those who do it effectively make progress in their relationships. Those who do it poorly are frustrated and feel diminished in their relationships.

5. *Symbols Deceive.* As a powerful activity, symbolizing is put to many uses. It serves to deceive, as when people use symbols that are falsely related to what they are supposed to represent, ranging from little white lies to the great imposter. As a general human activity, all symbolizing may be somewhat false, in that any substitution for or condensation of an event must to some degree violate it.

People make precise discriminations among what degree of departure from "fact" is acceptable or moral. A certain degree of exaggeration or distortion is usually allowed, for example, for emotional expression, as in saying, "The outfit was just ghastly. I could have died." The average churchgoer is permitted a conventional amount of hypocrisy. In some areas there is confusion with mixed values as to what symbolic departures are acceptable. Many people feel that abstract modern art is excessive in its symbolic movement away from the realities it is supposed to "represent," while others think such art "really" captures the essence of modern life.

6. *Symbols Clarify.* The felt goal of symbolizing is usually to clarify, to explain something about oneself or about life by some kind of analogy. The child is saying, in essence, "My skipping steps are somehow similar to the gay, cheery way I feel inside." The executive says, "The several phones on my desk say that my importance has multiplied, as my voice and avenues to reaching people are multiplied." A housewife feels that a broom makes her a drudge and ill-tempered, transforming her by symbolic analogy into a witch. Such analogies have always been necessary to make the universe comprehensible, whether by believing sea sprites animate the waves, or by comparing the particles in the atom to the solar system.

7. *Symbols Gratify.* Making symbols is a gratifying activity. Be-

yond its necessity for forming thought patterns, people do it to find pleasure. Symbolism is especially manifest in the processes and mechanisms of the mind that are thought of as literary and artistic in character. Then it shows its magical, fantastic character in being able to ignore logical rules of time, space, orderly sequence, or normal causation. These qualities of symbolic activity make possible poems, puns, and stageplay devices that move us readily through time, arousing laughter and tears in quick sequence.

All thinking may be basically symbolic, and every object may be a symbol. But there are different kinds and levels of symbolism. Certainly some symbols are more obvious than others, more easily recognized or agreed to, whereas some are difficult to analyze and can lead to mixed or conflicting interpretations. A few major principles and categories can be distinguished.

8. *Symbols Are Multiple.* First there is the problem of multiple meanings. Every object can have many meanings. The same person may see several meanings, and different people may see different meanings. For instance, hot cereal offered for breakfast as a sign of nurturing may be taken as old-fashioned pressure to be a good, obedient child.

What determines which meanings are taken? Context, inclusion of other objects, who the observer is, and other factors will affect the interpretations made. In any given situation the person has to select what seems important, appealing, or appropriate under the circumstances in order to understand the event or communication in some way that seems adequate.

Some of the factors that affect such emphasis, selection, and reactions are the public and private nature of symbols; their universality; the groups for whom they have special significance; their degree of formality; their placement, apparent source, and supposed purpose.

9. *There Are Private Symbols.* A main distinction is between public and private symbolism. Each person develops a world of symbols that are peculiar in reflecting a specific pattern of experience. Like Citizen Kane, one may attach intense feelings to a sled named Rosebud; or popcorn may stand for Zanzibar in someone's mind; or Kleenex tissues may symbolize a beloved aunt. Such private or personal symbols are quite important to people, being components of their individuality and special character. These private symbols tend to flourish at less self-controlled or less rational times (meaning that the rationale is not

easily perceived or sensible to others), when people are disordered or when dreaming, or are interpreting ambiguous stimuli, and freer rein is given to personal meanings. Private symbols will be at work more covertly at other times, as well. While they may not be relevant to general studies in marketing, it is useful to be aware of their existence (since their presence affects how public messages are received) and it is necessary to take account of their influence in one's own communications.

10. *There Are Public Symbols.* Public symbols are those that command some broad degree of consensus, that tend to arouse in people's minds similar interpretations, feelings, and responses. The size of the public may vary but the symbol has a general character that is learned by those born or trained into particular groups or societies.

Some public symbols have such a generality of meaning that they suggest that universal symbolism may be at work, possibly based on a biological response (the stimulating effects of color, for example); or perhaps a powerful and inescapable analogy impresses most people. Maleness and femaleness have such strong associations with certain forms that it is hard to imagine people wrongly interpreting which of these lines is "male" and which is "female."

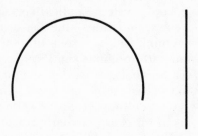

Some people believe that there is a universal phonetic symbolism, and that, for instance, if given the choice between such syllables as *mal* and *mil* to signify a large and a small table, most people will agree that *mal* is larger than *mil*, on the ground that the *a* sound is symbolically "larger" than the *i* sound.[2] Similarly, living usually teaches people that relative largeness suggests power and strength — as grownups are stronger and more powerful than children. The relationship of high to low seems recognized in most societies as symbolic of status. Thrones are elevated, and inferior or deferential people lower themselves in prayer, in bowing.

Universal meanings of this sort transcend the different languages to the level of basic forms, relationship, and objective experience. It is less likely that one would see a circle as representing disorder or diversity, or that light would mean death (and darkness life), except as a technique for rebelling against conventional understandings.

11. *Religion Uses Symbols.* Religious symbolism is close to universal symbolism because it attempts to understand and explain universal phenomena. The "substitutive" character of religious symbolism is usually recognized as such, by way of demonstrating the "unreal" nature of experience in contrast to the greater spiritual reality it symbolizes.

Religion deals especially with the mysteries of coming into and leaving life. It expresses awe, reverence, and submission to the supernatural forces presumed responsible for the nature of the world and one's destiny in it. Its symbols are orderly techniques for showing what the beliefs are and for representing how people relate to the divine forces. Once established, the complex of symbols and symbolic acts turns into rituals and ceremonies wherein the symbolic language is only partly understood by the congregation. Numerous objects are drawn into sacred symbol systems, such as a book, water, candles, special clothing, stars, crosses, fish, cats, cows, and trees—the list could be multiplied endlessly—since anything can be drawn into the sacred symbolic drama and be vested with religious significance.[3]

12. *Cultures Have Symbols.* A particular range of symbols are those that might be called anthropological. These are symbols characteristic of a given cultural group or nation. Americans recognize many objects or ideas as peculiarly related to a distinctive way of life. The meanings aroused in Americans by the American flag are not the same meanings observed elsewhere (where it may signify "imperialistic capitalism"). The American eagle may quicken the citizen's emotion with pride, with feelings of staunchness and fierce freedom, whereas elsewhere it stimulates fear and hatred of a predatory bird.

Flags and national birds are defined as symbols. There is no problem in interpreting them, since they are explicitly ways of referring to the country. By definition, the 13 stripes stand for the first 13 states, and the Great Seal stands for the United States.

These meanings are arbitrarily assigned as originally agreed upon or are a natural historical reference. The same is true of Uncle Sam, of the political elephant and donkey, of Minute Men, and of the Statue of Liberty.

Other things are also taken as national or anthropological symbols without having this historical public character. The automobile and all that it represents to Americans make it a powerful contemporary symbol. Only recently has there been much self-consciousness about the car as a symbolic object. Until now it was merely *used* as such. The same is true of telephones, houses, education, appliances, and the whole array of things that are increasingly being sought after, not only because of their inherent benefits, but because they are also ways of expressing dominant American values.

13. *Social Groups Have Symbols.* Very important are sociological symbols, those that have special meanings to subgroups in society, or which vary in meaning from group to group. Some symbols have particular meanings to only a limited number of people. They may use technical symbols which are jargon to those outside the group, or they may attach an additional particular significance to a symbol widely known for other meanings. This occurs commonly among all professional groups, age groups, social-class groups, and regional groups and between men and women.

For instance, among physicians certain Latin phrases or newly coined drug names are understood, but most lay people will not grasp them. Abbreviations may be used casually among the initiated, such as Ca for cancer, or among waitresses BLT for bacon, lettuce, and tomato. A teenage girl was heard to tell a friend she would not be coming over to stay because she "had a visitor last night," meaning she had started her menstrual period. Many Northerners are not aware that "Bubba" is widely used in the South as an affectionate symbol for a young boy, or brother. Fashion and style create special modes of conversation. Clothes act as a vocabulary in themselves; some have general cultural meanings, while others speak primarily to women. Tailored suits say such things as professional woman, masculine woman, or club woman. Sweaters say teenage girl or college woman, upper middle class, suburbs. Women know that sweaters are not objects to be worn for warmth alone, but are to be combined with skirts and blouses for a "total look."

The language of hair is also part of the sorority. Women talk of ratting, backcombing, guiching, and stripping their hair—most men do not know what these expressions mean. Among men, different objects are understood to symbolize different kinds of men and the kinds of masculinity they seek to express. Straight-edge razors hark back to a time of staunch masculinity. They say that a man is conservative, rural, possibly a tough, no-nonsense middle-of-the-road, conventional, ordinary Joe. An electric shaver implies middle-class status, modernity, expense, a softer, gentler personality.

14. *Symbols Are Formal and Informal.* The meanings of objects and activities are formal or informal, depending on whether or not the implication is supposed to be an indirect one. Formal symbols are those that are usually recognized and defined in everyday understanding as "symbolic." Whereas a tailored skirt is an informal symbol of diminished femininity, a wedding veil is a formal symbol of virginity.

The function of formal symbols is relatively limited to communicating the familiar and publicly understood meaning. For example, institutional symbols are usually formal ways of signifying the identity of the institution and its purpose. The lamp of knowledge does not mean that lamps are sold but, in one instance, that merit scholarships are available. The lamp is a formal symbol of the light of knowledge. The formal purpose of the GE symbol is to stand for the company name; it acquires additional informal meanings through time.

On the other hand, an automobile functions as an informal symbol of status. Its formal purpose is transportation; and in addition people have come to feel that choices made among cars may reflect other symbolic meanings such as technical interest or striving for higher social status. As informal meanings become publicly recognized, they tend to take on a more formal character, since the object or activity is then more like a badge signifying the symbolic meaning that people recognize. A mural of a boat, a train, a car, and an airplane is formally symbolic of "transportation," of human triumph over distance, even of "progress." A red convertible with leopard-skin upholstery, festooned with fox tails and a hanging plaque reading Moontown's Maniacs, is informally symbolic of more than the owner's wish for transportation.

References

1. Heinz Werner and Bernard Kaplan, *Symbol Formation* (New York: Wiley, 1963).
2. Edward Sapir, "A Study in Phonetic Symbolism," *Journal of Experimental Psychology,* 1929, pp. 225–239.
3. W. Lloyd Warner, *The Living and the Dead* (New Haven: Yale University Press, 1959), Part IV, pp. 321–444. This is a fascinating account and interpretation of sacred symbol systems.

Appendix B

Products as Symbols

THE MOTOR GOD[1]

The devotion of Americans to their automobiles is legendary. The modern American society can be seen as having come into being with the production techniques that made the Ford car available to Everyone by manufacturing them in quantities and by paying the workers the five dollars a day that allowed them to buy the machines they made. The millions on the road (shortages or no) are testimony to the full flowering of that devotion. Its roots are diverse and at times seem to have the compelling, inevitable quality of being part of human destiny. Just as eating animal protein increases in linear fashion with rising income among the countries of the world, so has the lust for cars grown as nations develop.

The interest in locomotion that turns people from pedestrians into riders is ancient. It is a dream that has many parts, making the automobile a complex satisfaction. An object of fantasy, of practical purpose, and of symbolic richness, the car is the fulfillment of so many aims that it is hardly surprising that people identify intensely with it.

The car falls on a continuum of locomotion values that range from walking to such means of locomotion as donkeys, boats, horses, carts, carriages, trains, automobiles, airplanes, and space-ships. To be able only to walk means to be earthbound, to be in the dust, slow, exposed, and vulnerable. Walking is a form of work, fatiguing and uninspired. The word pedestrian has come to mean having the characteristics of a drudge or plodder, unimaginative, and commonplace. To be able to ride anything at all is a step upward in social importance even if it is a bicycle where the rider still does the pedal work, or is a poor woman on a donkey receiving the mixed recognition of her supposed weakness and of her femi-nine refinement. More generally, the master rides, the serf walks; the child bicycles, the adult drives a car; the average citizen rides mere cars (for 85 percent of vacation trips), the executive flies in private Lear jets; and a chosen few orbit the Earth at 15,000 miles per hour.

The ancient Greek story of Daedelus and Icarus and their at-tempts to fly shows the early eagerness to soar like the birds and the gods. The interpretation of the ride of the sun across the heavens as a Sun Chariot is common to most mythologies of the world. Here, the idea of the chariot is one of splendor, power, a glorious daily trip. It is a vision of a hero controlling a great fiery vehicle with incredible horsepower, strong and beautiful. A Pol-ish folktale makes the three horses of silver, gold, and diamonds. In the thirteenth century, Roger Bacon wrote that "cars can be made so that without animals they will move with unbelievable rapidity." Three hundred years later, Leonardo da Vinci devel-oped the idea for a military vehicle very much like a modern tank. The potentialities of an automotive vehicle for military pur-poses was an obvious and quick encouragement to seeking to re-place animals. An artillery tractor powered by steam was created by a French major, Nicholas Cugnot, in 1769. When the horseless carriage finally struggled into being in the late 1800s and early twentieth century, it was welcomed with some mixed feelings, but the War Department bought three in 1899.

As the car ramified into the fabric of American life and emo-tions, its importance to people grew, changed, and went through various stages. When expensive and rare, autos were toys of the rich, with criticism and resistance by horselovers and city gov-ernments. But the desire for the glamorous object was an irresist-ible force that seemed to pave the nation with concrete and as-phalt as in time all bowed down before the idol of the motor god.

Prior to the burgeoning of the suburbs and the interstate high-way system, the automobile went through a relatively idyllic stage. It meant picnics, family drives in the country on Sunday, a challenging kind of struggle with its fallibility—cranking it to start, changing tires frequently, cleaning spark plugs, and all the other joys of tinkering. The car and American lifestyles became more and more interwoven. The vision of the heroic chariot took its peculiarly American forms—the jalopy for youngsters clanking around town, the roadsters and convertibles at the country club, the salesman and his coupe, the plant parking lots filling up with workers' earnest sedans.

Cars were especially a man's thing: his beloved machine to be cherished, polished, and displayed, a proud exhibition of his masculinity, an assertion of his manhood, the manhood of a success in the United States.

The car seemed particularly appropriate to a free society, a society opening up and out, from East to West, from farm to city, hoping to move up, with geographic and social mobility for all who could make it. The freedom was of many kinds. It was freedom from being a mere pedestrian and from being a localite. A larger perspective became available to those who drove, who could drive out and away. Part of the vision of the chariot is the deep and impelling urge of the journey. Founded on journeys, the nation drew those who were fleeing and seeking, who established a tradition of pioneering and restlessness. The car facilitated the journey to freedom and adulthood, to get away from the house with its immigrant mother and puritanical mores, to find sexual experiences, competitive races, and chances to show your daring, power, and skill, and whatever is your private quest. Like the medieval suit of armor, the car encased you and encouraged sport, aggression, and the mentality of a surging force.

The sense of contemporary dependence on cars reflects the long way they have come from luxury novelties. People feel they need them for work, for security from the hazards of public transportation, for their convenience in spontaneous use. No longer restricted to masculine pride, the car attests also to women's competence as family chauffeurs or in driving to their jobs. With two, three, four cars, the family is free to disperse in all directions.

All along, it is evident that cars have been imperfect as well as sources of difficulty. But even when the freedom gained is illusory or offset by enslavement to problems of financing, defects, service, traffic, parking, pollution, and gas shortage, millions want to buy and drive them. Where they *must* yield to car pooling, public transportation, conservation, smaller cars, and fewer trips, they will but they will resist hard, and yield with profound regret for the senses of social substance, of freedom, of personal style, and of sexual maturity that the automobile provides and represents, that are being diminished or lost. Can these gratifications be replaced by other means of self-expression, by other forms of heroic address to the chariot, and of ways of making both the mundane trips and the secret journey? For those of you who have been revved up by this discussion on cars, there is a list of suggested readings at the back of the Appendix.

ON THE EATING OF MEAT

The definition of meat and attitudes toward it provide an important and striking example of the symbolic meanings of products in the marketplace as powerful forces that reflect and influence the states of mind of the individual and social groups that make up society. Meat is a very provocative product. People feel strongly about meat the world over. Many complex ideas and emotions have developed about the eating of meat. It has general appeal and a high place in popular esteem. As a society becomes increasingly affluent, its meat consumption tends to increase in direct proportion (see Figure 6 in Chapter V). In the United States, for example, the pounds of meat consumed per capita rose from 136.0 in 1920 to 188 in 1974.

This interest in meat is often grounded in practical ideas about health, related to the nutritional content of meat and its specific effects on the human body. Observers point out striking differences in physique and state of health among neighboring peoples that correlate with the amount of animal protein consumed. The people of northwest India who eat more foods of animal origin than people in other regions of India and have a higher protein intake, are generally healthy, vigorous, and well developed, while many peoples of the south and east are poorly developed, disease ridden, and lacking in energy. The pastoral Masai of Kenya, whose diet includes substantial amounts of milk, blood, and flesh, also are tall and vigorous, whereas their agricultural Kikuyu neighbors who live almost exclusively on millet, maize, sweet potatoes, and yams are smaller, weaker, and less resistant to certain tropical diseases, as well as to tuberculosis and pneumonia. In fact, it is said that the average Masai woman is as strong as the average Kikuyu man. Stefansson points out that no people of the past or present are known to have had freedom from tooth decay unless they were hunting, fishing, or pastoral in their way of life, and got little or none of their food directly from the vegetable kingdom. For many people, the only reason for not eating more meat than they do is that it is scarce or expensive.

American meat eaters consider nothing superior to meat, and enthusiasm for it is pronounced and easily elicited:

My husband and I love meat. That's our favorite subject: steak or a nice roast.

It's important, it's full of iron and protein. It provides the basic protein needed in the diet.

It gives about 75 percent of the nutritional value of the meal.

Meat eaters are healthy looking, none are sickly.

I couldn't do without it. I crave it, I don't feel the meal is complete without it. I serve it because I know my family likes it. We have it at least twice a day, it's that important to us. I take it for granted that it's important. It's the way I was raised.

Nevertheless, meat is not regarded as totally good. The fact that it involves the slaughter of animals and the eating of creatures that can be regarded as having some type of kinship to the eater introduces feelings and attitudes that are very powerful. In some places, this attitude has led to an emphasis on vegetarianism. Pure vegetarianism is followed in some groups, especially among clergy and devout people whose religious belief says that killing animals is wrong and that eating flesh is a contamination. Even among meat eaters there is commonly the wish to have professional butchers who take the terrible responsibility unto themselves, and who may then be regarded with some dread or distaste. These feelings may be expressed with intensity:

The sight of animal food is unnatural and disgusting. Meat reminds the thoughtful person of a dead body along the road being eaten by vultures or ravens, or perhaps even of a cannibal feast.

Among those who have less qualms about animal food, as such, there is often the unwillingness to countenance the killing and eating of animals whose acquaintance has been made, who seem to have some individuality of personality.

Meat eating takes its strength not only from its healthful effects (since these can be denied by the vegetarians), but also from its psychological implications. There is a profound recognition of the idea that *you are what you eat.* One becomes what one has taken in. Many people take this quite literally, in the belief that when they eat of a certain animal, they acquire its characteristics (strength, endurance, power, vitality, cunning, sexual potency, grace, and the like). The animal may be revered for its special qualities, and eating it then may be either forbidden as too dangerous or encouraged as a way of having a special relationship to a deity and its nature, being like it and gaining its favor. Gandhi abhorred flesh as food, but at one point in his struggle with the British, he decided to try to be like them, if it might help his cause. He said:

> It began to grow on me that meat eating was good, that it would make me strong and daring, and that, if the whole country took to meat eating, the English could be overcome . . . it was not a question of pleasing the palate. I did not know that it had a particularly good relish.

He tried to eat goat's meat, but it made him sick.

Traditionally, meat is a man's food, and a food of high status. What are usually regarded as the best kinds or parts of meat are reserved for the men. The system of distribution of meat expresses and reinforces the prestige of the men in the society. Among some groups this principle is so strong and so common that many women are denied an adequate supply of protein, although as bearers of young they need it particularly. More dominating is the man's need to feed his maleness, his muscular force.

In American society, attitudes of aversion toward eating meat are not widespread, but there are still many nuances expressed in how meat ought to be prepared and about the degree of refinement in the people who eat it, and the ways they eat it. In seeking to be removed some step from the grosser aspects of meat eating, it is of course common to cook the meat. This makes it taste better and easier to eat. In his amusing story, Charles Lamb points out how the delicious taste of an inadvertently roasted pig led to such preparation as a routine thing. But it is clear that more than just taste or flavor is involved. Eating raw meat is too close to elemental and animalistic behavior to suit most modern Americans. Asked about this, housewives showed strong resistance to the thought.

> I don't like it, and the family doesn't like it. To me, we're civilized people. It's for the Africans. I don't think it's good for a person to eat raw meat. From what I understand, they claim raw meat can cause worms.

> We don't eat it. I don't like the looks of blood.

Forget it! My little one tries to eat raw hamburger because my sister and father do it—yuch! I think of getting worms. I feel cannibalistic if I see blood. Forget it! I like my food done—I'm no cannibal.

I'm against it. Just for esthetic reasons. The thought of it—just considering raw, unprepared, unseasoned meat—is unappealing. Cooking enhances the flavor and is more edible, easily digested.

But if the meat is to be cooked, what does proper preparation mean? Here are other nuances. Logically speaking, to get meat furthest away from its raw, cannibalistic state, it should be cooked extremely thoroughly. Curiously, the most refined people come full circle here. They want their steaks rare. In fact, some of the most fastidious restaurants will refuse to cook a piece of meat to the well-done stage. It is enough that the meat be raised a notch above the state of rawness: "We simply don't like to see blood running in the dish." The woman who said she thought raw meat was unesthetic does not want to go too much in the direction of artificiality. She wants her meat "medium rare—I feel you have most natural flavor that way."

Doing other things to meat, besides simply broiling or roasting it, is in some sense to depart from the preparation that Americans regard as optimal, to be the best blend of the natural and the civilized. Still, civilization makes other demands. It provides for freezing, precooking, grinding up, and canning. Each of these forms of preparation is regarded with mixed feelings, as apt to do something undesirable to meat, and probably as a consequence to make it less suitable for men, therefore more suited to women, children, and effete, overly refined types.

Canning especially takes on the meaning of being overly civilized and made soft and immature. As one woman said, "Meat loses all flavor, loses all identity. You don't know what you're eating." "Canned meats seem overprocessed." "I think it softens it too much, makes it mushy. It isn't like real meat." Canned meat is no longer something to sink one's teeth into in some degree of aboriginal fashion. It may even come to hint at the worst aspects of animals—their intestines, glands, genitals, and who knows what—implying that one is given the leftovers, or has developed perverse tastes, beyond the sturdy, honest enjoyment of conventional muscle.

To sum up, food is deeply symbolic. This symbolism is highly rationalized by notions of taste and is mixed with the many symbols attached to money, status, and how one's lifestyle is expressed. People do what seems natural to them, even when this is the mixed-up symbolism of eating relatively primitively. Picture a chicken liver wrapped in bacon impaled on a toothpick being eaten by a person dressed in very proper fashion at so "refined" a human event as a cocktail party.

Even canned meat products constitute a complex experience. The merit of canned meat products is that they do refer to the requirements of an elaborated and developed civilization in which people can store meat for long periods rather than killing animals daily. They can spend whole days in socially elevated activities and come home to a quick, easy meal. On the other hand, canned meats are too removed from the more fundamental, ideal experience people speak about embodied in a fresh roast or steak just this side of bleeding carcass. From cannibal to canned is to move far from the ideal goals that are located in the vigor, power, and aggressiveness of meat.

The discussions of cars and meat are not formal marketing studies of the nature and meaning of products. Rather they are vignettes, sketching in an interpretive overview that may help to orient one toward the product area, and foster further discussion and inquiry into specific contemporary problems.

At another level is the analysis of the bathroom by Alexander Kira, described as an intensive $100,000, seven-year study, which examines bathroom facilities in a 233-page report. It includes a perspective on historical and cultural aspects of personal hygiene and facilities, social and psychological aspects, physical and anatomic considerations, and the consumption system and design elements, and offers numerous criticisms and implications for product improvement.[2] The close, thorough analysis is formidable in its detailed explanation of the inadequacies and primitivity of the contemporary bathroom and the constructive manner in which Kira tries to solve problems. Most marketing product analyses are limited to smaller investigations and are more circumscribed in their aim.

How to interpret the meanings of products poses a problem. There is no single best way because there is no one way that suits everyone. Often people scoff at interpretations that smack of the Freudian: The prune is a witch, soap washes off sexual guilt, taking a cake from the oven is like delivering a baby, and so forth. But some people do find such ideas useful and think these metaphors reflect valid emotions or deeper realities. Even if the symbolism is taken at a more general level, linked fairly directly to the things people say about the products, some such inferential process goes on, and must go on, if the analysis is to be meaningful. This analytic process may be further illustrated with a few brief examples.

WRISTWATCHES

A study of wristwatches showed them to be objects that are richly interwoven into important life experiences and expectations. Watches relate to the passing of time and thus have to do with an awareness of one's fundamental being and mortality. To be oriented to the issues posed by taking formal and systematic account of time, to have a watch, then, implies maturity, the achievement of significant levels of responsibility. Some comments made in interviews about watches show these ideas.

> As soon as a child is able to tell time or can learn to tell time — about six years old, I'd say. It teaches children to be on their own.

> My first watch was a present from my family when I graduated from high school. It probably didn't cost a lot, but it meant a great deal to me. It made me feel like a man.

The giving of a watch, even an inexpensive one, is not a light matter, because it is usually not done casually or impersonally. It expresses respect and affection.

> It would have to be somebody very important for me to buy a watch.
> It would depend on the closeness of the friendship.

The watch is also technical and executive in character, a kind of mechanical taskmaster, pointing up the inexorability of time's passage, the demands of scheduling.

"I'm always looking at the time. I do everything like clockwork." Watches are also jewelry, potentially a beautiful adornment, precious and assertive of wealth. As a consequence of these various issues, foci of concern with watches can vary. They may orient to *compulsive* concern, referring mainly to the time-binding and demanding aspects of promptness and accuracy. They may elicit interest in *technical* features, involvement with the internal and device nature of the watch. *Exhibitionistic* concern may dominate, referring to common wishes to display possession, to show off the merits of the watch in design, cost, brand, or to call attention to the achievement, affection, or special status implied.

PEANUT BUTTER

Peanut butter is a product that has a lively, provocative character. Its flavor, texture, and appearance make eating it a strongly individual experience that people tend to love or hate. It is a food not normally found on restaurant menus, but most enthusiasm for, and consumption of, it go on between 6 and 12 years of age or so. Most often, peanut butter is viewed as a casual food, that is, a substantial snack. It plays a central role in some light meals, most usually at noon. While the stereotyped use of peanut butter is in peanut butter and jelly sandwiches, its potential variety is apparent in its being eaten uncombined, as a spread; combined with cream cheese, bacon, bananas; spread on waffles, french toast, pancakes; in making confections; and as a salad trim.

The texture sensations of peanut butter are a special part of its appeal or repellence, being rich and complex. Eaters emphasize the feel of the food as the tongue plays over it on the teeth, on the roof of the mouth. There is a sharp awareness of contradictory smooth-sticky sensations. Many people claim that "stickiness" is the worst thing about peanut butter; yet there are indications that this is not just a demerit, that it draws the kind of congenial carping complaint one makes about a cherished drawback, the blemish that is enjoyed. This paradox stands out in the remarks adults make.

> I would say it tastes like peanuts and looks like a spread. It's brown, very hard to eat, sticks to your mouth, smells like peanuts, and I love it!
>
> It's certainly sticky to spread—sticky and smooth too. I'd say it was smooth to spread and sticky to the roof of the mouth. But I enjoy it, myself.

Children are especially likely to outright approve the hard-to-eat qualities.

> It makes your teeth feel furry.
>
> It's good, and oh gee, how would you say it?—It feels "ushy" [he shivers].

Peanut butter is perceived to have certain social characteristics. While not in the category of hamburgers, hot dogs, popcorn, and Cokes, peanut butter seems an American food. Like other American foods, it is for "ordinary" people, for everyday occasions. It has an air of heartiness, goodness, and wholesomeness, of simplicity and lack of complication. Given these qualities, it is a highly approved family food. Homes with children consume more peanut butter per capita than homes without children. Even though children account for the bulk of its use, adults do not want it defined as not suited to themselves.

One of the general psychological meanings of peanut butter is independence for children and mothers. In the self-assertive, energetic days of middle childhood and pre-adolescence, peanut butter has a special appeal because it serves admirably as an acceptable badge of freedom (from depending on mother for feeding). Kids can help themselves and are freed somewhat from the ordinary restraints of polite eating. Peanut butter can be eaten out of the jar and fingered, and it is used for a certain amount of smearing pleasure, compatible with the anal associations that some people snicker about and others openly comment about.

THE SIGNIFICANCE OF BOATS

Boating offers another example of the intricate interweaving of symbolic meanings. The reasons people want to go boating can be answered at many levels. They are feeling restless. Things around the house are not so interesting lately. Fishing from the shore is boring, and the bay is dotted with sails. A friend offers a boat ride. Somehow the family needs a new activity. Explanations of this kind are not too helpful. They mainly repeat the fact that people want to go boating. Behind such reasons are broader ideas and meanings that influence people toward or away from boats.

In the background is the historical image of boating. It is thought of as something with a tradition, not as a recently devised activity. It has an aura of elegance, glamour, and adventure. Boats seem as old as history, and different kinds call forth different ways of life and identification—the proud Spanish galleon, the quick Indian canoe, the embracing Eskimo kayak, the luxury liner to Europe, the expensive yacht lazing through the Caribbean or the Mediterranean.

At the physical level, there is the question of how people want to use their bodies when they get out on the water. What sensations are looked for? Some just want to loll and soak up sunshine, while others want to get soaking wet. Some want to struggle with ropes and canvas, to tinker, polish, and paint. Others want wind and spray and stars. Buying a boat means buying a great diversity of possible experiences.

There is a body of shared ideas about the tradition and sensations of boating. From this background are derived the many kinds of satisfactions boaters seek. They can bask in the pure leisure tradition—the idle rich sport and special social outlet now made available to the masses. This proves the average person is as good as anybody, even J. P. Morgan, almost. As one woman commented:

More and more of the middle-class people go for things that were at one time considered a rich man's possession.

It is cause for marvel how democratic boating has become, considering how aristocratic a sport it used to be.

We always go to the boat shows when they're in town. Most anybody goes for boating these days. I know several people who own boats and they're just ordinary people.

Boating has sexual and impulsive meanings. Part of the glamour of boating lies in its glittering associations with sex. Yachts are traditional locations for seductions at sea. A classic burlesque of this was shown in the movie "Some Like It Hot" where Tony Curtis masquerades as a yacht owner who is cold to Marilyn Monroe's kisses. A suggestive news item tells of a 44-year-old man arrested for buzzing a beach after repeated warnings by the lifeguards—and with him was a 19-year-old model.

The sexy, impulsive aspect of boating has its high-class social side represented by the larger boats, where wild parties and offshore gambling can go on. People can get away—if only in imagination—from normal restraints and conventions; the boat is a symbol of this freedom from routine morals. This may include the idea of businesspeople using boats to entice and influence customers.

I have made many friends and business acquaintances, which resulted in some good accounts.

Another version of the impulsive motives is the smaller boat that youngsters use to chase around the shore line, showing off noisily and dangerously to swimmers, irritating people fishing, tossing beer cans overboard, and offering rides to shapely sunbathers. These boaters give outboard motors and small boats a bad name. Their problem is that unlike other boaters, they do not want to get away from it all. They want an audience and a way of calling attention to themselves.

Part of this complex of commanding an audience and an impulsive sense of excitement comes from water skiing. This is an activity that harnesses the power of the motor for the sake of the skier's thrill, giving the skier a vivid experience. It creates a sense of being caught up by a terrific force and mastering it for a while.

The cult of sailing. On the whole, sailboat enthusiasts tend to bring more energy, vitality, and precision to boating than other groups. Sailing is attractive to people who are seeking a special degree of challenge and adeptness. Here there is an emphasis on skill. The basic assumption that the sailboater is taking nature on its own terms and turning it to personal ends in a smoothly coordinating way, leads to tremendous feelings of pride and superiority. Sailboaters look down on other boaters the way car drivers who manually shift gears look down on people with automatic transmissions. Sailboaters are apt to be the most fanatic about going boating, the most eager to race, to find people who will help them sail, and to help others. This man's comments show some of the typical values of the sailboater.

> *Especially sailing—I think it's more relaxing. It's not as hazardous as on the highway. There are people who have accidents but they're usually the ones that don't belong there. They don't abide by the laws of the water and they are the ones that cause the trouble. I've had more experience with sailboats and that's the kind of boat I like. It's more of a challenge. You're getting all you can out of the wind. In a power boat you're—well, just like driving a car.*

Fishing is a manly art. In addition to the luxury and excitement themes in boating, and the elegant dedication of the sailing crowd, there is the ancient emphasis on masculine occupation that finds special expression in the fisherman. The man who goes fishing draws upon deep motives whether he goes after perch or deep sea monsters. He is making a private arrangement with nature. He will throw back the little ones—or traditionally catch nothing useful at all, if he is allowed to get away from civilization and its refining influences. The fisherman seeks fundamentals. He wants to vanish to quiet, primitive spots. To him a boat is heavenly transportation to his retreat. This state of affairs still exists for great numbers of men, but they are steadily losing out.

Domestic symbols come to the fore. Boats used to be For Men Only. A woman on a boat was bad luck, an evil omen; she meant disaster. But she was not to be kept out. The men yielded slowly. Many still insist that a boat is no place for a virtuous woman, anyway. And some of their wives agree with them, refusing to get wet or to live on fish.

Nevertheless, one of the basic trends in boating is its domestication. The family has joined the movement to water. As soon as children are old enough not to topple overboard, the unit is complete; and in many people's eyes the boat has become an outstanding symbol of modern togetherness. Asked about the effect of this activity on the family and its relationships, they say:

That's why I don't play golf. I'd rather have a boat so we can all be together. Our children are two boys and where one is a devil, the other is an angel. But I like them both. We all get along together just fine. The boat has brought us closer together. Everyone in my family enjoys the boat and that's what counts, isn't it?

We used to go to the motorcycle races. . . . Oftentimes my husband would become involved in the technical discussions of motorcycling and that left me out. Here is a sport [boating] that a husband and wife and family can enjoy and it creates amongst a family an even closer union than a home. It seems everyone wants to learn about boating and they enjoy participating.

We are all together, we each don't go our own way. At one time we did. The boys love the boat. It has brought a togetherness to our family and most of all I can easily share in my husband's interest.

Womanly motivations are often the same as men's. Many women enjoy boating and fishing, but a wife's yearnings easily turn in domestic directions. She is willing to live the outdoor life, but she hopes it will be more homelike all the time.

I'd have a large-size motor boat. It wouldn't be anything elaborate. It would have a sun deck, a kitchen area, and a bathroom. I would want to be safe. I'd like to have some portable bunk beds.

These examples illustrate how objects transcend basic utilitarian definitions, developing personal and social meanings and complex symbolisms. These meanings are influential in determining attitudes when it comes to making choices, in having a broom but being slow to replace it; in deciding on what kind of mattress is needed for the kind of sleeper one wishes to be; in ordering a new computer system; in being a fussy eater or a dedicated cook; in going fishing, sailing, or both. This is true for all activities and objects, and any may be studied to find out the important meanings relevant to effective communications about them.

References

1. **Sidney J. Levy**, from keynote remarks presented at conference, *The Automobile and the Future of Denver*, Colorado Women's College, Denver, Colo., Jan. 10, 1974.
2. **Alexander Kira**, *The Bathroom: Criteria for Design* (New York: Bantam Books, 1967).

Suggested Readings on the Motor God

Hughes, J. R. T., *Eight Tycoons: The Entrepreneur and American History* (Boston: Houghton Mifflin, 1966).

Jerome, John, *The Death of the Auto* (New York: Norton, 1972).

MacManus, Theodore F., and **Norman Beasley**, *Men, Money, and Motors* (New York: Harper & Row, 1929).

Pound, Joseph Horace, *Civilization and the Motor Car* (Houston: Rice Institute Pamphlet, 1924).

Rae, John B., *The American Automobile* (Chicago: University of Chicago Press, ——, *The Road and the Car in American Life* (Cambridge, Mass.: MIT Press, 1971).

Schneider, Kenneth R., *Autokind vs. Mankind* (New York: Schocken, 1971).

Shenu, Robert, "Paradise Lost—The Decline of the Auto-Industrial Age," by Emma Rothschild, *The New York Times Book Review*, Oct. 28, 1973.

Spivak, Alvin L., *The Immoral Machine* (San Jose, Calif.: Milieu Information Service, 1972).

Index

256 INDEX